THE VIEW FROM
Brindley
Mountain

A MEMOIR OF THE RURAL SOUTH

SECOND EDITION

EUGENE SCRUGGS

STRATTON
—PRESS—
Publishing Life

THE VIEW FROM BRINDLEY MOUNTAIN
Copyright © 2020 **Eugene Scruggs**

Stratton Press Publishing
831 N Tatnall Street Suite M #188,
Wilmington, DE 19801
www.stratton-press.com
1-888-323-7009

ISBN (Paperback): 978-1-64895-060-5
ISBN (Hardback): 978-1-64895-062-9
ISBN (Ebook): 978-1-64895-061-2

Printed in the United States of America

Other books by this author

For Lindsay, Erin, Alex, and Shannon

Contents

Preface

How hard it is to escape from places.
However carefully one goes, they hold you.
You leave little bits of yourself fluttering
on the fences—little rags and shreds of
your very life.

—Katherine Mansfield
From *Collected Letters*

Regardless of where our journeys take us, neither place nor time erases the thoughts and actions of youth. Memories—ghosts from the past—find their way to the surface at unexpected times. A simple smell, a sound, a voice, a face, a taste stirs our recollections into action. In the words of noted sociologist Eric Hoffer, "Smell is the closest thing human beings have to a time machine." A *Madeline* cookie created a flood of memories for French novelist Marcel Proust. The smell of a baking cherry pie stimulates a similar reaction for me. In this way, memories bridge the gulf between what *was* and our nostalgia for a more perfect past.

Unfortunately, over time, memories tend to fade into each other in a jumble of confusion. Additionally, it is tempting to embellish our recollections, and the greater the lapse of time, the greater those embellishments tend to be. Mindful of this phenomenon, in the following pages I strive to avoid creating new stories to replace the "real" ones I witnessed and lived.

These little vignettes cannot, and should not, be considered *the truth* about life in the 1940s and 1950s near the little town of Cullman, Alabama, at the western edge of Brindley Mountain (or any other specific area in the rural South). The images pass through the filters of my senses, my emotions, and my concept of reality. Melded together, they offer glimpses of my *world view* as it was then and now.

The journeys of adulthood separate us from family and friends. We leave behind the familiar as we choose paths that lead to a wider world. With apologies to Robert Frost, I attempt to capture in verse this seemingly random nature of life's choices.

> Diverse paths fan out along
> the mountainside,
> While peering down first one
> and then another,
> I wondered which I should travel
> when I became a man.
> Curiously, I watched each fade
> in space and time.
> And yet the path I chose seemed

> much less traveled by,
> And who can know what difference
> that choice has made?

Memories are not measured in days or hours, but in fleeting snapshots. Our mental "scrapbook" is stuffed with *clichés* of moments, good and bad, when we experienced heightened consciousness, replete with times when we felt great highs and deep lows, spectacularly happy moments and moments painful and traumatic.

In the following vignettes, I share experiences that began at a specific point in time and in a specific place. Consciousness of my surroundings began in the late 1930s. While the location was inauspicious, the era was momentous. The world was dashing headlong into a titanic struggle between fascism and freedom. In the first eight years of my life, I witnessed many tears of joy and sorrow. Our little clapboard house was in earshot of bugle taps and armed salutes, unforgettable symbols that the wider world was a very dangerous place indeed.

My first conscious experiences were inside the walls of that little clapboard house, yet very soon, my world encompassed the yard and the fields around this house and barn. Then came neighbors, men in overalls, women in bonnets, a big collie dog; next the town, with all its sights and sounds and smells, its delights and its frights. Eventually the circle widened out far enough to include the world.

Prologue

Life isn't about finding yourself.
Life is about creating yourself...

—George Bernard Shaw

L ate one Friday afternoon in mid-October of
1956, I strolled into the basketball gym at
Transylvania College in Lexington, Kentucky.
This was registration day for freshmen, and the time
had finally arrived when students with surnames
beginning *S* through *Z* were permitted to enter. The
room was nearly empty. Seniors, juniors, and sopho-
mores had arranged their class schedules over the past
three days, and new, incoming students had been
warned that the pickings might be rather slim during
the final hours of registration. Obtaining a desired
class schedule would be a case of perseverance.

Looking around for the Foreign Language
table, I hoped to register quickly for an intermediate
Spanish class to build on the two years I had studied
that language in high school. A rather cosmopolitan-looking gentleman sat behind the registration
table, leisurely smoking a pipe. No students were in

line, so I sauntered gingerly up to the pipe-smoker and asked if I might register for Spanish 201.

"I'm sorry. All beginning and intermediate Spanish classes are full," he replied.

"Darn! I was really hoping to continue Spanish. I studied two years in high school and made good grades. Couldn't you possibly squeeze me in?"

"No señor. Estoy triste, pero no hay más asientos en esa clase," replied the professor. (I am sorry; no seats remain in the classroom.) "However, I have openings in Beginning French. Since you've studied Spanish, you could do quite well."

"No. Thanks. I *do not* want to study French," I replied, and began looking around for another department.

Transy, as the college (now university) is affectionately known to intimates, offered classes on the quarter system, and a full academic course load consisted of three classes, meeting daily, Monday through Friday. Based on my advisor's suggestion, I hurriedly registered for the only section remaining of English composition. This was followed with a class in Western Civilization, again only one section was available—at 8:00 in the morning!

Now, I needed to enroll for one more class. Hopefully I could register for one that met during the morning hours. I walked around the gym looking at the various departmental stations. I checked in with Art History—nothing available. I tried Philosophy— all sections filled. I stopped at Natural Sciences— nothing remained except Beginning Biology, and that section met at the same time as my just acquired English Composition class. I was stymied. Finally, I was forced to slink back over to the Foreign Language table to the handsome, pipe-smoking professor.

"All right," I said. "I guess I'll have to take your Beginning French class!"

That seemingly inconsequential decision was the genesis of a new and exciting journey that eventually led me to my life's career. Having spent many previous hours in farm fields, I was now destined to make frequent visits to the *Elysian Fields* (not the one in the afterlife, the one in Paris, better known as the *Champs-Élysées*).

Actually my decision on that fateful fall day in 1956 took me from prior days of picking cotton to eventually being picked by the prime minister of France for the highest order in the field of education awarded by that country: *Chevalier de l'Ordre des Palmes Académiques*, Knight of the Order of Academic Merit.

Unfortunately, the professor who had faith in my abilities, who helped me in my self-creation, who pushed me along my career path, the pipe-smoking Dr. Edwin Alderson, did not live to see me honored by the country he loved so much; however, I am sure he would have been delighted. After all, he tapped me to fill a vacant seat in an intensive French Institute program, which he organized in the summer of 1957. I was the only member of the group not preparing to travel to Africa as a missionary to the Belgian Congo.

All members of the class were required to take an oath to speak only French for the entire ten-week program. My classmates and I met classes together. We ate together. We enjoyed evening activities together. We sang together. We even slept together—in the same dormitory, not in shared rooms. This was, after all, the 1950s; nothing risqué was very likely.

After weeks of heavy-duty study, we all began dreaming in French. I was ten to fifteen years younger than the other participants and had studied French for much less time than any of them. Yet despite a great deal of anxiety, I was able to pass that intensive program and develop a passion for the language and literature of France—something I had not anticipated in any of my various *reveries* as a youth in the rural South. I was creating an entirely new and unexpected path.

Within a few weeks after completing this intensive course in French, I underwent another life-altering experience that would lead me irrevocably beyond the views on Brindley Mountain. In the early fall of 1957, I was working a part-time job as dishwasher at the local YWCA cafeteria. One day I met a young freshman coed also attending Transy who had just been hired to work the steam table. This young girl from a blue-collar family living in Cincinnati, Ohio, would spend the next fifty-seven years challenging me to expand my worldview. This young lady, who had the melodious name of La Donna Loescher, invited me to a Sadie Hawkins Day Dance a few weeks later, and, as they say, all the rest is history.

The Clapboard House

Who am I?
How did I come into this world?
Why was I not consulted?

—Søren Kierkegaard

I was born in a frame house in the rural South—literally "born in" since giving birth in a hospital was rare for rural women at that time. Ole Doc Daves (I am told) came to the house with the tools of his trade early on a Tuesday morning, and I made my appearance a couple of hours later. My brother Glenn recounted a different story. He maintained that Doc Daves drove up to the back porch of the house and, after giving me a spanking, presented me to the family. Glenn was five years old at the time and had gotten things a bit mixed up.

When I arrived on the scene in Cullman County, Alabama, on the sixteenth day of November 1937, planet Earth was on the brink of a second major world war within a quarter century. Fascism was rampant in much of Europe. Mussolini swaggered in Italy, Franco was destroying freedom in

Spain, Hitler was forging a powerful war machine in Germany, and Stalin was overseeing the murder of millions in Russia. In Asia, Japan was raping China with a ruthlessness that is hard to imagine.

Many reasons to be pessimistic about the menacing "new world order" were in evidence, but Americans, still in the throes of the Great Depression, seemed little concerned with the problems facing other countries. Isolation was the order of the day. The rest of the world could fight if they wished. America viewed itself as self-sufficient and determined to stay out of the fray.

The year I was born, life expectancy for a male child was just under sixty years. Life-prolonging medicines and medical techniques were in relative infancy. In that year, the average annual household income was approximately fifteen hundred dollars. A modest new car could be bought for less than eight hundred dollars. New bungalow-style houses were being built and sold for around six thousand dollars. Gasoline was selling in most areas of the United States for ten to twelve cents a gallon. Milk was more expensive at twenty-five cents a quart. A loaf of bread was nine or ten cents. The DOW hovered around the 150 mark.

Social and racial injustices were generally accepted as facts of life. Despite the prowess of Joe Louis in boxing and Jesse Owens in track and field, black athletes could not dine in the same room with whites. Yet white Americans took great pride in the fact that Owens had beaten Hitler's super race of athletes in the 1936 summer Olympics and that Louis had beaten the best white boxers the world had to offer.

Joe Louis became world heavyweight champion in the year of my birth by beating James Braddock. Even the most prejudiced of white men listened avidly to radio accounts of Louis's boxing matches. During the early 1940s, like so many others, my dad sat with his ear glued to the static-filled radio, straining to hear the blow-by-blow accounts of Louis's fights, always rooting for him.

The world I joined was quite different from the world of the twentieth-first century. So much of what we now take for granted did not exist: no fast-food restaurant, no diet drinks, no air-conditioning, no television, no computers, no cell phones, no internet, no dot-com, no Walmart, no video games, no ATMs, and no credit cards! Cars were manual shift, with no power steering and no power brakes; the interstate highway system was fifteen years from conception. And these are just a fraction of things unavailable or unheard of at the time. Luckily, when an item hasn't yet been discovered or invented, it is not missed. For example, no one missed watching television or talking incessantly on cell phones. Plenty of time existed for real conversations and real personal contacts. The virtual world was years away.

In my early years in the little clapboard house, in the sloping shaded yard, in the fruit orchard, in the barn lot, in all the contained spaces that encircled our house, I was quite content. As I grew older and more constraints were placed on me and my activities, I began to reevaluate. When the first of several major disciplinary actions occurred, when I was asked to assist with chores, when I was denied previously granted pleasures, I began to question my place in this little microcosm of a world. One day when I was five years old, in a fit of anger, I put a half-eaten peanut butter sandwich in my pocket, put on my straw hat, and left home. Mother watched me walking south through the cotton fields. When she thought I had gone far enough, she sent my brother to retrieve me.

A few years later, as I slowly ventured into a larger circle and was amazed by the seemingly huge white-columned houses with indoor plumbing, enormous flower gardens, glistening swimming pools, large gym sets with swings, slides, and monkey bars, I questioned my luck at having drawn the family I had and the little house with odiferous outdoor "plumbing" and the stifling interior. Eventually I began to ask, in the fashion of Kierkegaard, but only internally, *How did I come to be in this place? Why do I have these parents? Why was I not consulted about the place I wanted to live?*

Of all the locations where I could have been born, looking back on the various branches of my family tree, there seems little reason to suspect the location would be a small farm south of the town of Cullman. Nevertheless, the modest clapboard dwelling that was to be my home for the next sixteen years was constructed by my dad in 1931. The architecture was typical for that period and that region of the country. Over the years, Dad had worked at various occupations, including farming and construction, and he was an accomplished framing carpenter. He had been fireman first class while in the US Navy during World War I when he tended boilers on the minesweeper *Chattanooga* off the coast of New England. The crew was searching for underwater enemy explosives. After the war, Dad worked for a short time in an automobile assembly near Cincinnati, Ohio.

In the mid-1920s, Dad and his first wife, Candace Morgan, returned to Alabama, the home state for both. At first, Dad was employed as a switchman by the Louisville and Nashville Railroad in Birmingham, Alabama. He was small of stature (five feet seven inches tall and weighed scarcely one hundred fifty pounds), but Dad had a strength acquired through years of farming, shoveling coal, cutting crossties, and other labor-intensive occupations.

In those days, Birmingham (often called the Pittsburg of the South) was heavily polluted with industrial smoke, sulfur fumes, and coal dust. Unfortunately, Candace became ill with asthma, and the couple was obliged to move to a cleaner climate. For a time, Dad worked on construction projects at the Arsenal in Huntsville, Alabama.

Eventually Dad, Candace, and Edna (their six-year-old daughter) settled on forty acres of land acquired from Jerry Morgan, Candace's father. This property was located just south of Cullman, the bustling county seat nestled on the western slope of

Brindley Mountain, a ridge of the Sand Mountain Range. Most of the purchased acreage was forested, so Dad immediately began to clear the land manually using a double-bladed ax and a single-handle cross-cut saw to fell the trees. Afterward, he used dynamite to blow out the stumps. The logs were eventually hauled to a nearby lumber company and milled into framing material for the farm buildings.

The first structure Dad built on the property was a barn, which, for the first year, served as living quarters for the family as well as shelter for the livestock—animals on the ground level, humans on the floor above. Candace couldn't say to my dad when he forgot to wipe his feet, "What's the matter? You think you live in a barn?"—a phrase my dear mother was wont to use with my brother and me on many an occasion.

In order to have a supply of drinking water, Dad dug a well about seventy-five feet north of the barn. Within a year, new living quarters were constructed one hundred feet up a slight grade from the barn. The primary building material was wood, even the interior walls—no drywall (or Sheetrock, as it was once called) was used. After the main house was completed, Dad dug yet another well closer to the new kitchen. Shortly after the completion of the house, Candace gave birth to a son whom they named J. Glenn. She did not survive the birth.

Dad set about the task of raising this infant son and his seven-year old daughter. At first, he had rotating help from Candace's sisters, but soon he realized that if he was to keep the children, he had to find a suitable wife. My mother-to-be, Ora Mae Smith, a thirty-year-old who was assisting her widowed mother with four younger siblings at Gum Pond, Alabama, became that wife. Following a short courtship, Dad borrowed a neighbor's Model A Ford and drove to Gum Pond on May 27, 1934. Mother was waiting with suitcase packed. Back in Cullman, they were married by a justice of the peace. In fact, the two eloped since Grandmother Smith did not want her "assistant housekeeper" and "babysitter" to leave. It did not take Mother long to convert Dad's little clapboard house into a well-scrubbed home.

The dwelling consisted of three bedrooms, a living room, a kitchen, a screened-in back porch, and an open front porch. Later, the back porch was enclosed to create a dining area. Eventually another open porch was added off the dining area. The house sat on stone pillars about a foot and a half above ground.

The crawl space under the house allowed air to flow, helping to cool the inside of the house in the summer. This also made the house more difficult to heat in the winter. It also created a hiding place for little boys, nesting places for chickens, and a cool location for lazy snakes. Eventually this crawl space was enclosed.

The house had a simple dug-out "root cellar" with dirt walls and dirt floor. The cellar stayed relatively cool even on the hottest summer day. This cellar functioned as the family's first refrigerator, becoming the storage place for items that needed to be kept somewhat cool: eggs, vegetables, milk, butter, and fruits. For a few months during WWII, we had the luxury of a "real" refrigerator lent to us by Mother's youngest sister, Evelyn Rains, who was away on an army base with her new husband.

The living room in the house was far from plush. It contained a couch, one "easy" chair, a rocking chair, a child's rocker, a cane-bottom chair, and a small table on which sat a kerosene lamp and a Bible. A potbellied stove (in winter only) completed the furnishings. This cast-iron stove was called a *Warm Morning*, but it was warm only after my dad built a fire in it.

One print hung on the wall. The only other item eventually hanging on the walls of the living room was a knickknack shelf, which I built for my mother's birthday when I was twelve years old. The living room contained no books except the well-read Bible. My dad read a few verses from the *Good Book* every night before going to bed. Mother darned socks or crocheted. (Mother was never much of a reader.) I thumbed the Good Book a few times myself in later years after hearing exhortations by revival preachers who came our way, but I couldn't make sense of what was written. I never got past the "begats," or if I did, I got hung up on the "thou shalts" and the "woe to him that doth not heed." Dad's Bible was a red-letter King James Version, which I eventually discovered to be quite poetic. In my Sunday school years, I memorized many verses contained in that melodious translation.

My parents occupied one bedroom of the house. My brother Glenn and I shared another after I reached age five and graduated from a baby bed. My sister Edna used the third bedroom until she left home in 1942 to attend vocational school. Linoleum covered the floors of the living room, kitchen, and dining area. The bedroom floors were bare pine boards (tongue and groove). Mother hated those floors because the cracks trapped the lint and she had a hard time sweeping it out. Why she wanted to sweep lint around every day was beyond me. She seldom left enough in the whole house for me to gather and roll up with the aid of a bit of spit into what I called an indoor silent marble to flick across the room. As far as I could tell, all Mother's sweeping on the linoleum in the dining room just helped to wear it out.

My parents' bedroom was modestly furnished with a double bed, a tall chest of drawers (they called it a *chifferobe*, apparently a combination of *chiffonier* and *wardrobe*), a dresser and mirror, two cane-bottom chairs, a navy trunk, and a *Singer* sewing machine. Occasionally a quilt frame was slung from the ceiling so Mother and her friends could quilt and chat (a quilting bee). The two windows in this bedroom had diaphanous curtains, but there were no decorations of any kind on the walls.

The bedroom that my brother and I shared until he left home to seek the riches of the North had one double bed, one cane-bottom chair, a small closet, a small chest of drawers, and a wooden toy box. One picture hung on the wall—a tinted photograph of Glenn's deceased mother, Candace Morgan Scruggs.

The guest bedroom contained a wardrobe and a double bed, but this room was used mainly for storage. In the winter, the door to the room was kept shut; consequently, the temperature inside the room remained cool, and at times, even cold. Since we seldom had overnight company, this bedroom served as a refrigeration unit. My mother stored dried fruit and apples, pears and pecans in the room. During Christmas season, the room was an excellent place to preserve oranges, peppermint canes, chocolate candy, and fruitcakes.

An icebox sat in one corner of the "dining" room and a metal hutch in another. The icebox was a superfluous appliance that had been useful in Birmingham. However, the ice factory did not deliver beyond the city limits where we lived. Mother sat a flowerpot on the icebox to brighten the corner of the room.

The dining area also contained a "pie safe"—a wooden cupboard originally intended for pies and cakes, but which enclosed a variety of cooked items to keep them "safe" from flies, dust, and other hazards. A stove-wood box and a small closet completed the furnishings in the dining area. The floor was laid with linoleum, and the table was covered with an oil cloth. Four cane-bottom chairs were placed around the table.

The kitchen held a wood-burning cookstove that furnished heat to the kitchen and dining room in winter months. This cookstove had four "eyes" (equivalent to burners on an electric stove) and a large oven. It also had a side reservoir that held five gallons of water warmed by the heat from the stove. A slop bucket sat to the left of the stove and was the "garbage disposal." All food scraps ended in that bucket and were recycled to the pigs. There was no waste on this farm!

A sink was installed under one window of the kitchen with cabinets built beneath. This sink drained used water out through a pipe that descended to the cellar and then out through an underground pipe that surfaced by the barn lot. Before running water became available, water for cooking and washing dishes was hauled in by bucket from the outside well. My dad eventually built counter space and cabinets on the north wall of the kitchen. The final item in the room was a cane-bottom chair that sat under the small window that opened onto the front porch.

From a swing hanging from the ceiling of the front porch, I had a great view of Bremen Road, composed of dirt and gravel until "Big Jim" Folsom's first term as governor when the county road crew arrived and the fun began. (After all, Big Jim *did* live in Cullman.) I watched the bulldozers and the road grader for hours at a time. I had my own windup tractor, which I received for my third Christmas. It was a good imitation of the big bulldozer working on the road. I could wind up my toy bulldozer, and it would travel the length of the porch floor. Sometimes it would curve and go head-over-end off the porch and down the wooden steps. However, nothing ever seemed to damage it.

When our house was eventually wired for electricity in the early nineteen forties, the wiring was quite elemental. The living room had three outlets for lamps and appliances. The other rooms had but one outlet each. However, this was not a problem, since the only electrical appliances in the house before 1952 consisted of a *Frigidaire* (the name everybody used for a refrigerator) and a table-size radio receiver made of inexpensive *Bakelite* plastic.

The radio was a gift from my mother's brother, Captain Cephas Smith, who was serving at the time in the US Army in Burma. Despite any inconveniences with reception, we were very proud to have this radio. In those days, to complicate matters, the tubes in radios burned out frequently and had to be replaced. You could take the back off the radio by removing a couple of screws. When the back was removed, you could see the entire innards of the set. A technician could repair such a simple radio in a matter of minutes.

During lightning storms, our radio had to be unplugged. Sparks were visible as the lightning followed the wiring into the house and spewed out the sockets. We were careful not to sit near any outlet. The little radio picked up static from lightning, even from flashes too far away for us to either see or hear. At such times, there was little point in trying to hear a program. Even at the best of times we had trouble bringing in the three closest stations, all in

Birmingham, some fifty miles away. Eventually, the city of Cullman acquired a radio station of its own with the call letters WKUL (*We Keep You Laughing*, as it was dubbed by an early creative disc jockey).

In addition to radio programs, we learned of national and world news via the daily newspaper. My parents subscribed to the *Birmingham Post*, a newspaper that arrived by RFD (rural free delivery) each morning around 7:30 and was placed in our mailbox on Bremen Road along with any letters or catalogs for that day. Dad also received the *Woodman of the World* magazine and the *Ford Times* (after 1948). The latter was a polished small-format magazine with great watercolor illustrations, short stories, jokes, and naturally, publicity for the *Ford Motor Company*.

In the nineteen forties, this was the extent of reading material in our house, other than the *Sears and Roebuck* quarterly catalog, the "Wish Book," which could entertain a person for hours. After receiving a bicycle for my ninth birthday, I began to ride to the Cullman City Library to borrow books. At that time, the library was housed in one room in the basement of the Fuller Building. The books occupied an area about thirty by fifty feet. The librarian was a very kind lady who was eager to help youngsters find good books.

By the time I was ten years old, one of my daily chores was to chop pine slabs into "stove wood" (foot-long pieces about three inches in diameter). I brought armloads into the house and stored them in the wood box near the kitchen. For some reason, chopping stove wood was one of my favorite chores. I used a double-bladed ax, holding the slab with my left hand atop a three-foot-high oak chopping block. Usually a slab would require three or four chops to create the right size pieces to fit into the stove. Only once did I miss the wood and hit my hand. I still bear the scar on my left index finger.

At our house, as well as at most rural residences in the forties, Monday was designated as wash day. This was a day-long affair. My mother did not own a washing machine; all the work was done by hand. Consequently, washing, scrubbing on a "scrub board," rinsing, and wringing by hand took an entire morning and much effort. After the washing process, the clothes were hung outdoors on a line to dry and were taken in the house in the late afternoon.

Tuesday was ironing day. Before we had electricity, Mother ironed clothes with two flat irons, which she warmed on the cookstove in the summer and on the *Warm Morning* heater in the wintertime. Ironing was quite a process. She first sprinkled the clothes with water using an old quart bourbon bottle with a cork sprinkler-head. She then rolled the clothes into bundles. When all the clothes were sprinkled, she began to iron. A flat iron did not hold heat for very long, so Mother kept changing irons and reusing the hot one from off the stove. If an item to be ironed became too dry, Mother gave it another sprinkle with her bourbon water bottle.

Before the Rural Electrification Act made it possible for us to tap into a power line, we used coal oil (kerosene) lanterns and lamps to light the house at night. Most work in the barn was completed before dark. The barn was not wired. Therefore, if a cow was in labor or a young colt required attention during the night, the only light was from a lantern. Even after we acquired electric lighting, we kept coal oil lanterns and lamps handy. Electricity to the house was unpredictable. Power was frequently knocked out at the transformer about a hundred yards away on the Bremen Road. When lightning hit the transformer, sparks flew in all directions, and the popping noise sounded like a dozen shotguns going off simultaneously.

This was the signal for the coal oil lamps and lanterns to be hastily retrieved. The sulfur smell as the kitchen matches were struck, combined with the odor of burning oil, imprinted powerful olfactory memories. Flames from the coal oil threw off dark smoke if the wick was not properly trimmed. Even at best, the globe of the lamps required frequent cleaning to keep the light from becoming progressively duller as the globe blacked over.

These smells go hand in hand with eerie shadows formed by the flickering flames of lanterns, frightening flashes of lightning, and loud claps of thunder. Lightning hit the ground frequently in our fields. Where it struck, all vegetation was burned to a crisp. The locals said the frequent lightning strikes in our fields were due to iron deposits in the soil. This seemed a feeble explanation to me, since I never found a single piece of iron.

If an electrical or windstorm appeared to be a danger to our little frame house, my dad would signal that we all needed to head for the storm pit (cellar). With no local radio station, we were unable to receive local weather reports. Even if there had been a local station, the reception would have been drowned out by static, and we would have been unable to hear a report anyway.

In lieu of radar, my dad "read" the clouds and made a judgment about the severity of the weather. The main concern was high wind and tornadoes. While we were not precisely in "tornado alley," our area was not exempt. A devastating tornado hit near Dad's birthplace in Morgan County in the nineteen thirties, and this event was ever on his mind. He remembered an acquaintance who was blown through the air for several yards during that tornado. Dad recalled that pine needles were embedded in tree trunks by the force of the wind.

At least two or three times each summer, we descended into the storm pit, usually at night when the rain and wind were already strong and lightning was flashing close by. Those were traumatic moments—to be aroused from bed and taken out of the dark house and into the damp and musty-smelling cellar. The floor was clay and was slick and muddy. Snails hung about on the dirt walls, and spiders had webs in all the corners. The light from the lantern flickered and sputtered and created magic shadows on the dirt walls.

The Coal Oil Lantern

The yellow-blue lantern glows
In waves and flickers, smelling
Strongly of half-burnt oil.
Tongues of light echo wall to wall
Leaving dark and lonely corners
Where the boogie man may hide
Or some old ghost from ages past...
...Perhaps a tiger or even a bear!

Electrical storms have a particularly acrid aroma. This, combined with the damp clay-earth of the cellar walls, created a very pungent smell. Add to this the odor of burning kerosene and sulfur and you have quite a distinctive aroma, to say the least. The space between the ground and the floor of the house made the building susceptible to lift from strong winds. Once when my family was huddled in the storm pit, the wind lifted our house slightly from its stone pillars. After this rather frightening incident, the crawl space was enclosed.

The dug well near our house had very "sweet-tasting," cool, clear water. The bucket brought up an occasional bug or frog, but these nuisances were simply dipped out and tossed away. All visitors to our house commented on the quality of the water. Many wells had mineral-tasting water; thus, a well with "pure" water was quite a treat. The well became known to work crews from the county prison who periodically cut grass and weeds along the Bremen

Road. The convicts loved to fill their jugs with our well water when they were in the area. The guards picked one man to come to the well—the prisoner least likely to try to escape, I imagine. He was a large man with a jolly laugh who loved to tease and frighten little boys.

One of the frequent sounds in our house in the forties and fifties was the humming of a *Singer Sewing Machine*. In those days, one of the finest compliments you could pay an automobile was to say it ran like a Singer. Using a foot-pedal to work the action, Mother made our sheets, pillowcases, and towels from guano sacks (pronounced *gyou-aner*) that had held the hundred pounds of natural fertilizer used on the crops. (*Guano* is a French word for *wanu*, a South American Quechua expression for bird droppings, of which this fertilizer was composed.) Sheets made from guano sacks were a bit scratchy until they had been boiled in the wash kettle several times. Mother also made dresses and shirts using the colorful cotton sacks in which twenty-five pounds of flour were sold.

At the risk of readers' skepticism I should mention bathing practices at our house in the early 1940s. I speak of the Saturday night bath that became stock-in-trade humor in movie and television shows such as *Ma and Pa Kettle*, *Yee Haw*, the *Grand Ole Opry*, the *Beverly Hillbillies*, and other such "country" fare.

Before indoor plumbing was available in our area, we used a large corrugated number ten washbasin as our bathtub. This washbasin was partially filled with well-water mixed with water heated in the cookstove reservoir. Each in turn, family members took a rather simple bath standing or sitting in the tub.

The expression, "Don't throw the baby out with the wash!" resulted when baths were taken according to seniority and gender. The father went first, then the older male children, then the mother and the older girls, then the youngsters and finally, the baby. If the family was rather numerous, by the time the baby was put in the tub, he or she could easily be "lost" in the opaqueness of the dirty water. Let me hasten to say that in my family, each person had his or her own fresh water from the cookstove reservoir, even though that required a good bit of time and lots of effort. For my mother, cleanliness was the ultimate virtue.

Naturally our house had no air conditioning other than the natural breeze. As a consequence, during the summer months, after supper, we sought the cooler air on the front porch swing. We created our own breeze by swinging. The only drawback was mosquitoes, since the porch was not screened. Luckily, mosquito bites had no effect on me. However, the buzzing in my ears and eyes was very annoying. We kept a rolled-up piece of newspaper or a fly swatter handy to try and kill as many of the critters as possible. We did not know about mosquito repellents (if any existed at the time). We had not heard of candles to burn or the power of lemon scent to keep mosquitoes at bay. We tolerated the mosquitoes and assumed that this was only natural.

When bedtime arrived (usually around 9:00 p.m.), we went into the house, undressed, pulled on pajamas, and climbed into bed. During hot nights, we kept cardboard "Jesus" fans handy (fans given out by churches or funeral homes with pictures of Jesus and a bit of advertising for the institution). My brother Glenn and I would quarrel about whose turn it was to fan first. Since I was almost six years younger, I could usually talk him into fanning me more often than I fanned him. He was always a kind and good-hearted soul.

Since I have made it clear that our house did not have indoor plumbing for the first six years of my life, I should make a few passing remarks about the proverbial "two-seater outhouse." This outdoor "privy" was quite an institution, offering a wealth of folklore and scabrous tales. However, it is definitely not an object to be remembered fondly. Hardly larger than a phone booth and with no ventilation, the privy was hot in summer and cold in winter and always odiferous. The only light inside was what filtered through the little moon-shape slot cut into the front door. A night visit required a flashlight or a lantern. Then came the logistics of where to place the light once inside.

The classic "toilet tissue" was the *Sears and Roebuck Catalog*. Four issues a year came in the mail, and each contained well over a thousand pages. The *catalog-as-toilet-paper* has also become a standard joke—as well as humor regarding the use of corncobs for hygiene. Corncobs were used as a last resort by many poor families, and mainly, it would seem, among sharecropper families. These folks could even talk "quality" and "softness" in the manner of Mr. Whipple, the pitchman for *Charmin*. The white cobs (I am told) are much smoother than the red cobs. Luckily, the corncob crowd was farther down the socio-economic ladder than my mother would allow us to fall.

A less touchy topic concerns how we heated our house in winter. In early November, my dad brought out the *Warm Morning Heater* from the spare bedroom into the living room and hooked up the flue piping to the chimney. We were then ready for heat. The coal-burning heater had a pan underneath the grate that caught the ashes. The pan had to be emptied every couple of days.

Dad always built a fire in the early morning (around five-thirty) using lumps of coal, paper, and a few sticks of pine kindling. On a cold day, that fire was not allowed to burn out until after we had all gone to bed in the evening. Each morning, before starting a new fire, Dad shook the grate to get rid of the ashes and clinkers from the previous fire. However, if the coal lumps were not of sufficiently high grade, the impurities within the lumps would fuse into large clinkers that had to be removed with a scoop.

After shaking the ashes into the catch-pan using an iron rod that was jerked left and right in a vigorous manner, Dad added paper and pine kindling. As the fire caught, he added a few small lumps of coal. In a few minutes, the rest of us tumbled out of bed and dressed near the warm stove. The linoleum on the floor was icy cold on our bare feet, so my brother and I hopped around on first one foot and then the other to slip from pajamas into overalls. Sometimes the stove would draw too fast and become overly hot, the black iron taking on a reddish glow. A damper in the stovepipe controlled the amount of draw, and thus the amount of heat generated.

Once while poking my legs into long-johns, I lost my balance and fell against the stove, catching myself with my hands against the iron belly. As a result, I lost considerable skin on both palms. After that unpleasant incident, I was always leery of falling again. When dressing or undressing, I stayed farther back from the stove, despite the chill in the air.

Cold Nights, Warm Mornings

Cold nights we got undressed beside the cast iron
    stove,
Peeling layers 'til we reached our long-john
    underwear,
Then dashed to bed across the cold linoleum floor

Y'all better git them slippers on
'for ye freeze yore toes!

Plowing under covers on the wrought-iron bed,
Pressed down with Mama's homemade quilts.
Dead still we lay 'til sheets thawed out from body
    heat.
No fancy warmers, no irons heated on the stove,

The View from Brindley Mountain

Just extra sheets wrap the head-board 'round.
To ward off chilly drafts which cause the colds
    and flu.

> *Better put them nightcaps on*
> *They say its goin' down to freezin'!*

Through the knotty pine-wood walls, the north
    wind
Whistled bleakly, making window curtains flap
    about.
When morning was announced by faint first light
Staying a-bed appeared the wiser thing to do.

> *You boys gonna sleep 'til noon?*
> *Them chores ain't gittin' done theirselves.*

We feigned deep sleep until the scraping grate
And clank of coal lumps 'gainst a metal scuttle
Made a mockery of our 'tempted sham of sleep.

> *Who done forgot to fetch the kindlin' in?*
> *How'm I supposed to start this fire?*

The pungent whiff of sulfur from a kitchen match
The sounds of ice chopped from the pantry pail,
And water splashing in the cookstove reservoir
Gave signals clear that hibernating time was o'er!

> *Ain't nobody gonna he'p around here?*
> *We ain't got all day, ye know!*

With Mama up, the crackling sound of salt-cured
    ham
And smell of biscuits baking in the cookstove
    oven
Help the mind o'er come the numbing morning
    cold.

> *Y'all gonna miss the bus*
> *If'n you don't git a move on.*

With haste to dress behind the red and roaring
    stove
(Dubbed "*Warm Morning*" by some patent wit)
We left behind the night of cold, and broached
The sameness of another day of school and chores.

Soon after purchasing and clearing the land near Cullman, my dad planted a variety of trees around the house and barn: red oaks, water oaks, sycamores, mulberries, willows, peach trees, cherry trees, apple trees, pear trees, sweet gums, and black gums. All these trees were useful in their own way. The mulberries, sycamores, and fruit trees were great for climbing. The water oaks grew fast and created excellent shades. The red oaks produced large acorns that could be collected, carved, or simply tossed. When a gash was cut in the sweet gum tree, a chewy resin seeped out like rubber from a rubber tree. The black gum also furnished toothbrushes for our snuff-dipping visitors.

One of the apple trees produced tart fruit that was not very good to eat. However, they could be used as ammunition to fire at any target, but best of all, these apples were my source of juggling material. I spent hours practicing juggling two apples with one hand or three apples with both hands. I ultimately became rather proficient at this little pastime.

A grape arbor near the washhouse flourished with golden Loudons and deep blue Concords. Dad once made wine for his personal use, but during Prohibition days, he ceased and did not resume after the repeal of that idiotic piece of legislation. Mother used the Concords to make grape pies that were famous among the extended family and the neighbors. She also canned grape juice each year, storing the liquid in Mason jars.

However, for me the grape arbor was a place to gorge myself with the sweet and juicy Loudons. I could eat a pound of grapes at one time, seeds and all. At first, I swallowed the entire grape except the hull, but when I was told you could get appendicitis from the seeds of grapes, I became proficient at eliminating the seeds from the pulp with a quick action of my tongue and the space between my front teeth.

In addition to our domestic grapes, my brother and I sought out the wild varieties in the late summer and early fall. The woods near our farm were replete with thick vines of scuppernongs and muscadines. Those wild grapes were so sweet that "muscadine" became a slang word for "kiss." Adults asked little children to give them a muscadine. (They pronounced the word *musky-dime*.)

Finding the wild grape vines was an easy task, but getting to the good, ripe grapes was much more challenging. The best grapes were always high in the trees. This meant shinnying up the trunk of an oak, black gum, or sourwood tree and grabbing a branch and pulling up far enough to get a solid and secure foothold that would allow one hand to be free to pick the grapes and drop them down to an assistant below.

On the farm, we grew two additional domestic berries—dewberries and strawberries. Dewberries look much like raspberries, only larger and darker in color, resembling the blackberry. The bramble or stalks of the dewberry are replete with spiny thorns. Picking the berries is not much fun, but the effort is worth it when tasting a cobbler made from those delicate and juicy berries.

My mother was a great fruit-cobbler maker, and the dewberries were so juicy that her cobblers were heavenly. My mother was always best at baking desserts, and we were regaled with pies, cakes, cobblers, puddings, or cookies at both the noon and evening meals.

By far and away, my "most" favorite dessert was rhubarb pie. Indeed, this taste must have been shared by many Southerners because rhubarb was very frequently referred to simply as "pie plant." I was not aware that the plant was called *rhubarb* until I was an adult. For me, the word *rhubarb* meant a *fight*.

As I mentioned, the dug-out cellar beneath a portion of our house was very functional. A drain to the outside allowed the water in the cooling trough to be emptied out on a regular basis. Fresh water was continually added. At first, the drain pipe caused a problem. When eggs began to disappear, their absence was traced to a wily possum that had squeezed its way up the narrow drainpipe and into the cellar. A heavy-gauge screen wire solved the problem.

I was never fond of going alone into the damp and dark cellar. I imagined all sorts of ghosts and goblins lurking about in the shadowy spaces under the house—snakes and other critters, as well. One day, in full light, a black racer snake tried to squeeze into the cellar through a narrow crack in the concrete foundation. My dad grabbed it by the tail, yanked it out. and cracked the snake like he cracked a rawhide whip. The head of the snake became the "cracker," and it popped "clean off the snake!" I was quite impressed, and though I could crack a whip, I doubted I had the stomach to grab a snake by the tail.

We didn't have running water in our house until we and the other farmers paid to have a main line installed down the Bremen Road in the mid nineteen forties. What a happy time for me and my brother. We no longer had to draw what seemed like endless buckets of water to haul into the kitchen or take down into the cellar. Before the main line was run past the house, the number of daily buckets increased dramatically on washday. Water had to be drawn and carried about fifty feet to the iron kettle and the tubs in the wash house. What a life-changing experience when we were able to turn a tap and have instant water.

My dad quickly installed a hot-water tank in the house, and an even greater relief occurred. No longer did we have to warm our water in the reservoir of the cookstove—hot water came directly out of a tap and into the sink. As soon as Dad sold enough cotton, he purchased a bathtub, commode, and sink, which were installed where a walk-in linen closet had been. We felt like we were now "uptown" folks. The two-seater outhouse was torn down, the hole was filled, and the wood burned. No more trips outdoors in all types of weather. No more swatting flies and spiders. No need for periodic bags of lime. Our little clapboard house had become rather upscale and comfortable.

Growing Up with the "Funnies"

Little Orphant Annie's come to our house to stay.

—James Whitcomb Riley

Before I could read, my dad sat me on his lap and read newspaper comics to me. (For us they were the "funnies.") If he was in a hurry, Dad would say, "Look at the pictures and try to figure out what's being said." I found this a lot more difficult than he seemed to think. Dad's favorites funnies were *Snuffy Smith*, *Alley Oop* (the *B. C.* of that era), and *Andy Gump*.

When Dad was in a mood to doodle, he often sketched out a silhouette of *Snuffy* or *Gump*. Snuffy was (and still is) the archetype of the Appalachian hillbilly. His manner of living hasn't changed in seventy-five years. Snuffy, an inveterate moonshiner, is constantly being chased by the Sheriff. The epitome of laziness, Snuffy prefers to sit in his rocking chair and smoke his corncob pipe, wearing his frumpy old black felt hat. In just about every way, Dad was the opposite of Snuffy. Maybe that was what attracted him to the strip.

Other favorite comics included *Lil' Abner*, *Jiggs and Maggie*, *Dick Tracy*, and *Popeye the Sailor Man*, and *Gasoline Alley*. The latter didn't make much sense to me. The only thing funny was the name of the young soldier—*Skeezix*. I mean, what kind of name is that?

Alley Oop, on the other hand, was a fascinating character. He had such an outrageous appearance, with his high brow and flat head and his elephantine legs. He wore a "loin cloth" made of some sort of fur, and for a weapon, he carried a monster-sized hammer. Even though Alley Oop was a caveman, he thought and behaved much like a twentieth-century man, and his trials and troubles were those of our contemporaries. Oop's kingdom of Moo was in perpetual conflict with the rival kingdom of Lem. In the midforties that seemed a rather natural state of affairs.

The names of Oop and his girlfriend, *Ooola*, sounded funny to me; however, I had to wait several years before I understood the linguistic puns embedded in their names. After living in France for a while, I became accustomed to hearing *Oo-là-là* and *Allez hop*. The latter expression translates something like "let's get moving" or "up and at 'em." Obviously, the creator of this strip was an *aficionado* of the French language

Other facets of pop culture were influenced by the popularity of Oop. In the nineteen sixties, a song with the title *Alley Oop* rose to number one on the pop charts. Basketball athleticism made possible a high pass and dunk shot labeled an *ally-oop*.

My imagination was peaked by Oop's voyages into the past via a time machine invented by Dr. Elbert Wonmug. The latter's name illustrates once again the cartoonist's love of linguistic puns. This time, the play on words involves German: *Won* (or one) plus *mug* are translations of *ein* and *stein* (think beer stein/mug). Changing *Elbert* to *Albert* is a no-brainer, and *voilà*, Dr. Elbert Wonmug becomes Dr. Albert Einstein.

Imaginary time travel and space travel were not new fascinations in the nineteen forties. As far back as the seventeenth century, Cyrano de Bergerac imagined space travel via propulsion rockets, making it possible for men to visit the moon and the sun. Mark Twain's Connecticut Yankee traveled back to fifth-century Camelot via a time machine. Jules Verne created fantastic voyages to worlds previously unknown. Certainly, in the late nineteen forties, young imaginations were spellbound with visions of space travel, although we could not envision that rocket science would make possible a trip to the moon within twenty-five years.

Pop culture also embraced cartoons of the little sailor man with the pipe and the can of spinach. Popeye was the champion of good, healthy eating, but he was not much of a role model for English grammar. "I'm strong to the finish 'cause I *eats* my spinach. I'm Popeye the sailor man."

His pal Wimpy, the hamburger addict, was always hungry and always looking for a handout. Wimpy seemed never to get his fill. He continually sought to obtain just *one more* burger, even after devouring a half-dozen or more. *"I'll gladly pay you Tuesday for a hamburger today,"* was Wimpy's comment to anyone willing to listen. Unfortunately, devouring hamburgers, à la Wimpy, has become the downfall of many Americans.

This fanatical love of the juicy burger gave the name *Wimpy* to one of the early fast-food chains in Europe. In the Latin quarter in Paris, long before *MacDonald's* made its debut, Wimpy Corporation (headquartered in England) had a restaurant at the corner of Boulevard Saint-Michel and Rue Souflot, near the Pantheon. In 1967, when my wife and I and our two young daughters were living in Paris, we laughed to see the French eating burgers with a knife and fork in Wimpy's restaurant. At the time, French etiquette was not prepared to tolerate picking up food with one's hands. It's barely acceptable today.

On the comics page of the newspaper, my dad never missed checking to see what weird subjects were depicted in *Ripley's Believe It or Not!* However, it seemed that he got the biggest laugh from reading *Blondie and Dagwood*, especially when Dagwood's boss, Mr. Dithers, threatened to put Dagwood's little finger in the pencil sharpener after Dagwood pulled some stupid trick or fell asleep at his desk.

My imagination was greatly strained at the thought of a little finger being made into sausage.

Luckily for Dagwood, Mr. Dithers never carried out his threat. The *Blondie and Dagwood* comic strip furnished our culture with the name for an oversized sandwich—the "Dagwood sandwich." Unfortunately for the body mass of Americans, some restaurants now offer super-sized sandwiches that rival Dagwood's.

The reader's sympathy was usually with Dagwood and his troubles. He was the "little man" who was not appreciated by his wealthy industrialist boss. For example, Dagwood continually pleaded for a salary raise, but he never received one. Actually, in the very earliest of strips, Dagwood is depicted as the son of an industrialist who disowns him for marrying Blondie, whom the father considered to be much beneath his son's station. (Blondie, an airhead with the family name of Boopadoop, began her life in the strip as a flapper girl.)

Dagwood was frequently late for work because of his tendency to oversleep on the living room couch. Many of the strips depicted Dagwood running out of his front door still putting on his hat and coat and hurtling square into Mr. Beasley, the postman. Naturally the letters and packages go flying in all directions. This oft-repeated gag never failed to evoke a chuckle.

As a young child, I enjoyed the drawings of Baby Dumplings, Blondie and Dagwood's child. Baby Dumplings was the epitome of the "girl with the little curl right in the middle of her forehead," and she was forever crawling around in a sleeper that had no legs so that she resembled a fat worm with a human head.

Switching genres, *Dick Tracy*, the detective comic strip, was very different from the humor of *Blondie and Dagwood*. The story line in *Dick Tracy* was often harsh and at time brutal, with frequent gun play and fisticuffs. The strip was something of a *comique noire*, if I may be allowed the expression (thinking of *film noir*).

However, most young boys were excited by the two-way wrist radio that Dick Tracy used, and they wanted a toy replica. The idea of such wireless communications seemed such a wild and futuristic idea in the forties. Of course, today, young kids find nothing unusual in wireless gadgets of all kinds.

A new excitement was generated in the strip when Dick Tracy finally married longtime girl-friend, Tess Trueheart. Their first child was a little girl named Bonny Braids. Obviously, the cartoonist was also an *aficionado* of puns. He created not only Trueheart and Bonny Braids (a pun on *bonny braes*), but such characters as detective Sam *Catchem*, the fat inventor *Diet Smith*, and the hillbilly family of *B. O. Plenty*, *Gravel Gertie*, and *Sparkle Plenty*. I found the subplots involving B. O. Plenty and his gang more interesting than most of the plots involving Dick Tracy. Perhaps that was because I observed more B. O. Plentys in real life than I did Dick Tracys.

One of the most successful comic strips of all times was *Little Orphan Annie*. It received a significant boost when the musical became a major Broadway production. Annie of the comic strip was placed in foster homes and continually forced to run away because of mistreatment. Her only true friends were her doll, her dog, Sandy, and a wealthy industrialist known as Daddy Warbucks. The latter's name was a puzzle to me. *Roebucks* I understood (half of a catalog title), but not *Warbucks.* Later, I realized that Daddy made his money during the war as a member of the military-industrial complex.

The problem of orphans and street children loomed large in the nineteenth century on the heels of the European and American industrial revolution. Many writers brought the need for social justice to the forefront, the need for child labor laws and shorter working hours for adults. The most popular literary figure to expose the issue was perhaps Dickens in his *Oliver Twist*, which illustrated the problem in London and other cities in England. I was fascinated with Oliver's exploits when I read a children's version of the classic when I was ten years old.

In the major industrial cities of the Eastern United States, thousands of street urchins and unwanted children and orphans became a major problem by the 1880s. A systematic effort was initiated to place these children in homes in western states. Farmers and tradesmen in the West who needed labor were given the opportunity to either adopt or indenture children from the East, especially from cities like New York, Boston, and Philadelphia.

Consequently, the children sent west for adoption or indenture became known as *orphan train riders*. My wife's mother was one such rider, leaving New York for Arkansas sometime between 1900 and 1908. She, too, like Little Orphan Annie, ran away from her foster home to escape physical and emotional mistreatment. It seems probable that the poet James Whitcomb Riley had orphan train riders in mind when he wrote the first stanza of his poem *Little Orphan Annie* in 1885.

> Little Orphan Annie's come to our house to stay
> An' wash the cups an' saucers up
> an' brush the crumbs away.
> To shoo the chickens from the porch
> and dust the hearth and sweep
> And make the fire and bake the bread
> to earn her board and keep.
> While all us other children, when
> the supper things is done,
> We sit around the kitchen fire
> and has the mostest fun,
> A listening to the witch tales that Annie tells about
> And the goblins will get ya if ya don't watch out.
> (James Whitcomb Riley)

Little Orphan Annie has become an icon, with her red dress and red hair and wide open and blank eyes. Her difficulties never seem to end. She is constantly in some jam or other, but she has the virtues of resilience and perseverance that Americans love. No wonder the comic strip has been so well received for so long. All those old "friends"—Annie, Gump, Oop, and Tracy played roles in developing my young imagination and my early constructs of "reality."

Preschool Days

Spare the rod and spoil the child.

—Folk wisdom

Mother's best friend in the vicinity of our farm was Mrs. Guy "Ruby" Hodge. I remember her very well. Before I began attending elementary school, I often accompanied Mother to visit with Mrs. Hodge, who lived about a quarter of a mile north on the Bremen Road. There was no one at the Hodge house for me to play with. However, better than a playmate, Mrs. Hodge had *Ritz Crackers*! At our house, we only had ordinary old saltine crackers. "*Ritz Crackers* are too expensive," my mother would respond when I asked her to buy a box. Consequently, I couldn't wait to arrive at Mrs. Hodge's house to have a few delicious Ritz Crackers to eat! The first few times I would ask her for some, but my mother soon made it clear to me that I should wait for Mrs. Hodge to offer some to me. Luckily Mrs. Hodge knew very well my reasons for sitting restlessly on her couch with an anticipatory look.

When I was three years old, Santa Claus brought me a tricycle for Christmas. That was the best gift I ever received in my young years. I rode that tricycle for the next three years. My dad had to raise the seat and handlebars ever so often until they could not be raised anymore. The tricycle was in great shape even after I was too big for it, and it was passed on to one of my younger cousins, who destroyed it in less than a year.

At a very young age, I learned to avoid unnecessary conflicts with my parents. That meant "minding" them and not begging for something after they had said *no*. They were implacable disciplinarians who did not spoil the child by sparing the rod (or switch). I could see that my parents were frugal by necessity. It was clearly useless to ask for anything beyond the ordinary necessities of life. I seldom pitched a fit when I couldn't have something I wanted.

However, there is one major exception, which I vividly recall. One day my mother took me shopping in downtown Cullman when I was five years old. We stopped in Kuhn's on First Avenue. The sign above Kuhn's indicated that items inside could be bought for five, ten, or twenty-five cents.

Mother had probably wanted to buy thread or buttons. However, this being a day near the Fourth of July, Kuhn was selling small American flags. The flag was about five by eight inches and on a two-foot dowel stick. For some reason, these flags tickled my fancy, and I felt I had to have one. My mother said no. I began crying and screaming that I wanted a flag.

It must have been a very embarrassing moment for my mother, because rather that giving me a spanking on the spot (her normal reaction), she gave in to my request and bought the flag. I was surprised and very proud, but she later shamed me so much that I did not try that stunt again. I kept that flag for a long time. I believe it was still in my room when I left home for college.

Mother returned to her home at Gum Pond periodically to visit her mother, called Mama Smith by all the grandchildren. Mother always took me with her, and we stayed several nights. Mama Smith's youngest son, Herman, and his wife, Vera, and their two children lived with her in the "old home place." The oldest child, Jerry Charles, was born one month after me in 1937, although he swore for years that he was older than I. How he got that idea, I could never figure out. In any case, we were good buddies but something of rivals in those early years.

Jerry and I tried to outdo one another in all things. One incident stands out as though it happened only yesterday. Once when mother and I were visiting Mama Smith, Jerry and I were playing out in a pasture. Another cousin, James Robert Smith, was along with us. James Robert was a year or two older than Jerry and I. It was rare that I would see him on my visits to Gum Pond, even though he lived on a farm just down the road. But that day, the three of us were running through the pasture. Recent rains left large puddles of water in one low-lying area. J. R. and Jerry decided we would jump over this puddle.

J. R. went first and splashed across. Jerry followed. I hesitated to try to jump, knowing that if I got mud on my clothes my mother would give me a scolding and maybe make me sit in a chair for half an hour.

As I hesitated, wanting to be as bold as the other two but fearing the consequences, Jerry taunted me from the other side of the puddle, "*Fraidy cat, 'fraidy cat! Come on and jump!*" When I hesitated, he added, "*Come on, chicken. Don't be such a crybaby!*"

Well, that was more than I could take. I looked down at the ground and found a small rock. I picked it up and threw it straight at Jerry's head. I would show him who was a baby and who wasn't! The rock hit Jerry on the forehead, right between the eyes. He grabbed his head and burst into tears. I was afraid I had hurt him, and I really hadn't intended to. I only wanted him to stop taunting.

When I saw the effect of my David-like throw, I took off running to find my mother. I wanted to get to her first and tell her why I had thrown the rock. She and Mama Smith were sitting on the front porch. I came running up crying, "I didn't mean to. I didn't mean to." It took a while for Mother and Mama Smith to find out why I was crying and what I didn't mean to do. Once it was understood, Mama Smith wanted to know why I was crying if Jerry was the one conked on the head. "I don't want a whipping. I didn't mean to hit him," I sobbed in my mother's arms. Now, for some reason which will forever remain a mystery, I did not receive the punishment

I expected. Mother and Mama Smith seemed almost sympathetic.

The next morning, Jerry came into the kitchen for breakfast when I had almost finished my bowl of oats. He had a huge bump on his forehead that was turning half the colors of the rainbow. "Look what you did!" he whimpered.

My dear sweet Aunt Vera joined in the scolding. I knew what I had done was wrong, but deep inside, I was kind of proud that I had put a stop to the taunting. However, all I could do was repeat that I was sorry. Mother said she would have to tell my dad about the rock throwing. That put the fear of the Lord in me. When Dad was angry, his punishments were not to be taken lightly.

My anxiety grew until we arrived home, but Dad did not punish me. Instead he told me to always stand up for myself and not be afraid. However, he added, I should never take unfair advantage of someone else, nor should I fight just because of a few silly words. I was very grateful to receive only a lecture instead of punishment. As for Jerry, he soon forgot the incident.

Kerosene and Quarantines

The metal headboard of my
Bed served as a gong.
Listening for the gong
Was my mother.

B efore the age of nine, I experienced chicken pox, whooping cough, diphtheria, scarlet fever, and German measles. During the second grade, I missed twenty-three days of school because of whooping cough and scarlet fever. Each time, the County Health Department nurse was sent to our house to tack a quarantine notice to our door. In those days, physicians still made house calls. Old Doc Daves drove out to the house with his mysterious bag, looked in my eyes, ears, and throat with a tiny flashlight, took my temperature, listened to my lungs with his stethoscope, and poked around on my neck and chest.

After his diagnosis, the Doc shoved a spoonful of horrible-tasting liquid down my throat and gave my parents a script to take to People's Drug Store for more of the same. During those particular illnesses, my fever ran through the roof. My hallucinations were impressive. I watched the walls of the bedroom close in on me, a sensation that stayed with me for a long time.

My mother was not prone to pamper; however, with these childhood illnesses, she was very attentive. Three of her brothers died in childhood from one of these dreaded illnesses. She stuffed me with aspirin, fixed lemon and vinegar toddies, placed cold washrags on my forehead, placed poultices of *Vicks* on my chest, and made homemade chicken and noodle soup. Nothing helped. In those days, a person's immune system basically had to overcome the illness. For the less fortunate, the cases were occasionally fatal.

My bed had a metal headboard. When I struck it with my knuckles, it sounded like a gong. That gave me the idea to create a code to use when I needed something. One knock meant I wanted water. Two knocks meant I wanted a cold washcloth. Three knocks meant I wanted a glass of pineapple juice. Four knocks meant I wanted a toy. Mother tolerated the game until I began to improve. With no antibiotics available, parents tried to keep their sick children as comfortable as possible. Not much had changed since the childhood of the poet Robert Louis Stevenson.

When I was sick and lay a-bed,
I had two pillows at my head,

And all my toys beside me lay,
To keep me happy all the day.
("The Land of Counterpane")

Cold compresses were used to try to break a fever. Aspirin was given for aches. I am not speaking of children's aspirin (they did not yet exist)—these aspirins were the quick-dissolving, grainy, yucky-tasting, variety that were very hard to swallow. My gag reflex kicked in every time I tried. The solution was to dissolve the aspirin in juice before drinking it.

For less serious health issues—colds, flu, stomach aches, cuts, bruises, and sore throats—an array of home remedies was stocked in the kitchen cabinet. Salt in warm water was gargled for sore throats. Lemon juice or vinegar in warm water was an alternative. If these two remedies failed, there was always a drop of coal oil on a lump of sugar held in the mouth until it dissolved. If the soreness in the throat was not too severe, options included Luden's or Smith Brothers cough drops. For chest colds, a poultice of *Vicks Salve* was the standard recipe.

Several old patent medicines (over-the-counter drugs) were stored in most rural medicine chests: *Phillips Milk of Magnesia* was the mild laxative, but *castor oil* sat on one shelf daring a young boy to complain too much. *Castor oil* was frequently used as a threat in case a child had an idea about faking intestinal problems to avoid school or work. "Stop complaining or I'll give you a dose of *castor oil*."

Pepto-Bismol was administered at the first sign of upset stomachs—for example, after eating too many green apples. In case of diarrhea, horrible-tasting *Paregoric* was brought out. This latter product contained a tiny bit of opium mixed with water, alcohol, oil of anise, camphor, and benzoic acid. Yuk!

Rubbing alcohol or coal oil was used to cleanse punctures from cuts and rusty nails. *Mercurochrome* was a must for scratches and abrasions. For worse cuts, the hard-burning *Absorbine Jr.* or iodine was applied. That stuff burned the germs right out!

Hiccups were quickly cured with a spoonful of sorghum syrup or honey. Baking soda took care of bee or wasp stings. *Epsom salts* mixed in warm water was the answer for tired, sore feet.

My mother had several prescriptions for keeping a child healthy. Most important was to add a couple of drops of *cod liver oil* in a teaspoon of milk every morning after breakfast; another was to serve a bowl of hot oatmeal each morning. Mother had obviously heard of the efficacy of fish oil and oats—long before nutritionists took up the mantra.

The great progress in medical science in the last fifty years means that youngsters today do not have to experience the childhood illnesses that were common in the forties. Unfortunately, diseases that appeared to be conquered are reappearing in the twenty-first century because some parents are failing to have their children immunized. To complicate the situation, many drugs appear to reduce an individual's ability to fight illnesses.

Accidental cuts and bruises usually were treated at home using over-the-counter (or patent) medicines. For example, one day my brother, Glenn, was hoeing cotton in a small patch where a chicken house and lot had once stood. The soil was very rich, and the cotton stalks were as tall as Glenn and much taller than I was. I was six years old at the time and was playing around among the stalks, hiding from Glenn. He was chopping out cocklebur plants and was using a *scovil* hoe (a heavy-duty hoe).

With one wild whack, Glenn brought the hoe down on top of my head instead of on a cocklebur. The blade of the hoe cut a slice across the top of my head, and the blood began to flow down the sides of my face. The weight of the hoe was almost enough to knock me unconscious, but the sight of blood scared both Glenn and me into fast action. He grabbed me up and ran to the house with me bawling at the top of my lungs. Mother came screaming out of the side door when she saw blood dripping from my head.

Since we had no phone and no car, it was up to my mother to act. She carried me to the kitchen sink and began to wash my head with cold water. Then she held a dish towel tightly over my head until the bleeding stopped. At that point, she reached for the coal oil and literally poured it generously all over my head. The burning was enough to start me bawling again. Mother patted my head with a clean towel until she had dried off the excess coal oil. It turned out that the cut was not as deep as originally thought.

The many capillaries in the scalp were causing the profuse bleeding.

During this time, poor Glenn was white as a sheet and trembling with panic. He thought he might have killed me. Mother made me sit quietly in the "easy chair" in the living room for twenty minutes. It felt like an eternity. Although my scalp was sore for a few days, I was no worse for the wear. This appeared to be proof that I had a hard head—which my mother had always maintained.

Pain from a scovil hoe was nothing in comparison to having a tooth pulled by the dentist. The science of dentistry had a long way to go in the nineteen forties, at least in rural areas. Instruments were very primitive. Electric drills were slow speed. The bits were easily dulled and created enough friction to cause smoke (if not fire). The drills made a loud noise, much like today's carpenter drills or jigsaws.

There was no hygienic suctioning of oral fluids by an assistant. As a matter of fact, I don't recall there being an assistant. The patient had to spit into a ceramic dish, which was located on the left side of the chair and which had a drain with constantly flowing water that made a gurgling sound as it eddied around in the basin.

Dental chairs were made of hard metal, and the backs were almost upright. The height of the chair could be adjusted by pumping a pedal. The first time I saw a dental chair that reclined to a horizontal position parallel to the floor was in Paris, France, in 1967. At that, time the French dentists were using masks and rubber gloves. I was amazed at how different the procedures were from those stateside.

Dentists were once among the most hated of professionals. They were aware of this dislike, and probably because of this, dentists had a high suicide rate. Just about everyone had disparaging labels for dentists. "Old jawbones" was one of the best (or worst). Many jokes were passed around at dentists' expense, frequently about surnames—Dr. Paine, for example, or Dr. Akers, or Dr. Pulliam. However, I doubt if anyone can top the name of my childhood dentist: *Dr. Bledsoe*. Honest! No joke! And when Dr. Bledsoe got through with you, I guarantee you *bled so*!

In the forties and fifties, fluoride treatments were given to schoolchildren with parents' permission. This provoked a good deal of controversy among the naysayers. Many people believed (and some still do) that this was part of a conspiracy to harm young Americans. It was seen by Joseph McCarthy's "ditto heads" as just one more Communist plot. Fluoride turned out to be a great boon in the fight to prevent cavities. There seem to always be naysayers and screwballs who attack each new medical or scientific discovery. The smallpox vaccine was opposed by a majority for many years and even by a few mistrusting souls today.

In the summer of 1947, after a serious bout with German measles, I began to complain of headaches and blurred vision. The local optometrist tested my eyes and noted that I needed glasses. From that point on, spectacles have been resting on my nose except when I am asleep. At that young age, I quickly acquired the nickname "four eyes." That was not nearly as bad as the crimp those new glasses put on tussling with the boys on the playground. My glasses were frequently twisted out of shape.

That same year (1947), my tonsils and adenoids were removed at the Cullman Hospital by none other than good old Doc Daves, the man who brought me into the world. Anesthesia was primitive at the time. A rag was soaked in ether and held to a person's nose. The smell was very unpleasant, and the aftereffects were worse. An assistant held me down while Doc Daves covered my nose with the ether-soaked cloth. He told me to start counting backward from one hundred. I never reached ninety.

In the hospital room where I spent the afternoon recovering, I looked out my window and watched a man plowing land just a couple of hundred yards to the east. I watched the mule pull the plow back and forth, back and forth in mesmerizing motion in my semi-etherized state. In 1954, when my parents sold the farm, they bought a house that had been built on the very land this man was plowing. How bizarre is that?

In the later afternoon, after sufficient recovery, a nurse brought me ice cream. It not only tasted good, but it felt good on my sore throat. For some reason, my throat didn't heal readily, and I was given considerable amounts of the new drug penicillin. Finally, my throat healed, but I continued to have problems with strep for the next fifteen years.

In the fall of 1951, Dr. Bledsoe informed my parents that I should have braces on my teeth. The nearest orthodontic practice was in Birmingham, so my dad drove me fifty miles once a month for the next couple of years. Orthodontics was very much in infancy. The wiring hurt my gums. The rubber bands I wore during the night caused jaw pain. When the wiring was finally removed, no retainer was prescribed as a follow-up, so my teeth became somewhat crooked again in a few months. As far as medical and dental care is concerned, my peers and I did not grow up during the "good old days."

Whatever the city or town, the greatest fear of mothers of young children in the forties and fifties was not a nuclear attack by the Russians, although we had an occasional drill in school and most towns had a so-called bomb shelter. Polio was far and away the number one concern for mothers. We youngsters were constantly reminded, "Don't go down to that dirty swimming hole, you might catch polio. Don't be running around so much in this heat, you might have a sun stroke and get polio." Despite the fear, only one boy among my classmates suffered from the results of this debilitating disease. The very courageous Ralph Johnson came to school in braces and did his best to keep up with the rest of us. I remember how very strong his arms were from years of walking with crutches. A dozen years after we graduated from high school, Ralph was able to witness the eradication of polio in the US and in most developed nations. Rapid medical advances meant parents no longer feared the potentially life-threatening child-hood illnesses witnessed in the years before nineteen fifty. Now, if only research can create a cure for the pesky cold and flu viruses that plague today's children and adults.

Crawfish and Dry Flies

Time… There was always too much.
Always… Then too little.

—Louise Glück

Time often seems to move slowly for a young child and rapidly for an active adult. Within the framework of his relativity theories, Albert Einstein concluded that time is not *static*, but *dynamic*. The human psyche perceives time in relation to movements, activities, space, and—more importantly—to strong passions (danger, suspense, competition, intimacy). In Einstein's words, "When you sit with a nice girl for two hours, you think it's only a minute. But when you sit on a hot stove for a minute, you think it's two hours. That's relativity."

A young child is absorbed for short periods, but tiring of one activity, immediately seeks other excitement. A child's innate desire for instant gratification leads to impatience with the "slowness" of time, and the unwelcomed word *later*, which often stands between the child and his or her desire. Most healthy adults keep rather busy with work or entertainment and thus pay less attention to the passing of time—except to note that there never seems to be enough.

My childhood was punctuated with seemingly endless days and with multitudes of "laters." I played alone most of the time, since few children lived in the vicinity of our farm. My mother's work in the house and vegetable garden did not allow her the freedom to entertain me very often. Consequently, I was ever in search of ways to "kill" time.

By the age of five, I was convinced that attending elementary school would provide exciting new things to do and would make life more enjoyable. I fully expected to begin the first grade in September of 1943. Unfortunately, my mother discovered when she took me to register that I had to be six years old before September 30 in order to begin the school year. Unfortunately, I did not have my sixth birthday until November 16. Kindergarten would have been an option except that the city of Cullman did not offer free kindergarten classes, and private programs were economically beyond the reach of my parents.

I had learned to read a few words and perform simple addition and subtraction, so my mother petitioned the principal of the school, Mr. R. P. Johnson, to waive the birth-date requirement. A waiver was not granted in my case, although a few had been permitted in the past. My parents did not live within the city limits and were not members of the established

Cullman middle-class. Consequently, they could exercise no leverage.

What a disappointment to wait another whole year (a forever later!) before beginning the first grade. It irked me that one of my cousins, Jerry Smith, whose birthday was in December, was permitted to begin the first grade at Gum Pond in Morgan County when he was only five years old. Rules were apparently more lax in small rural schools.

Once when staying with my maternal grand-mother who lived at the Gum Pond crossroads, I visited the first-grade class with Jerry. This little country school had only two rooms. The first through third grades met in one room, and the fourth through sixth grades met in the other room. By coincidence, the first through third grade teacher was Miss Gwendolyn, wife of first cousin, Rufus Murphree.

In Miss Gwendolyn's classroom, students performed activities that were familiar to me: reciting ABCs, calling out flash-card numbers from one to ten, sounding out words and short sentences in a little picture-book called *Fun with Dick and Jane.* One of the first sentences that millions of us learned to read was "*See Spot run!*" which came from the pages of that little book. That day of class at Gum Pond was exciting and made me more anxious than ever to attend school on a permanent basis. In the mean-time, I kept on the lookout for challenging ways to pass the time.

In addition to the few little farm chores that a six-year-old was expected to perform, I found plenty of amusements. I whittled away a goodly amount of time using my Barlow knife and a few pieces of soft wood or twigs from the willow trees growing along the creek in our pasture.

At this age, tree-climbing became one of my favorite activities. The most challenging tree on our farm was a mulberry in the upper part of the pasture. This tree had three trunks, each one over a foot in diameter. The first branches were six feet above ground level. That meant a young, short climber had to shinny up one of the trunks with no grip for the feet.

It was much easier to climb the fruit trees growing close to our house, but my dad scolded me if he caught me doing so. Apparently he was afraid I would break off limbs that might otherwise produce fruit. (However, he didn't seem to mind breaking off a limb to use as a switch to apply a moral lesson to my brother and me.) Both my parents subscribed to the philosophy that if you "spare the rod, you will spoil the child." The threat of being whipped with a razor strop always hung over our heads, but it was never used.

I discovered while still quite young that sycamore trees are not especially good for climbing during the time of year when they produce fuzzy little balls. On one hot, humid day, some fuzz from a sycamore tree dropped down behind the collar of my shirt and trickled down my back. The itching was ferocious. I took off my shirt and ran to the house. Mother scrubbed the fuzz off with a wash rag, but the itching continued for several more minutes. Afterward, I was careful not to climb a sycamore in "bloom." In Sunday school class when the teacher told the story of short, little Zacchaeus sitting up in a sycamore, I was convinced he had made a poor selection of trees to climb.

Of course, trees weren't the only thing young boys climbed. The storm pit (cellar) door offered another time-killing sport. The storm pit was about fifteen feet from our house. The door sloped down three feet and was covered with tin, creating a good slide.

One summer a cousin, Jim Scruggs, from near Rochester, Pennsylvania, was visiting and decided to run down the cellar door standing up, rather than sliding. He had not noticed that my mother's five-foot high clothesline ran very near the base of the slide. Jim caught his chin on the wire as he reached the bottom of the door. The tension in the wire threw him backward, and he hit his head on the corner of the cellar door. This created quite a gash and a lot of blood. A few other kids were around at the time, and we were all terrified when Jim lay still on the ground. We were sure he was dead or dying. Luckily, our neighbor, Mr. Graham owned a pickup truck. He drove Jim to the office of Doc Daves who sewed up the wound in Jim's head with a few stitches, gave him a "lockjaw" shot (tetanus), and sent him back to our house.

Jim had been sent by Uncle Dewey to work on our farm for a few weeks during the summer months, presumably to build discipline and endurance. Luckily for Jim, he was unable to do strenuous work for a week or more. He loafed around under the shade trees and sipped "cold drinks." He called them "pop" and "soda." These labels seemed strange to our Southern ears.

The rest of us continued to work in the broiling sun, and Jim's hours of repose didn't endear him to us in the least. In Jim's defense, he had a difficult time adapting to the heat and humidity on Brindley Mountain. He had spent most of his years in the cool mountains of western Pennsylvania. My dad realized that Jim would not be able to do the field work, and he sent him back north where he spent the remainder of the summer in Flint, Michigan, with Dad's youngest brother, Carlton Scruggs and his family.

Meanwhile, that old storm pit offered other less hazardous possibilities. From the top, which was flat and made of poured concrete, you could jump and catch a low limb on a nearby pear tree and swing for a few seconds. This was a great way to build coordination and arm strength.

Another game that reinforced balance and coordination was "jump board." This was a poor kid's seesaw or teeter-totter. All that was required was a good length of board (eight to twelve feet), at least six inches wide, balanced on a makeshift fulcrum (a rock or cinder block). One kid stood on one end of the board, and the other kid jumped off the storm pit and tried to land square on the raised end of the board.

If all went well, the kid opposite went sailing in the air. (Well, maybe sailing is a bit of an exaggeration!)

Swinging from a rope tied to the limb of a tall oak tree was an even better "workout." You pulled the rope back and got a "running go" before flying through the air. This was a Tarzan-like activity without the hazard of being many feet high in the trees. The sheer joy of swinging as fast as possible—to stir up a mighty rush of wind—is captured in verses by Thomas Hood:

> I remember...where I was used
> to swing, and thought the air
> must rush as fresh to swallows
> on the wing.
>
> ("I remember")

On the other hand, for a "gentle" motion, the front porch swing with its monotonous squeaks was a perfect place after dinner.

Once sated with swinging, sliding, and tree-climbing, other time-killers were only an imagination away. During the early summer, lazy June bugs besotted themselves by gorging on rotting apples. In that state of inebriation, June bugs are very easy to catch, but you have to tolerate a rather unpleasant smell. The object is to catch a June bug and tie a lightweight string around one of its back legs. The June bug can then be prodded into flying, and you run along beside or behind as though flying a kite.

If a kid wanted a much greater challenge and a lot more flying time, a better playmate was the "dry fly" or, as it is known outside of Southern Appalachia, the *cicada*. A June bug tires out rather quickly, and its legs are prone to pull off its body and allow it to escape. However, if you managed to trap a wary dry fly and tie a string around one of its back legs, you had yourself the 1940's equivalent of a remote-powered toy airplane. A dry fly has enough stamina to remain flying for several minutes before tiring out and landing, and it seldom loses its leg.

We had a large lilac bush near our back-porch steps. This bush attracted dozens of bumblebees. These fat stingers would become so enthralled with nectar-gathering that they were rather easy to catch in a glass jar. A lid with a few nail holes covered the jar, and you could watch the bumblebee buzz for hours. One other sport I practiced at the lilac bush was a little riskier. I would come up close to a bumblebee and flip it with my index finger and send it flying off the bush in a dazed state. The fun came by knowing that if I was not very fast and very careful, I would be stung by the bumblebee. This only happened once. The pain was too great to allow it to happen a second time.

Catching lightning bugs (fireflies) in a jar at dusk was not dangerous at all. If you could get about twenty or more in a jar at one time, you had almost continuous light. Unfortunately, lightning bugs, like June bugs, have an unpleasant odor about them.

When not molesting nature's small creatures, singing and whistling were very relaxing time-killers for me. Singing in solitude was always best, and a way to avoid erstwhile critics. On a farm, there are plenty of places to be alone: wash house, woodshed, smokehouse, barn loft. I practiced singing gospel songs and Negro spirituals that I heard frequently over the radio, and hymns sung repeatedly at revival meetings and weekly Sunday worship.

For years, I hesitated to sing in public, even as part of a group, but when I finally overcame my insecurity, I already knew the words and melodies to hundreds of songs. A favorite gospel tune I some-times belted out at full voice from the barn loft door went something like this: "*I'll fly away, O glory, I'll fly away, in the morning, When I die, hallelujah by and by, I'll fly away.*" Not only was the tune catchy, the words were very intriguing to a youngster, sparking visions of Superman zipping through the sky.

My dad was innately musical. As a young teen-ager, he built a banjo and accompanied his fam-ily during Saturday evening song fests. The family eventually included ten children—six boys and four girls. Along with the parents, they sang together for entertainment in the days before electricity (and thus radios) was available in rural areas of the South.

When Dad's older sister, Velma—the designated family pump organist—married and moved away, Dad took over the organ playing duties. During my childhood, we had neither piano nor organ in our house, so Dad was limited to playing a harmonica when he was in a musical mood.

Prior to joining the US Navy in 1917, Dad taught shape-note "singing school" during several summers when public schools were not in session. These singing schools gave rural children an opportunity to learn the rudiments of music and prepared them to participate in church services where no organ or piano was available or desired. My mother, seven years Dad's junior, was a pupil in his class one summer. At the time, nothing would suggest that twenty years later the two would marry.

When I was in my teen years, my dad was in his late fifties, in poor health and with little patience or stamina. He was treated for pernicious anemia, but unknown to local physicians, he was suffering from acute hyperthyroidism. After a hard day's work, Dad didn't have the energy to sing. He had long since given up trying to teach my brother, Glenn, to recognize and imitate pitches. Dad swore that Glenn couldn't carry a tune in a slop bucket. This humorous but harsh criticism turned out to be self-fulfilling. Glenn never sang, even though for many years he was a faithful member of church congregations that forbade instrumental music in their sanctuaries.

My dad was an inveterate whistler, and by mimicking him, I learned to whistle at an early age. I soon began to imitate bird calls and songs. With practice, I eventually was able to produce sounds reasonably close to the main calls of a dozen or more birds. The mockingbird offered a major challenge. That loquacious fowl repeated a short tune two or three times and then quickly switched to a different set of notes.

In my view, mockingbirds are among the most perfectly adapted natives of the South. They appear to be totally unaware of the oppressive heat in summer and the cold in winter. When most other birds are taking midday siestas in the shade trees, the mockingbird sits atop the highest tree or pole singing a repertoire of notes with the gusto of an Italian tenor performing an aria before an audience of hundreds.

During the nesting season, the male mockingbird claims all the territory in proximity of the nest and lets every creature know that this domain belongs to his family. The mockingbird doesn't stop singing at nightfall as other songbirds do. That show-off may decide to tune up any time of the night, breaking the silence with impressive volume.

Midnight Tune-Up

Late March for mockingbirds is nesting time.
From highest perch, at midnight, one a.m., or three
The hardy male makes certain life of every kind
Knows that his spouse is nesting in a nearby tree.

He's tireless with his loud and cheery call,
And, like a concert master ere the curtains rise,
He's tuning up as though he's ready for a ball!
In fact, his tuning up could surely take a prize.

His repertoire, it seems, would fill a hefty score
But never does he play beyond a bar or two.
He sings three notes, and seldom any more
Indeed, that's all this jolly fowl will deign to do.

In dark of night, when all is quiet, his notes begin!
I want to scream: "Shut up! And let me sleep!"
Yet for the neighbors' sake, try nodding off again,
Counting changes in his notes, in lieu of sheep.

The drab catbird gives the mockingbird plenty of competition. The two species are similar in size and color and have some very close note patterns. However, the catbird usually repeats a call only once or twice. The funniest, in my view, is its imitation of a meowing cat (giving the bird its name). In the cool of the morning, the catbird is at its most prolific, but I've never heard one sing in the middle of the night.

Some birds are "name-sayers." The crow, the barred owl, the bobwhite, the whip-poor-will, the mourning dove, and the killdeer are among the better known. All are easy to imitate because their distinctive vocalizations invoke their names. On the other hand, the thrush family simply cannot be imitated. Those gifted musicians are able to harmonize with themselves, something the human vocal cords are incapable of performing.

In my view, no more beautiful singers exist in North America than the hermit and the wood thrush. The only comparable sounds occur in the dead of night in Europe when the complex melodies of the nightingale may be heard in rural areas. It's no wonder this legendary bird stars in poems and love stories.

Robins are some of the most human-tolerant of songbirds. As they hop around on a lawn, it is not uncommon to come within ten feet of a robin. They produce a rather lengthy singsong that is pleasant but not very melodious. They have a call note that is a kind of clucking, but if they are frightened, they produce what I would term a whinny-like sound. My mother's two favorite bird species were robins and eastern bluebirds. The latter has a light, airy tweeting song. We always had a family or two in boxes by our garden where they had plenty of insects available. These birds definitely aided in lowering the worm and insect population that fed on the vegetables.

Some birds simply are not gifted with melodious voices. The blue jay doesn't sing; it screeches at the top of its lungs. To increase the volume, the jay squats down, then jerks its body upright, apparently to give more force to the call. In the woodpecker family, two species have loud, raspy, and easily recognized calls. The pileated woodpecker (a large, crested specie, also known as the "Indian hen" in Southern lore) has a rather lengthy clucking sound that rises and falls and can be heard for great distances. The flicker or yellowhammer (the State Bird of Alabama) has a similar cluck, but with less rise and fall and less volume.

Whistling to attract or imitate birds can be enhanced with simple instruments. When I was still quite young, my dad taught me some homemade devices. The easiest requires only a piece of bark from a willow twig. He cut a section roughly the diameter of a soda straw and about two inches in length. He tapped all around the bark in a gentle way with a knife handle, and eventually the bark pulled free from the wood yet remained in one piece. The bark was now hollow like a straw. With appropriate pressure and air flow, one can produce sounds similar to a duck's "quack" or a crow's "caw."

Whistles were carved from soft pinewood, but that process took more time than most boys were willing to dedicate to a project, especially since, for less than a quarter, a plastic whistle could be bought in the five and dime stores. These had the advantage of looking and sounding like the whistles used by professional referees.

Of course, a perfectly good whistle can be made just with the hands and takes very little effort. I learned to fold my hands together in a single fist, leaving a tiny slit between the two thumbs. With a little practice, a flute-type sound can be produced. The pitches change by varying the size of the aperture.

My brother and I often passed the time by playing with the sharecropper's kids who lived on the Fred Lessman farm adjoining our land about a quarter of a mile to the east. Our only free time to visit these neighbor kids was usually Sunday afternoons. My parents didn't work on the Sabbath, except for those chores that could not be skipped (milking cows, feeding chickens, slopping hogs, and throwing hay to the cattle).

This Puritan-like sabbatical observance meant that we boys had an afternoon of playtime. My mother was not too keen for us to play with sharecropper kids, who (it must be admitted) didn't always wear the cleanest of clothes and were very likely to have snot running out their noses. Mother was rather class-conscious. She considered sharecroppers to be well below us in social respectability.

My parents were quite proud of the fact that, while living on the economic edge, they were purchasing their own farm. In particular, the family kept a clean house and a neat yard—no abandoned cars, tires, old washers, or other "yard art" were permitted to gather around our place. In my mother's view, yard art of that kind signaled the presence of "white trash" to any and all passersby.

A water hole was conveniently located near the sharecropper's tin-roofed house. The creek that meandered through our farm was joined by another branch at the edge of the Lessman land. A man-made dirt and rock dam had been constructed to create a water hole. We could jump into the water from the limb of a nearby oak tree, or we could swing out over the water on a rope with an inflated inner tube tied to the end. As the tube reached the center of the water hole, we dropped in with a big splash.

The hole was not big enough or deep enough to swim in, but it was a great way to cool off on a hot August day when the temperature in the "bottom land" could reach 105 degrees Fahrenheit. The only caution was to keep an eye out for the ever-fearsome water moccasin.

The two creeks and the water hole teemed with minnows, tadpoles, and crayfish (we called them *crawfish*). Another great way to kill time was to catch minnows and tadpoles and transfer them to jars of water. Crawfish were more of a challenge. The larger ones had good-sized pinchers, and it wasn't too funny to have one hanging on to a thumb or finger. We were told that if a crawfish grabbed you with its claws, it wouldn't turn loose until it heard thunder! But we were brave young boys and were willing to take the risk.

If you can snatch a crawfish quickly between your thumb and index finger and hold it behind its front claws, it cannot pinch. This is the same principle as picking out a lobster from a tank of water. Lord only knows, as my good mother would say, how many crawfish I caught in my youth and brought to the house in Mason jars filled with water. Thinking back on this pleasure years later, I penned the following lines:

Winding Creeks

Creeks wind lazily throughout the land
With invitations for a bold an active mind.
Willows bow above the rain-drenched sand,
And teem with squirming life of every kind.

Narrow creeks form gentle banks for leaping;
Nifty water hazards guaranteed to please;
Shallow ones are great for knee-deep wading,
Tossing shoes aside along with books and keys.

Mighty crawfish forged in silent combats past
Peer out from under semi-buried stones.
When attacked they scurry with a mighty blast,
Swirling water into ochre-colored tones.

Mothers don't enjoy such creek-side joys,
Nor crawfish lurking in a makeshift rink,
Nor mud tracks left from feet of little boys,
Nor tadpoles swimming in the kitchen sink!

Between the ages of nine and fourteen, my favorite outdoor pastimes included bike riding, cut-throat games of marbles, "hunting" with slingshots, and stalking "big game" with a BB Gun. Playing catch with a soft ball was great fun but unfortunately required a second person. Occasionally my dad or brother would deign to join in; otherwise, I was left to bounce a rubber ball off a wall of the barn. That was good practice in trapping "grounders," but soon grew boring.

Indoors, my favorite pastime—other than reading—was building architectural marvels with *Tinker Toys* or *Lincoln Logs*. But most of all, I loved to spend hours perfecting "tricks" with a fifty-cent yo-yo—creating actions like "sleeping yo-yo," "walking the dog," "rocking the baby," "going around the world," or just sustaining a spin of the yo-yo at the end of its string for fifteen seconds or more.

Since Glenn was six years older than I, he had little interest in my games. He wasn't into playing marbles, so I often played that sport alone. Such practice prepared me to play "keepers" with the Styles boys. Donald and David were twins and lived about a half mile from our house. They were fierce competitors at marbles. We each won some and lost some, but in the end, each of us usually had about as many marbles at the end of a session as when we started. Most boys traded aggies, taws, and immies (shooter marbles) as frequently and as avidly as baseball cards or comic books.

Each day on the way to elementary school, I rode my bike past an automobile repair shop. The shop kept a pile of used inner tubes taken from all the tire-changing that was done in those days. When an inner tube was so worn that it could no longer feasibly be patched, it would be thrown out on a trash heap with old worthless tires. Those rubber inner tubes could be cut into strips and made into useful objects. One of the best uses for the rubber was to make slingshots.

There are two basic types of slingshots. One is the type that David used to slay Goliath. This type of slingshot is made of long leather cords and a pouch. A stone is placed in the pouch and the throwing arm rotates in a three-hundred-and-sixty-degree arc. At the proper moment in the arc, one of the cords is released, launching the stone toward the target. This is no easy feat and requires considerable practice.

A more "user-friendly" slingshot can be made with a Y-shaped branch from a tree, or a Y carved from a piece of pinewood. Two narrow strips of rubber are cut from an inner tube. These strips are cut eight to ten inches in length. One end of each rubber strip is attached with string to the top of each branch of the Y. At the other end of the rubber strips, a pouch made of leather is connected with good stout string. The best pouches are made from the tongues of old work shoes.

Using small stones, a good shooter could learn to hit a tin can from twenty-five or thirty feet away. A slingshot is a serious toy and can be a harmful weapon. Adults cautioned us never to shoot at another person. The best targets were glass bottles, dinner bells, or any object that made a clanging noise when hit—or anything that would shatter (windows in vacant houses, burned-out streetlights).

Strips of inner tube could also be used to make "rubber" pistols. The most primitive form called for two pieces of one-inch-by-one-inch wood strips cut to approximately nine inches and four inches in length and attached at a ninety-five-degree angle. A nail brad was hammered into the end of the longest piece, and a spring-action clothespin was attached to the shorter or handle piece. A strip of inner tube was cut four inches long and a half inch wide. A hole was pierced in one end, and the strip was hooked on to the nail brad. The other end was stretched back and clipped with the clothespin, which served as the trigger. Pressure applied to the clothespin released the strip of rubber, which then flew (hopefully) to its target.

Making objects of any sort was always fun. My dad was a handyman who believed he could make just about anything from wood, tin, rock, concrete, fiber, or bark. I tried to emulate him in this respect. On rainy days when I couldn't play outdoors, I spent hours in the woodshed using my dad's carpentry tools. I used his fold-up ruler and T-square to measure out pieces of scrap wood. I used his handsaw to trim off the excess. Plenty of nails of all sizes were available to be hammered into these scrap pieces. The danger was leaving a piece of wood lying about with the exposed point of a nail protruding from one side. A bare foot was inevitably going to find this nail.

When I came hobbling to the house with a nail in my foot, be it new or rusty, my mother quickly pulled it out, washed the hole with cold water, and poured a few drops of coal oil on the wound. No thought was given to tetanus. I was an adult before receiving an immunization. Apparently, the burn from the coal oil was enough remedy.

During ramblings in the Lessman's Woods south of our farm, I always kept a lookout for straight hickory saplings. They made excellent walking sticks, but even better, they could be used to make long plaited whips. The process required soaking an eight- or ten-foot sapling in water for several hours and then stripping the bark back in thirds from the small end to about eight inches from the larger end. The wood underneath was cut about six inches from the tip of the large end, leaving just enough wood for a handle. The three long strips were then plaited, and *voilà*, you had a whip. Unfortunately, such a whip didn't last very long. But so what? I had plenty of time to make another whip when the old one dried out or broke.

Hickory saplings could also be used to make archery bows. A very straight sapling was cu about four feet in length, the ends notched and strung with heavy twine. The bow had to be kept unstrung when not in use. Otherwise, it would soon lose its elasticity and remain curved. The difficulty lay in finding good material for arrows. If the arrow was not perfectly straight, it did not fly true. Bird or chicken feathers were glued to the notched end of the arrow to help create a more correct flight. Of course, if you wished to be a serious archer, you needed to purchase a bow and arrow set from the sporting goods section of a department store. Since this was a considerable financial outlay, the average farm kid in my day made his own equipment, regardless of the inefficiency of the product.

Southern craftsmen had a practical use for hickory saplings. When the seat of one of our cane-bottom chairs wore out, my dad used strips of hickory bark to reweave it. Such a seat would last for years, safely bearing the weight of the heaviest guest.

On a dull and boring day, some slight respite from youthful *ennui* could be had by catching flies.

Yes, I said catching house flies! Now, this sport really requires patience, fast reflexes, and an understanding of the flight patterns of flies. When a house fly sees an object coming toward it, the fly automatically leaps away on a horizontal path, not a vertical one. That's why it's so difficult to hit a fly with the hand. If you slap straight down, the fly will leap off at an angle—right, left, or forward—from the spot you are striking. The secret is to come at the fly sideways. As your hand sweeps toward the fly, the creature will leap away from the movement of your hand. If you have good reflexes, you can grab the fly in flight. Try it sometime. But do it when no one is around. It isn't good etiquette to catch houseflies in public. When folks are in the vicinity, use a flyswatter.

In my youth, kids whose parents weren't allergic to noise were permitted to run around the yard, and even through the house, firing off cap pistols. To my chagrin, my mother was one of those with low noise tolerance. She refused to buy a cap pistol or permit me to buy one for myself. However, when I was far enough away from the house, I could place a roll of caps on a rock and hit the dots of powder one by one with a hammer. The tiny bit of powder made a popping noise. Sparks flew. and a little puff of blue smoke rose up. It's hard to realize why that activity was particularly fun. I guess it was mainly for the noise.

From our front porch swing, I had a great view of the Bremen Road. It was dirt for the first few years, but then the road crews arrived, and the fun began.

I could watch the bulldozers and road graders for hours on end. When they weren't in action, I could emulate them with my little wind-up tractor.

March began a season of kite flying. For years, beginning at the age of eight, I made my own kites. The ribbing was very strong because I used the wooden strips that were sewn into the bottoms of cheap roll-up window shades. For the body of the kite, I used a heavy-grade, brown wrapping paper. This paper was more tear-resistant than the flimsy material used in the store-bought kites sold at Kuhn's Five & Dime in downtown Cullman.

I painted designs on my kites—stars and stripes, a big yellow sun, the face of the moon, an eagle, or a few stars. The tail of the kite was made from scrapes of cloth tied in knots. The tail served as a stabilizing weight; otherwise, the kite would quickly plunge to the ground in a strong breeze.

The larger the kite, the longer (or heavier) the tail had to be in order to maintain stability. Also, the stronger the wind, the longer the tail had to be. String wound in a roll could be purchased at Kuhn's Five & Dime. However, one roll was not long enough to permit a kite to sail very high in the sky. I usually bought three or more at a time, if I had enough money.

In order to handle this amount of string and avoid a messy tangle, I needed something to wind the string on. At first, I just used a short length of wood. My dad decided that this was not very satisfactory. To solve the problem, he built a little hand-cranked "wench" out of wood that kept the string from slipping off or tangling.

One spring when I was eleven years old, Woodrow Graham, our farm neighbor to the south, took a serious interest in my kites. Now, Woodrow was probably midthirties and apparently had never flown a kite, at least a homemade one. He wanted to see just how far my kite would fly. He went into town and bought several rolls of string. A couple of days later, with a strong and steady wind blowing from the southeast, we launched the kite and started adding string. We had enough tail on the kite to keep it stable and kept adding string. I was amazed how far into the sky the kite soared. Soon the kite was almost out of sight. The tug on the line became too much for me. It took Woodrow's muscles to keep the line from jerking loose.

The tension eventually became too great, and the string broke, and the kite sailed away. We were never able to find any remnant of it in the trees. It may have flown into the next county! To make matters worse, all our string was now stretched for a half mile or more across pastureland and into a swampy area. We could only salvage a small amount. Nevertheless, we were both satisfied with our little kite-flying experiment, even if we didn't prove any new law of physics as old Ben Franklin had done.

In the colder days of winter, even in the South, we had to find indoor activities. My parents weren't very interested in playing games, but I could occasionally talk them into Dominoes, Chinese checkers, or a card game like Rook or Old Maid. My dad was unbeatable at Dominoes and Chinese checkers, and when we played Old Maid, I always got caught with that pathetic-looking old gal. This limited my desire for that game.

Dad had several ideas for fun during long dark evenings before bedtime. He whittled out tops that spun wildly on the cold linoleum floor. He made Gee-Haw-Whimmy-Diddles that could keep a kid occupied for several minutes at a time. It was amazing what Dad could do with a long piece of string. He showed me how to create designs using my hands and fingers. These figures had names like "cat's cradle," "witch's broom," and "Jacob's ladder" all just using a loop of string and ten fingers. My favorite figure was the "crow's foot," because even I could make it.

Believe it or not, games can be created with a length of string and a large button. With the string looped through two holes of the button and tied off, the button can be twirled around three hundred and sixty degrees several times. This keeps the string taut. By pulling the two ends of the loop as though playing an accordion, the button twirls rapidly making a great humming noise. Another trick I learned was how to make the button "walk" across the floor. These were foretastes of tricks that could later be done with a yo-yo.

One of my great uncles was named Bud Widener, affectionately call *Budweiser*. Now, Uncle Bud was a passionate checkers player. He played with anybody who came to visit, young or old, male or female. Uncle Bud played checkers on his front porch, which allowed him to spit tobacco juice and watch the world go by. He and his opponents pulled up cane-bottom chairs to his checker board lying across an old wooden cracker barrel serving as a table.

When my ,other visited Uncle Bud's wife, her maternal aunt Minnie, I was inevitably coaxed into a game or two of checkers with Uncle Bud. I could never beat that gruff but jolly old man. However, over time and many defeats, I became a rather good checker player in my own right. The problem then shifted to finding someone willing to play me. My peer group thought the game was only for old people.

All the time-killing devices practiced during my preteen years paid off. I made it through the periods of solitude missing little of importance except social skills. The next major hurdle would be to find a way to read, paint, and write my way through the awkward, shy, and acne-scarred teenage years.

Saturday at the "Picture Show"

There never was a horse that couldn't be rode; there never was a cowboy that couldn't be thrown.

—Cowboy proverb

On Saturdays, during seasons when farm work was at a lull, my brother and I often walked into town to see a Western at the local "picture show." The nineteen-forties were super years for matinee movies. Over the decade, admission varied from a dime to a quarter. What a fantastic entertainment bargain when compared to today's cinema prices. Another nickel (later a dime) would get you a bag of hot buttered popcorn, and five more cents a soft drink. These matinees were the premiere entertainment in pretelevision days. Boys never seemed to tire of the black-and-white Westerns starring Hollywood cowboys like Tom Mix, Roy Rogers, Gene Autry, Hopalong Cassidy, and the Lone Ranger.

Westerns were overt morality plays. Good struggled against evil—black hats clashed with white hats, and the white hats managed to win in the end. The clear message: *Do the right thing. Those who do wrong always lose.* No subtlety here. No gray area. No relativism. We received civics lessons while being entertained.

Gene Autry was a favorite Western star of that era. He was the singing cowboy, with his loyal horse Champion and his outrageous sidekick, Pat Buttram. Pat was a native Alabamian, so we could clearly identify with his drawn-out speech patterns. Not only did Gene Autry sing many well-known Western tunes, but he introduced the ever-popular Christmas tune "Rudolph the Red Nosed Reindeer." Gene was a clean-cut cowboy. He didn't smoke, he didn't cuss, he didn't chew tobacco, and he was always a perfect gentleman around the ladies.

Less clean-cut, but one of the most entertaining characters in all the Westerns was George "Gabby" Hayes. At various times, Gabby served as the foil for Hopalong Cassidy (William Boyd), Roy Rogers, and Gene Autry. Gabby came through the ranks of Vaudeville and was a master of slapstick and backwoods humor. In the movies, Gabby displayed a wild, unkempt beard and hair. He chewed tobacco and frequently spat a squirt on the ground or in the general direction of a brass spittoon. Some of the liquid always managed to roll down the corners of his mouth and onto his unkempt beard. His clothes looked like he had slept in them for weeks.

When Gabby cussed, it seemed funny and harmless. He didn't use four-letter words, or words with sexual innuendoes, or words that took the Lord's name in vain. His cuss words were original with him, or else imitations of the language of Western trappers who lived alone and talked to themselves the majority of the time. Gabby's words were colorful euphemisms—*tarnation, garchdarn, dadburn, consarn, heckfire.* There was something quite likeable about Gabby's character. His lack of conformity, his devil-may-care attitude, and his disregard for cleanliness made him attractive to most boys.

The "King of the Cowboys," Roy Rogers, was the type we all wanted to emulate. Before beginning his movie career, Roy had been a member of the singing group *Sons of the Pioneers*, perhaps the most popular group in the history of western-style music. Roy's wife, Dale Evans, had roles in his movies and sang music that she herself wrote. One of her big hits was "The Bible Tells Me So." Roy and Dale adopted several orphan children over the years and eventually came to epitomize the "Christian couple" for many viewers. Yet Roy could easily whip the desperados and outlaws he faced in his movies. He could always count on the aid of his dog, Bullet, his horse Trigger, and his comical sidekick, Pat Brady, also a professional singer and a former member of the *Sons of the Pioneers*.

Roy was okay, but I personally preferred the Lone Ranger, not only in the movies but on the radio. In the late forties, I listened to *The Lone Ranger Show* each week as soon as my chores were completed. I sat close to the radio so that I could understand the dialog above the static and poor reception. Keeping the dial on the station was a bit of a problem because the tuning string didn't have sufficient tension. Fortunately, that problem is unknown in the digital age.

The Lone Ranger's sidekick, the faithful Tonto, was a fascinating character. His broken but rather dignified English gave the impression of authenticity. Of course, we realized later that Tonto's speech was a caricature and demeaning to Native Americans. Consider a few lines of *simulated* dialogue between the Lone Ranger and Tonto:

Lone Ranger: Saddle up. We ride east.

Tonto: *Why we go this way, Kemo-sabe?*

Lone Ranger: The sheriff says a range war is breaking out over in the Badlands.

Later the two men see a dust clouds in the distance.

Tonto: *Plenty trouble ahead, Kemo-sabe.*

Lone Ranger: Yes, through my binoculars I see a dozen men riding this way with weapons drawn.

Tonto: *That plenty bad! What we do now, Kemo-sabe?*

Later, after capturing and taking the gang to jail, Tonto assures the Sheriff.

Tonto: *Me tell truth.* Pointing to a suspect. *Him leader of gang.*

Naturally we didn't worry about authenticity or "political correctness" in our youth. We innocently flocked to Western movies to be entertained. We could predict most of what would happen in every show. It was very comforting to know that *right* would ultimately defeat *evil.*

After their triumphs, Western heroes rode off into the sunset, either alone or with their "girl," a pure and diffident beauty. This was great symbolism. However, the Lone Ranger finished every show by jumping on his horse and belting out, "*Hi-Yo, Silver, awaaaayyy!*" No girl for him, at least as far as we could tell.

For many Westerns, Hollywood recruited country music singers to play lead roles. We moviegoers didn't see real, sweaty, working cowboys. Roy, Gene, and Hopalong were always spotlessly clean—clothes and body. They were out to fight for justice and the good, but they did not herd or brand cattle. Roy and Gene packed fine-looking guitars, but working cowboy did not have the luxury of taking such instruments on the trail. At best, the real-life cowboy packed a small harmonica while out searching for stray steers or mending fences.

However, seeing a cowboy strumming on a beautiful guitar didn't seem unrealistic to us kids. Living in the Southeast, I knew absolutely nothing about the West or about the life of a true cowboy. My friends and I knew only what we were seeing on the silver screen or hearing over the radio waves. We were witness to the construction of a myth but were oblivious to it.

The music of the Hollywood cowboys was mostly the music that issued from the Western lifestyle. The songs were about following the trail, rounding up cattle, and branding little doggies. The music had little in common with country-western music we hear today. Present-day country-western music is mostly composed of sad songs about drinking in the bar, depression over lost love, and telling the story to whomever will listen (a somebody-do-ne-somebody-wrong song).

If you lived through the cowboy music era (and it's not totally dead today for some *aficionados*), you will perhaps remember and maybe still hum a few bars of some of the old classic cowboy songs: "Tumbling Tumble Weed," "Ghost Riders in the Sky," "The Last Roundup," "Streets of Laredo."

In the nineteen forties, Westerns included worthy civic icons such as the schoolhouse and the school "*marm*" who encouraged education as a path to success. Hollywood sets often included a church with a kindly male pastor (usually Protestant) who encouraged the bad guys to reform their ways and seek redemption. The jail, the purgatory between heaven and hell, was the place where a person had the opportunity to confess and begin a path toward reform. Sometimes the bad guy saw the "light" (or was it the "white") and reformed and left the jail a new man. Otherwise, he was hanged and expedited to boot hill—the graveyard—where the unredeemed were buried. This was the dead end, literally and figuratively. This was hell.

Women had cameo roles in these morality plays. Most were "good" women (even if they ran a saloon, and even if they seemed in charge of activities that took place upstairs—of which we had no real inkling). For us, the upstairs of these saloons contained clean, comfortable rental rooms where tired and dusty cowboys could obtain a good hot bath after long days on the trail, perhaps even an innocent back scrub with a long-handled brush by one of the pretty women of the establishment. Just imagine the disconnect that exists between the historical role of women in the West who ran saloons and the idealized and wholesome image of a Miss Kitty in the long-running TV drama, *Gunsmoke*.

All the heroes, from Tom Mix to Hopalong Cassidy, from the Lone Ranger to John Wayne, were stereotypes. They were patient, strong, and fought for justice, even when they had to circumvent the law. They helped the weak, were chivalrous toward women, and respected the elderly. Indeed, these cowboy heroes had all the qualities it was hoped we kids would emulate.

The good guys in the old Westerns never provoked violence, either fisticuffs or gun slinging. The bad guys always started the trouble. And when the fighting began, the good guys never fought dirty. No poking out eyes, no kicking the groin or the shins, no hitting from behind. They never took advantage of an opponent who was down. They never drew their six-shooter first or shot an antagonist who was unarmed. The good guys settled their fights with well-place punches or well-placed bullets. However, the moviegoer never saw blood and never witnessed a horrible death. The bad guy always had the grace to die quietly and bloodlessly.

As a consequence, when we played *Cowboys and Indians* or *Cowboys and Rustlers*, we could imitate the shooting scenes pretty much to a tee. If we were "shot," we would grab our stomach and fall down on the ground and play dead—that is, if we were playing according to the rules, which so often we didn't, causing many arguments.

"I shot you."

"No, you didn't, I shot you."

"No, you didn't, I shot first. You're dead."

"No, *you're* dead."

More time was spent arguing about who did what to whom than in playing the game.

I once talked to some Navaho men living near Canyon de Chelly in Arizona about their childhood games. They admitted to playing *Cowboys and Indians*, too. However, according to them, none of the little Navaho boys wanted to play the part of Indians. Everybody wanted to be the white cowboy or the white cavalry hero. I use the term "white hero" because we almost never saw black heroes on the silver screen. At that time, we didn't notice that we saw few, if any, blacks in these movies. We weren't expecting any. We didn't know that in real life, many of the cowboys of the nineteenth century were black, nor had we ever heard of the black buffalo soldiers. We were innocent about ethnicity, and we were kept in the dark by Hollywood and by society in general.

Some of the Western heroes developed their own clubs and created codes of conduct. Initiates into these clubs swore to aid the weak and the sick and to be kind to all God's creatures. The young members learned to be courteous to their elders, to respect the laws and institutions of the nation, to love the flag of the United States of America, to always be truthful and fair, to avoid bad habits such as cursing, smoking, and mistreating animals, to work hard at their school studies, to be clean and neat in their dress.

An interesting thing about the oaths and creeds disseminated by the Hopalong Cassidy's *Troopers Club* and the *National Lone Ranger Council of Honor* and Gene Autry's *Cowboy Code of Ethics*—they all seemed a good bit like the Motto of the *Boy Scouts of American*: *"Be prepared"* and the oath that I recited dozens and dozens of times: *"On my honor I will do my best to do my duty to God and my country, and to obey the Scout Law; to help other people at all times; to keep myself physically strong, mentally awake, and morally straight."*

The Boy Scout Law requires that boys be *"trustworthy, loyal, helpful, friendly, courteous, kind, obedient, cheerful, thrifty, brave, clean, and reverent."* None of us lived up to these standards—either to the Cowboy Codes or the Boy Scout oaths and laws. However, we knew that these were honorable criteria for social behavior. We knew that we should try to live by these standards. We were reminded of them every time we went to a dime matinee, when we were present at the weekly Boy Scout meetings, and when we attended Sunday school and church. The message was constantly before us. Each morning in elementary school, we were again reminded of our relationship to our country and to a higher power. The school day opened with a prayer and was followed with the Pledge of Allegiance to the flag.

Most of us had some sort of religious training and had some notions of our Judeo-Christian culture. I doubt if we were outwardly as clean as today's youth, but we kept our mouths cleaner for fear of the ubiquitous bar of soap with which we were threatened by both parents and teachers. Even among our peers, we were less prone to use dirty words on a constant basis.

While Westerns were everyone's favorite movies, most boys I knew wouldn't think of missing a movie about *Tarzan the Ape Man*, the *Three Stooges*, *Abbott and Costello*, and the *Bowery Boys*. We always sat through the newsreels projected in theaters before the feature films. During WWII, we witnessed real-life battle scenes from the Pacific and European fronts. We cheered for the Yanks and hissed at the "Japs" and the Nazis.

On the walk to the movie theater, some of my friends and I passed a residence with a turret-like room with a conical roof. On the summit of the cone, a metal pole with a sharp, pointed tip reached another three feet in the air. We decided that it would be "neat" if Hitler or Tojo were dropped from and airplane and landed butt-first on that sharp pole. Such a gruesome and grotesque image shows to what extent our "innocent" heads had become filled with hatred for the unknown enemy.

Saturday matinees gave us an added bonus of *Looney Tunes!* We could laugh at the antics of *Tom and Jerry, Bugs Bunny, Porky Pig, Elmer Fudd,* the *Road Runner, Tweety Bird and Sylvester the Cat,* and *Donald Duck* and his nephews. The voices of these animal critters were very amusing. We often tried to imitate the speech patterns. "*Ehhh, what's up, Doc?*" replaced "What are you doing?" Then there was: "*I tawt I taw a putty cat.*" We learned to whine like Elmer and squawk like Donald. *The Looney Tunes* always ended with "*Th-th-th-that's all folks!*" and we clapped and cheered with delight. We didn't know and didn't care that a chap named Mel Blanc was behind many of those great voices.

These comic interludes offered up a constant spate of simulated violence or the threat of violence, but none of the characters in the cartoons were ever permanently hurt. No matter how far over a cliff they fell, or how crushing a blow they received with a five-hundred-pound weight, they always popped right back up, waiting for more.

For refreshments while at the movies, we bought "cold drinks" (soda pop) for ten cents a cup and a bag of popcorn for another five or ten cents. My brother and I usual had a couple of dimes each that our parents had given us or that we had earned in some way. But we always needed a few more cents in order to buy our drinks and popcorn.

We walked the mile and a half to the movie theater, and along the way, we stopped at the home of my brother's Grandpa Morgan. When Jerry Morgan was alive, he would give Glenn the loose change in his pocket. After his death, "Miss Nolly" (her real name was a mystery to me—but it may have been Magnolia) would give us a dime or a quarter. She was Grandpa Morgan's second wife. If for some reason Miss Nolly wasn't at home, Glenn could count on an aunt who lived close by and whom he called "Aunt Keneely," which was probably short for Cornelia.

When the movie ended, if either of us had an extra few cents, we would make a beeline to the candy counter at Kreitleins. *M&M's* hit the market in the midforties, along with *Tootsie Rolls* and *Life Savers*. These candies made it easy to share equitably.

Glenn had undiagnosed learning disabilities and never finished high school. In 1950, he left home to make his fortune in the automotive factories in Flint, Michigan. Soon afterward, *3D movies* made their appearance. What a fad! Barely lasting two years, but during that time movie houses were rocked with shouts and screams. Every B grade movie made for 3-D had an inordinate share of arrows, lances, spears, and other projectiles that came whistling over our heads as we ducked down behind the seat in front of us. No one could figure how this illusion was created, but after a while, the novelty wore off and the whole thing began to seem rather silly. We were becoming more and more difficult to entertain.

Special effects in the forties and fifties were very primitive in comparison with those that had become standard fare by the 1990s. Now our eyes and ears are unable to absorb the flashes, the flying objects, the animation, the noise, the kaleidoscope of colors that are part and parcel of twenty-first century motion pictures. These new pyrotechnics and spectacular animation techniques make the old Westerns seem mighty quaint...partner! Those wonderful old black-and-white movies are disparaged today as nothing but "oaters." But as Gabby Hayes would say, "I'll be dadburned if I care! I still like 'em!"

Where the Warriors Roamed

My grandfather is the fire; my
grandmother is the wind.
The earth is my mother. The
Great Spirit is my father.

—Native American verse

It is easy to pretend that the history of our great land did not begin with the settlement by Europeans in the 1600s. Like many farm young-sters, I found hard evidence of prior human existence each time the soil was turned in the spring. Along with a new set of rocks came flint arrowheads and small scraping tools. Walking along behind a turning plow, keeping a sharp eye, I spotted a few flints each year. I stored them all in an old cigar box.

I felt a special pleasure when I found a finely knapped arrowhead. In my imagination, this primitive craftsmanship was a link to a more exciting age. The flint belonged to a real person who lived perhaps hundreds of years before. Each had a story to tell if we only could learn it. Why had that arrowhead been abandoned? Had the flint pierced an animal that, not being killed, had run away, carrying the point along with it? Was this flint from an arrow that missed its target and was lost to the hunter?

Former President Jimmy Carter expressed these feeling in his little poem titled *The History of a Point.*

> Walking through a fallow field,
> I found an arrowhead
> More lovely than I'd ever seen,
> Upon an earthen pedestal
> Not packed by rain
> But sheltered by the point itself.
> *Always a Reckoning*

Carter continues by wondering if the point had hung around the neck of a chief's son, or if it had lodged in an escaped deer or if it had been the cause of death of a brave warrior. He ends the poem by wondering if the artist—the flint-knapper—had thought the work so perfect that he requested the point be buried with him when he died.

Longtime residents in our neighborhood reported that once a spring of water flowed on our land, but that earth had collapsed upon it. In years past, it was believed that Native American hunters stalked game in the early morning hours when animals came to this spring to drink. Several tribes used a northwest to southeast path that passed very close to the city of Cullman and very near our farm.

The trail was called the High Town Path and was used by Choctaw, Creek, Koasati, Alabama, and Chickasaw. Even some Cherokee hunters may have roamed into this area far from their villages as game became less plentiful. No more than ten miles to the south of our farm another trail passed roughly north-south through the county. That trail was the called the Black Warrior Path and was in close conjunction with the Black Warrior River, which has four forks that flow through Cullman County.

The territory that eventually became the new Cullman County was within the hunting grounds of the Koasati and the Alabama tribes who hunted and fished in the area. However, no permanent settlements were established in this area that is now Cullman County.

In the seventh grade, we studied Alabama history. The first few pages of our textbook dealt with the natives. The text had pictures that were not very flattering of the first American. The text narrated a myth concerning the naming of the state of Alabama. According to this myth, a tribe of nomadic Indians were traveling slowly through Alabama with their families and domestic animals. Each evening, the chief drove a spear upright into the soil. The next morning the tribe would set out in whichever direction the handle of the spear was leaning.

One day the spear remained totally upright. The chief proclaimed, "*A-la-ba-ma*!" which we were told meant "*Here we stay.*" Much later I discovered that scholars are not sure of the precise meaning of the tribal name *Alabama*. Some scholars agree that it may have meant "to camp." Others think the word or words may have meant "wild grass." So much for the nice myth!

Regardless of myth, a tribe that called itself Alabama (or something phonetically close) settled in the very center of the current state baring that name. This tribe had no rigid boundaries. Their northern territory appears to have been roughly the confluence of the Mulberry Fork of the Black Warrior River. The western boundary was the Black Warrior and the eastern boundary was the Tallapoosa River. Natives of the Alabama tribe erected four principal villages in the area, which now forms Autauga, Dallas, and Montgomery counties. In the seventeenth century, the tribe was observed as far south as the confluence of the Tombigbee and the Alabama Rivers by French and Spanish explorers.

According to folklore, every true Southerner can claim some Native American blood. In my case, oral history lends support. One of my paternal great grandmothers was Florida Henrietta Qualls. According to family lore, Florida was half Cherokee through her mother. Her father, a white pioneer in Eastern Tennessee, lived with a Cherokee woman for many years. Unfortunately, family tradition does not reveal the name of Florida's mother.

A maternal ancestor, Mary Hill, married Sherrill Smith Sr. Mary's father, according to family lore, was an escapee from the trail of tears who assumed white men's ways and gave himself a white man's name—

Micah Hill. If all this is indeed fact, then one of my sixteen great-great-grandfathers was a full-blooded Cherokee. If both these traditions are correct, and nothing has been discovered to dispute them, two of my eight great-grandmothers were full-blooded Cherokee.

Having nostalgia for the age of the *Noble Savage* and a wistful image of the Neolithic Age of simplicity, I welcome a few drops of Native American blood. Those so-called primitives had some highly prized virtues. They were at peace with nature (if not always with other tribes) and treated all forms of life with respect, even their enemies. They exhibited great discipline; they were brave in the face of danger, and they knew how to bear both pain and sorrow. Perhaps most importantly, they knew how to die with grace and dignity.

Making the transition from New Stone Age lifestyle to the level of European settlers was a formidable challenge for the natives; nevertheless, the Cherokee and other "civilized" tribes would have eventually blended into the fabric of American life if given some level of autonomy. Unfortunately, the white man did not wait to see if such a relationship could work. The natives were forcibly removed to the western lands. Only a hardy few hid in the depth of the wilds to resurface later.

The crushing of the indigenous peoples occurred elsewhere in the Americas. Once I was visiting a family farm in Belize located beside a Mayan *cenote* (water-retention pond) north of Belize City.

I walked across a plowed field and discovered a site used by a Mayan flint-knapper. Literally thousands of shards were lying in a pile. I kicked through the pile with my foot. In a moment or two, I found several imperfect ax heads that the knapper had obviously discarded as unworthy of his art. This site was probably no more than a hundred and fifty years old. Someone sat and worked at this place about the time the British seized the land to cut down and haul away the teak, mahogany and *zirakota* trees. Subtle and not-so-subtle exploitation of the present-day Maya, Alabama, Cherokee, Navaho, Miccosukee, and other tribal remnants continues even into the twenty-first century.

My wife and I, along with our grandchildren, once took a boat tour of Lake Lure in Western North Carolina. Our guide was a Cherokee. In a very eloquent and poignant manner, he told us the story of the rape of the sacred land beneath the waters of the lake. I was so moved that I wrote the following verses that evening.

Sequasicha

Sequasicha—a land of restful peace,
Stretched along Broad River's wandering crease,
Encircled all around by regal hills,
Renowned for herbs and artful, healing skills.

Sculpted into graphic shapes by glacial creep;
Here lies a princess deep in endless sleep.

THE VIEW FROM BRINDLEY MOUNTAIN

Yonder, poised unyielding from an era marred,
A monumental buffalo has charged.

O, land Great Spirit gave the Cherokee;
A place of holy mounds and mystic glee,
Reshaped in modern times by men of greed,
Scarred deep from rush for deadly golden seed,

Your lure is not yet lost; your present case
Invites a pause from modern frantic pace;
A call to recreate the peace-filled climes—
A Neolithic dream of former times.

Die Deutsche Kolonie

Each city, town and minor
crossroads has a story to tell,
though many are buried in the mists of time.

T he origins of Cullman, Alabama, are unique and historically significant. It's a story about the fulfillment of an American dream. The history books include many such stories, but I doubt if readers will have read much about this particular one. As a child growing up, I heard only a few vague sketches. It was not until preparations were being made for the city's centennial celebrations that I learned the entire background. The story starts in Bavaria, Germany, in the middle of the nineteenth century. A rebellious young man fought the tide of Germany unification that was being forced on the various principalities by Prussian strongman rule.

A couple of decades earlier a handful of hardy European pioneers had already drifted into the wilderness of north-central Alabama south of the Tennessee River. The area on which the town of Cullman would eventually be established was given the name Brindley Mountain by a sturdy pioneer named Thomas Pace

Brindley. Calling this low-lying plateau a mountain is a bit of an exaggeration. However, the region is located at the westernmost point of a long ridge called Sand Mountain, which in turn is one of the southernmost ridges of the Appalachian chain. The elevation at the highest point on the western slope of Sand Mountain is slightly above 1,100 feet. Not likely to impress a mountain climber.

The town of Cullman is located on the western downslope of Brindley Mountain and is slightly less than nine hundred feet at its highest. Nevertheless, the town is reputed to sit at the highest point on the Louisville and Nashville Railroad line between Louisville, Kentucky, and Mobile, Alabama. As a child riding into town from any direction, I was vaguely aware that we were climbing ever so slightly. The most evidence came when we approached Cullman from the north on US Highway 31. When we arrived about three miles north of the city limits, the spires of Sacred Heart Church stood out in prominent relief. It appeared the church was on a hill. A more spectacular descent from Brindley Mountain occurs as one drives northwest from the town of Arab. In this area, several businesses and churches sport the name Brindlee (a variation on the spelling).

The laying of railroad track through the relative wilderness of eastern Winston County played a role in the development of the communities on Brindley Mountain. However, the most important factor in the town's creation was the political struggles in Bavaria, Germany. The Prussians under the

Kaiser and his political and military leader, Otto von Bismarck, were forcing the unification of hundreds of little principalities that composed the long-existing German Empire (the so-called Holy Germanic Roman Empire) begun by Charlemagne at the dawn of the ninth century.

The Bavarians did not take kindly to Bismarck's forced unity. Some of the nobles and merchants launched a rebellion in 1855. One of the men who became heavily involved in this rebellion was the youthful Johann Gottfried Cullmann. He envisioned an independent Bavaria. For his pains, Cullmann was forced to flee his homeland. He left his wife and children in Bavaria and came to the United States, where he spent time in the highly Germanized town of Cincinnati, Ohio.

Although a well-educated engineer, Johann Cullmann worked for a time as a clerk and bookbinder in a Cincinnati bookstore. Little by little, he formulated a plan to create a "Deutsche Kolonie" in the US to be a haven for immigrants from Germany. He searched west of the Mississippi River for suitable land, but was concerned about hostile natives and severe weather in the Western Territories. Cullmann eventually read about large swaths of uninhabited land available in the South. At some point, he met a former governor of Alabama, Robert Miller Patton, who was promoting land development in northwest Alabama near the small town of Florence.

In 1871, Cullmann took a boat ride down the Ohio River to Paducah, Kentucky, and then up the

Tennessee River to Florence. Cullmann debarked at Florence and began to explore the land in north Alabama on horseback. He tried to buy property in the St. Florian area, but was met with hostility from the settlers who were suspicious of foreigners.

This big man with the funny German accent could not gain the trust of the Southerners whom he approached about funding his dream of a colony for European immigrants. The South was still in the throes of depression, both psychological and economic, brought about by the Civil War and the so-called Reconstruction, which was little more than exploitation by unscrupulous entrepreneurs (carpetbaggers and scalawags to use the vocabulary of the times).

Cullmann had a stroke of good fortune when former governor Patton introduced him to Louis Fink, a land agent, and later vice president, for the Louisville and Nashville railroad. The L&N had just completed laying tracks from Decatur to Tuscaloosa and sought development of the wilderness on either side of the tracks which would make the company more profitable.

This land was relatively uninhabited. Most of the Native Americans had been removed or had pulled back into remote areas and were trying to assimilate as much as possible into the white man's world. The land in question lay within areas comprising portions of the "Great State of Winston" and portions of Walker and Blount Counties. (If you want an interesting story, read some of the history of the *Great State of Winston*, an area that ceded from both the North and South during the Civil War.)

Johann Cullmann's dream of land in the South bucked the prevailing movement of peoples west to Texas, Colorado, Kansas, and California, but fit nicely into the needs of the railroad company. Consequently, officials granted Cullmann the title of colonel and gave him authority to act in their stead to sell the land. Soon Cullmann had options on 349,000 acres.

For his part of the agreement, Cullmann began recruiting settlers. He kept the proceeds of the sales, but he had to bear all the costs for recruitment including advertisement in the US and European newspapers as well as the costs of travel for settlers who needed financial assistance. Col. Cullmann advertised his dream in the *Cincinnati Enquirer* and in the *Louisville Courier Journal*, as well as in the *Chicago Tribune* and other midwestern newspapers. He included announcements in newspapers in New York and Boston. In addition, he advertised heavily in Germany cities.

In 1873, the first group of German emigrants arrived in the wilderness that would become Cullman County. The first year the "kolonie" consisted of only five families, but, thanks to the diligence of Johann, the following year, one hundred and twenty-three families had settled. Among these early families were names such as Dinkelbert, Stiefelmeyer, Richter, Kreitleins, Engelhart, Hartung, Schwerke, Brueninger, Klein, Burkhardt, Kleindienst, and

Quattelbaum. A walk through the Cullman City Cemetery further illustrates the town's German heritage. As many as two-thirds of the tombstones in the older sections of the cemetery bear German names: Ziegler, Peinhardt, Teichmiller, Feiertag, von Gerichten, von Lobstein, and Higginbotham. However, not all the early settlers in the colony had German roots. Irish, Scots, and English names appear as well. These include Sapp, Fuller, McAdory, Daves, Tucker, MacIntepe, Haynes. McMinn, Mitchel, Ratliff, Ragsdale, and Morgan.

Less than a decade after the founding of the County of Cullman, one of my great-grandfathers, Judson Scruggs, arrived from South Carolina with his family and settled on a homestead about a mile from Cullman County's northern line (about fifteen miles from the fledging town of Cullman). My three additional pairs of great-grandparents were already living in Morgan County and soon began purchasing supplies from merchants in the new town of Cullman.

By 1875, Colonel Cullmann's recruitment program was so successful that 1,500 residents lived in or near the new town. This was in the main due to the low cost of property. An acre of land averaged less than five dollars. Most folks purchased options for one hundred and sixty acres, which could be had for approximately six hundred dollars. Of course, that amount represented a small fortune to many of these settlers, but with their industriousness, many were able to pay off their loan within a few years.

These early pioneers begin by logging the forest and building cabins. In a short time, after a sawmill had been established, they could build more comfortable clapboard houses. Soon the merchant class began to build two-story frame dwellings for themselves. On the lower floor, they conducted business and on the upper floor they had their living quarters. True to their Bavarian heritage, most of these houses were constructed in what is called the gingerbread style. Around the porches, balconies, and eaves, carpenters carved lacy patterns, which gave the houses a frilly look.

Trouble developed between the new immigrants and the squatters who had come into the area with no legal right to the property they occupied. The squatters resented these foreigners who came to settle the land, immigrants who couldn't even speak English. The resentment of one squatter was so strong he tried to assassinate Colonel Cullmann with a Bowie knife. The attack was unsuccessful, but it left Cullmann with a huge scar on the right side of his face.

By 1877, the new town's population, combined with adjoining settlers, was sufficient to warrant incorporation and the creation of a separate county. The legalities moved at a very rapid pace, and in late 1877, a county was created out of portions of Winston, Blount, Walker, and Morgan counties.

The newly formed county looked like a triangle, with the hypotenuse being the Mulberry Fork of the Black Warrior River, which flows southwest into the main Black Warrior River at the southwestern corner of the county. The town of Cullman was chosen to be the county seat and the first courthouse was erected in 1878.

A German language newspaper was printed for many years. Several churches had worship services in German. The German language was taught in the schools. By the beginning of the twentieth century, as non German-speaking settlers moved into the county, the merchants in Cullman realized they had to learn English in order to serve their customers if they wanted to make money—and certainly they wanted to do that. Merchants began to use English when needed, albeit with an accent.

When I was born, sixty years after the formation of the county, the German language could still be heard, especially among farm families. They also peppered their English with German intonations, transliterated idioms and created a curious mixture of the two tongues. This made for some very colorful speech patterns, which my dad enjoyed trying to imitate: "*Ja, I to town am goink,*" and " *Eh, vat now?*" and "*Velkomen in our haus.*"

One of the most important legacies of Colonel Cullmann was the layout of the town. He insisted on a grid of rectangular blocks. Avenues paralleled the rail tracks, running slightly northwest to southeast and were called First Avenue East and First Avenue West. Then second, third, fourth, and so on were added east and west. However, the streets, running southwest to northeast began with First at the upper (north) end of town and followed in sequence down to the south. Later, streets to the north of First were given names such as Clark and Arnold rather than numbers.

Colonel Cullmann also insisted that each street or avenue be wide enough to accommodate four teams of horses traveling abreast (according to Stanley Johnson, the great-great-nephew of Colonel Cullmann). All the streets in the town center are at least one hundred feet in width. This created a problem in the early days before paving. When it rained heavily, the streets were rivers of water and mud.

As paving became feasible and popular, the cost for such wide streets was almost prohibitive. Originally only fifty feet in the center of the street were paved. However, by the second half of the twentieth century, and the increase in traffic, city officials were glad for Colonel Cullmann's foresight, and drivers were grateful for the easy pull-in parking spaces. No one needed to learn to park parallel. Eventually the original two lanes were easily converted to four lanes.

For the remainder of his life, Johann Cullmann continued to recruit emigrants. Many settlers arrived from other parts of the US. Unfortunately, Colonel Cullmann never received the kind of recognition he deserved for singlehandedly bringing more emigrants to the US to seek the good life than perhaps any other individual. When Johann Cullmann died in 1895, he was buried near the site that had been his recruitment office. His grave and marker are near the middle of the current city cemetery.

Eventually US Highway 31, a major artery for north-south traffic from Michigan to Florida, ran straight through the center of Cullman. This afforded the town a bit of recognition by the middle of the twentieth century. However, Cullman never flourished economically and industrially in the manner of its larger neighbors, Birmingham and Huntsville.

In the twenty-first century, the town remains dependent on local agriculture. Indeed, the county has the highest agricultural production per capita of any county in the State of Alabama. Cullman County is also one of the sixty counties in the US with the largest agricultural production in terms of dollars.

One of the early pioneer families had an impact on everyone who lived in Cullman in the first half of the twentieth century. A young man born in Velden, Bavaria, named Gottlieb Hartung married one of Col. Cullmann's nieces in 1878, and twelve years later, the couple emigrated to the new town of Cullman. Their son, Dr. Philip "Phil" Hartung, began the *People's Drug Store* in the early part of the twentieth century and operated it from 1915 to 1955.

In the days before the expansion of large chain drug companies, just about everyone shopped at Dr. Phil's place. The store became a central part of downtown life, with its soda shop and pharmacy. Dr. Phil was a major civic force and a stalwart in the First Christian Church (Disciples of Christ), which he helped to form and to nurture.

I suppose every locale has a lovers' story, and Cullman is no different. One of Dr. Phillip Hartung's sisters was named Minnie. At the turn of the century, Minnie became engaged to Reverend Lenk, the young pastor of the St. John's Evangelical and Reformed Church. Unfortunately, Minnie fell ill with malaria in 1901 and died from the disease. Reverend Lenk could not overcome his grief. One October day, he was found lying across her grave, dead from a self-inflected gunshot wound. He and Minnie are buried side by side in the Cullman City Cemetery. Their marker reads "*En Tode Verient*" (In Death United).

German culture in Cullman was impacted by the First World War. During and after that conflict, pride in the culture was dampened significantly. Over the next two decades of economic upheaval and rumors of German saber-rattling, celebrating the culture of Bavaria gradually became muted. The *coup de grace* came with the Nazi invasion of Poland, although all-out war in Europe did not begin until November 2, 1939, just a couple of weeks before my second birthday. This new conflict sounded the death knell to open use of German on the streets and shops of Cullman. The only time the German language could be detected was if you approached a home in the summer when the windows were open. You might then hear a few syllables before your presence became known. After that, only English was spoken. Even as a youngster, however, I could detect a slight accent among some of the elderly citizens that I couldn't describe or explain.

The US became fully engaged in WWII, following the Japanese attack on Pearl Harbor on the seventh of December 1941. Three weeks before this attack, I had my fourth birthday. By war's end, I would be a few weeks from age eight and becoming conscious of the greater world beyond my little cocoon.

Some Anglos may have been a bit suspicious of their German neighbors; however, for the most part, no one thought that these second- and third-generation folk were anything but patriotic Americans. Their young men were drafted or joined the services and fought and died like every group of Americans (except, unfortunately, the Japanese Americans who were interned).

Cullman suffered many military casualties during WWII. From a seat on our back porch or from my swing hanging from a limb of a plum tree, I could watch the military funerals occurring some two to three hundred yards from our farm. As the war progressed, more and more funerals for servicemen were conducted. What a moving spectacle for a young boy. First, I heard the mournful sound of taps. This was followed by the gruff voice of the squad leader belting out the signals "*Present arms. Read! Aim! Fire!*" With each command to fire, I heard a very sharp *crack*. Other gruff commands followed as the soldiers slapped their rifles and made rapid and graceful movements.

Finally, with rifles on their shoulder, the squad marched stiffly away. In a day or two, this drama would begin again. I was impressed with the way the US flag was folded and given to a person in the group sitting in a chair near the grave, dressed in black.

Men and women in uniform were visible everywhere you went. Uncles, cousins, and neighbors were fighting overseas. One uncle, Captain Cephas Smith, wrote a letter to me—the first letter I ever received. It was addressed to *Master Eugene* and was sent from Burma. I had no real notion of where this Burma was, just that it was "somewhere overseas." Captain Cephas counseled me to be a good boy and to help my mother with the chores. I was very proud of that letter and kept it for many years.

The name Cephas seemed unusual to me. I didn't know of anyone else with that name. I wondered how and why my grandparents chose it. Later, in a Sunday school class, the answer was revealed. The name Cephas is the Aramaic equivalent for Peter, the apostle. Only one other of Will and Mattie Smith's fifteen children was given a biblical name; the second oldest son was named Noah.

Many memories of Cullman during the war years remain vivid; for example, the ration book, with its little colored coupons. Every family, rich or poor, received these booklets. Inside the tan cover were blue coupons that entitled the bearer to buy foods that were in short supply: sugar, butter, and coffee, for example. Other colored coupons were for gasoline and tires. Since we didn't own a car, my mother traded gasoline and tire coupons for sugar and coffee coupons. Dad was a big coffee drinker, and Mother used lots of sugar to make preserves.

Following the war and the return of the millions of troops, the US population began "booming," and sociologists would soon begin to call the new cohort the "baby boomers." By 1950, the total population reached one hundred and fifty million. Immigration was at a high level. Ethnic diversity was rapidly increasing. However, since the outbreak of WWII, any talk of German heritage in Cullman was very subdued. Just as a small example of this loss of identity, the farm neighbors on either side of our farm began to call themselves Bill (for Wilhelm) and Fred (for Frederick).

Twenty-five years passed before a major effort was launched by citizens of Cullman to reintroduce the town's German heritage. A celebration was planned for 1973 to recognize the founding of the city. A renewed pride in the city's origins accompanied this celebration. A German language course was introduced in the high school curriculum after a lapse of over fifty years. An *Oktoberfest* became an annual event (experienced without beer!) This lack of legal beer and wine would appear very peculiar to the original settlers.

As a part of the centennial, a replica of Col. Cullmann's house was built and a museum created. A sister-city relationship was established with Frankweiler, a small village located in the southwest of Germany not far from the Rhine River. Frankweiler is the birthplace of Johann Gottfried Cullmann.

I recall tokens made of plastic and in various denominations from a tenth of a cent to a half cent. A tenth of a cent was one mil. If I remember correctly tokens were available in one, five and ten mils. I'm not sure why tokens were in distribution in Alabama or what real purpose they served.

The war years were a time of solidarity. Everyone felt a need to be helpful. Women saved grease from cooking. The grease was collected by local butchers and sent away for processing. The extracted glycerin was used in the production of a variety of items. One major invention during those years was synthetic rubber. Most "pure" rubber came from areas in Southeast Asia under the control of the Japanese. Another very welcomed synthetic product was nylon, which allowed such an improvement over cotton stockings for women.

In my teen years, I noticed that Cullman had some very beautiful houses. Many of these (I later learned) dated from the late nineteenth century. Many were wood frame houses painted a dazzling white with elaborate lattice work. Most were two story and some even three. These dwellings spoke of untold riches to me.

Many houses had large porticos and two-story columns in the style of antebellum homes observed in older sections of the South. I was a great admirer of these elegant old homes. I would walk by or ride by on my bike and imagine what they must look like inside. I tried to imagine what life would be like for those who lived in such magnificent buildings.

The house I saw and admired most often was catty-cornered from the elementary school. It had four wide columns with Corinthian capitals. This house had the look of an antebellum mansion. A glassed-in porch was on the east side and a large car port on the west. The building was all white except for dark green shutters on each of the two dozen or so windows. The house sat on a half acre of land with a manicured lawn and tastefully planted trees, shrubs, and flowers.

When we moved to town in 1954, I thought of making money by mowing some of the great lawns around some of these mansions. I thought that might also be a way to be invited inside. I was finally able to convince the housekeeper of the mansion by the elementary school (I never learned the family's name) to hire me to care for the lawn. I only worked there for one day and was never invited into the house. Afterward, I was told they had engaged someone else. I evidently didn't mow to suit the housekeeper or the owner.

Not all citizens of Cullman were wealthy. Outside the city limits things were different. In the 1930s, nowhere in America was rural life more primitive than in the basin of the Tennessee River, which included Cullman County. Ever since northern lumber companies had chopped down the virgin hardwood forests in the late nineteenth century, the areas closest to the Tennessee River had experienced numerous floods and erosion. Most of the region was mired in menial poverty.

A bill creating the Tennessee Valley Authority was signed into law by President Roosevelt in 1933. The hydroelectric dams on the Tennessee River would make the TVA the nation's largest producer of electricity within a dozen years. Seventy five percent of the folks in the area served by TVA had access to power by 1945 as compared with two percent in 1933.

Thanks to the Rural Electrification Act, a power line was stretched down the Bremen road. By 1943, we had electricity. The voltage transformer at the corner of our property was often put out of commission by lightning. A direct strike produced a loud bang and a shower of sparks.

Some sections of Cullman experienced significant poverty in the thirties and forties. Several city blocks located south of Fourth Street and west of Main were disparagingly referred to as "West Town." In the forties, West Town was wet, meaning you could buy alcoholic beverages. The area was reputed to be spoiled by the shiftless, drunks and prostitutes. This was the area to go to find day laborers.

In the nineteen-fifties, the Cullman chief of police was almost a perfect caricature of the Southern cop. He was a tall broad-shouldered man with a pot belly who wore a big bright star on his chest. A huge holster and pistol hung from his belt. In fact, the chief had a great name for a Southern policeman— Belt Edmiston. For wayward teens, Belt was a sobering sight, and I imagine he instilled fear in the petty criminal and the local drunks as well. Unfortunately,

Belt was allied with those who strove to keep the South segregated.

Despite my mother's loathing of West Town, it was an area we could hardy avoid. The nearest grocery was on Main a couple of blocks south of Highway 278. The only barbershop on that side of town was a couple of doors south of the grocery. We were obliged to walk through West Town when we visited Mother's oldest brother, T. A. Smith, who had a large white house a couple of blocks north of Highway 278 on Main Street.

The Brick Yard, the stockyards, a two-story wooden hotel and some rather seedy cafes and "juke joints" were also located in this section of town. The major business in West Town was Tucker's Store, a place to buy general merchandise, from horse collars to denim overalls. The store building was constructed of dark red brick. This two-story edifice sat at an odd angle at the corner of South Main and US Highway 278.

I remember very well many of the sights and smells of Tucker's store—the polished hardwood floors, the wooden counters, the slow-turning ceiling fans, and the dim lighting. The ceiling was constructed of stamped metal. The store smelled of furniture wax, kerosene, tobacco, tanned leather, and the dye used on denim overalls.

Folks in Plant City, Florida may be surprised to learn that Cullman was the strawberry capital of the world in the 1940s—or so the Chamber of Commerce proclaimed. In the late spring when the berries ripen, children whose parents grew large crops of berries were excused from school for up to two weeks with no penalties. On our farm we had only a small patch of berries, so I didn't qualify for excused absences. However, I was not jealous of my friends. It was more fun to be in school than in the berry patch.

At the height of the strawberry season, Cullman put on a big parade to celebrate. High school bands marched, civic groups marched, Boy Scouts marched, 4H Club members marched, the American Legion marched, and floats were constructed by several clubs and by local businesses. For a small rural town, this was quite a festive day. The spring when I was five years old (1943), my dad marched in the parade with other veterans. Mother was coaxed into marching with the Women's Auxiliary. Glenn was left on the sidewalk to watch me so that I would not be alone in the crowd.

When the Boy Scouts strutted by, some of Glenn's pals yelled for him to join them. He really wanted to take part, so it didn't take much encouragement. He ran to get in line and left me alone on the sidewalk with the remaining folk who preferred to watch the parade.

I stood for a few moments ogling the floats. When the parade passed me by, I became aware of my position. I was standing among towering adults whom I did not know. I began to panic and started walking in the direction of the parade, hoping to see one or more members of my family. I kept bumping into people in that forest of feet and legs. I tried to go faster, but I couldn't make much progress. I began to really panic and started to cry. I turned around and ran back in the direction I thought our house was located.

I had gone a couple of blocks when I saw Mr. Joe Cobb, who was a familiar face from our church. He stopped me and calmed me down and told me to stay with him and we would find my parents. In very short order, my mother appeared around a corner. She was nearly hysterical looking for me. Needless to say, Glenn was in deep trouble.

Cotton Gin, Icehouse, and Five and Ten

Sounds from the past resound in the mind:
the clank of a blacksmith's hammer;
the blare of an oil mill whistle; the
clamor around the cotton gin.

One of the more noisy and raucous businesses in Cullman was the cotton gin, owned by Jerry Morgan. The gin was located at the corner of Fourth Street and Fourth Avenue just west of the creek dividing the town. In its heyday, the cotton gin was a very busy place from September to November when wagons loaded with fresh-picked cotton queued up to be offloaded.

I accompanied my dad on the wagon when my mother gave her approval. We would pull up in line and await our turn to have the cotton sucked out of the wagon by a large circular vacuum tube. I was not allowed anywhere near the vacuum nor near the machinery of the gin. I was told, in unequivocal words, how dangerous the area was and how many men had lost hands, arms, and even their lives by being pulled into the blades of the gin. Dad's grandpa, Judson Scruggs, told of his younger brother who died in Denton, Texas, after his arm was mangled in a ginning accident.

The noise of the gin was deafening and quite unnerving. The mules and horses became jumpy and had to be controlled with tight reins. Dust, cotton lint, and pieces of dried bolls swirled in the air. The smell of sweat from men and mules was heavy. For a young boy, the gin was a wonderful, magical place. The animation was contagious.

Sometimes unscrupulous cotton pickers dropped a rock or two in their sack before weigh-in to increase their earnings by a few pennies. A rock might weigh two or three pounds and thus could earn the picker between six and ten cents if the trick was not discovered. Farmers tried to watch carefully as the bags of loose cotton were emptied onto the wagon. If a rock was seen falling from a bag, the guilty picker was usually fired on the spot. A rock of any size could wreak havoc on the gin blades. More than one ginner was hurt trying to grab a rock before it entered the machinery.

Another danger was a loose match in the lint. The friction of the gin could set off the match and cause a fire. Some years later, when very little cotton was grown in the county and gin owners were in difficult straits, idle gins were suddenly catching fire mysteriously. The joke went around that these fires were started when the insurance papers rubbed too hard against the mortgage papers!

For the visitor to the gin or the mule barn or any other business in town, very few eating places were available at noon. However, there was one great institution—the Busy Bee Café. This wonderful little shop occupied a small frame structure about seventy-five feet from the railroad tracks at the corner of Fifth Street and First Avenue West. This is the eatery where I enjoyed my first hamburger in the early nineteen forties. What a wonderful combination of smells—wood smoke, burning grease, singeing meat, onions, mustard, and catsup.

One Saturday my parents, my brother, and I were downtown shopping, when Dad decided that we would try one of those good-smelling burgers. The taste was unforgettable. It was like nothing I had ever eaten. The combination of broiled meat, condiments, and soft bun was like the ambrosia of the gods to me. I fell instantly in love with this taste. After eating that burger at the *Busy Bee*, I could understand Wimpy, the comic character, and his craving for that juicy and tasty treat. Even now, I measure burgers against that first one. None have ever surpassed it. As witness to this statement, the Busy Bee is still a highly successful business in the twenty-first century in the face of McDonalds, Burger Kings, Wendy's and other fast-food chains.

By the late forties, Cullman had its first drive-in restaurant. This should not be confused with modern drive-through restaurants. Werner's Drive-In was a place to come, park, and eat in the comfort of your own car! In the days when the love affair with cars seemed inexhaustible, you just drove into a parking space, and a young boy or girl would appear and take your order. The food was subsequently brought out to the car on a tray fashioned to hook over the car door with the window rolled down. (Yes, the car windows were manually rolled down with a knob, not powered down electrically.)

Ultimately, the desire to be in one's car caused the drive-in movie theater. Again, you just drove up to a post located at car-window level, rolled down the window of the driver's side, and took a speaker and hooked it on the window of the car and waited for the movie to be projected onto a large outdoor screen. Now, it didn't take long to realize the great advantages that this outdoor theater provided. For parents with young children, it meant being able to attend a movie without needing to hire a babysitter. For teens, it meant that some heavy petting could take place in the relative privacy of one's own car.

For the dating couples, the drive-in theater was safer than finding a place to park out in the countryside where a voyeuristic local sheriff's deputy could hardly wait to shine a flashlight on unexpecting young teens engaged in intimate contact inside their cars. Many of these zealous deputies seemed to get a vicarious thrill when they shined a spotlight on an embracing couple.

In the early forties, a blacksmith shop still functioned on Fourth Street by the muddy creek that ran through the hollow between the "upper" part of town and West Town. A muscular, sweaty, dark-featured man worked at an anvil partially covered by a makeshift roof that protected him from the elements.

For a young boy, few activities were more engaging than watching a blacksmith create horseshoes, plow shares, sickle blades, and hundreds of other items from random pieces of iron. The sound of the hammer striking the anvil was loud and sharp; sparks flew in every directions; the bellows blew breathy gusts of air; blue flames flickered in the charcoal fire; water sizzled in the cooling tank as the blacksmith immersed red hot pieces of iron; hot steam floated to the metal ceiling; the odor of sweat, smoke, and horse flesh permeated the air—all these sights, sounds, and smells mingled together to produce an effect I have not experienced in many decades. The poet Henry Wadsworth Longfellow sets the scene:

The Village Blacksmith

> Under a spreading chestnut tree
> The village smithy stands;
> The smith, a mighty man is he,
> With large and sinewy hands;
> And the muscles of his brawny arms
> Are strong as iron bands.
> ....
> And children coming home from school
> Look in at the open door;
> They love to see the flaming forge,
> And hear the bellows roar,
> And catch the burning sparks that fly
> Like chaff from a threshing floor.

A crowd of men and boys stood or squatted around the shop from morning to night, some of necessity, but many were like me, they just enjoyed watching. Gruff-looking, unshaven men conversed loudly over the din of the blacksmith's hammer. Although my dad could shoe a horse, he came to the blacksmith shop when he needed newly made shoes to fit his animals. Unfortunately, it was only a short few years until the smithy was gone the way of the candlestick maker.

In the 1940s, many commercial ventures in Cullman still bore German names. One of the best known was Stiefelmeyer's Dry Goods. This two-story wooden structure was one of the longest serving businesses in town. Here a person could find almost any items a farm family might need: brogans, overalls, denim shirts, long johns, work gloves, knee high socks, and house wares that were the envy of every homemaker. Creaky wooden steps led noisily to the second floor, a place where every child could check the sound of their latest pair of "Sunday go-to meeting" shoes. The well-trod floors gleamed with newly applied wax. Odors of snuff and tobacco smoke hovered in the air. Brass spittoons were pungent with ocher-colored juice. The aroma of boots, shoes, belts and other leather goods permeated the air. Stiefelmeyer's was *the* department store of the times, the place to come on a Saturday afternoon to hang out before the creation of malls.

The clerks at Stiefelmeyer's knew the patrons by name, and the patrons knew the clerks as well as each other. Greetings were exchanged, latest ailments discussed, the weather lamented. "Looks like it's gonna rain a week and then come a wet spell!" All items were cash only or layaway. At the cashier's stand, pocketbooks were rummaged for the last few coins. A dropped penny was quickly scooped from the floor.

Another popular business was Kuhn's Five and Dime. This great little store sold every toy a small child could imagine, including a varied selection of tops, marbles, and kites. For the women, bolt after bolt of cloth rose high on four-foot wooden counters. Drawers held buttons of every shape and size, and spools of thread in every color imaginable. Many items could be had for a nickel, or a dime, or a quarter. When a kid had acquired a few pennies, Kuhn's was the place to go.

Another favorite with kids was Kreitleins. This little store carried what seemed like an endless variety of penny candy: Uncle Remus Kisses, licorice twists, candy cigarettes, chocolate kisses, Jawbreakers, bubblegum. After school, kids walked several blocks out of their way to stop in and browse the penny candy counters. The owners were very patient with their young customers who might spend five minutes deciding on a one cent purchase.

George Ponder's Department Store was a bit more upscale. Men's, women's and children's clothes were rather pricy for farm families. Ponder's catered more to the Cullman middle class, the doctors, lawyers, and white-collar folks. Most farm families ordered their clothes from the Sears & Roebuck

Catalog or they bought them at Stiefelmeyer's or Joe C. Sapps.

Willy Monnie and Barney Chandler were the pharmacist's assistants at Dr. Philip Hartung's *People's Drug Store and Soda Shop*. A large majority of citizens had their prescriptions filled at Dr. Phil's place, a sure sign that they trusted him and his two helpers. The service was personal and sincere; these men knew their clientele intimately enough to know most of their ailments.

Some commerce came to us on the farm, but not for long. A medium-size van called a Rolling Store bounced down Bremen road ever so often, the driver tooting his horn to get the attention of the residents in the manner of today's ice cream trucks with their little jingles playing. It was a treat to run out to the side of the road with Mother to see what was available inside the van. She often bought mops and brooms and washing products. The Rolling Store also carried pots and pans, bottled sodas, Moon pies, crackers, cookies, gum and a few canned goods. I could usually manage to find a penny for a piece of bubble gum, if nothing else.

The Rolling Store served a very practical need in its day. You might say it was the convenience store of the 1930s and 1940s. Finding the time to go to town was difficult for many farm wives who had to spend most of their day cooking, cleaning house, washing clothes, ironing, sewing, and gardening. Within the town limits, salesmen came door-to-door with cleaning products and other sundry items, but these salesmen didn't normally sell in the country-side. Again, the Rolling Store disappeared soon after the Blacksmith Shop.

Professional photography remained a significant business in the forties. One summer day when I was five years old, my mother dressed me in my finest Sunday clothes and off to town we walked. We were going to Schlosser's Photographic Studio where I was to have my picture taken. As we neared the building where the studio was located, my mother stopped me and pulled a comb out of her purse and began running it through my hair. She used a bit of spit to try to force down the "cowlick" at the back of my head. Then she made a valiant effort to "roach" the front of my hair.

You may rightly ask the meaning of "roach" in that context. It's a rather archaic word meaning to create a mound of hair on the forehead (à la Elvis Presley). Mother always wanted me to comb my hair in that manner and was dead-set against the burr or the flat-top haircuts that became popular a few years later.

With my hair in some sort of presentable appearance, we entered Schlosser's studio. Mr. Schlosser, a gruff, fat man, sat me down on a stool and turned me this way and that. When he was satisfied, he began to make faces and tell jokes, hoping to wrest a good smile out of me. It wasn't easy, but eventually he did. The picture turned out to my mother's satisfaction. A framed eight-by-ten copy, slightly tinted, sat on her dresser for the next fifty years.

Buettner Brothers Lumber Company was less than a half mile from our farm. One of the brothers, Herman Buettner, was well-known to my dad. The business was originally begun by brothers Hugo and Max and later operated by sons Bill and Herman. I always enjoyed a trip to the sawmill portion of the company. Here the buzz of saws and planes filled the air constantly. Huge piles of sawdust and shavings lay about the floor and over-flowed several bins. The sawdust and shavings were for sale to whoever came to load up and haul away one or the other. My dad would load up the wagon with these shavings every couple of months. He filled the stable floors in our barn with the shavings as well as the floor of the chicken house.

A small grocery store in West Town was appropriately called the West Side Grocery, and was operated by Dewey Buchanan, a one-armed man. At this grocery, my parents bought items that couldn't be grown on the farm—salt, pepper, sugar, flour, soft drinks, lemons, an occasional "loaf" of "white bread." Mother would often send Glenn to shop for what she needed. She didn't have to give him a list. She simply told him what she needed, and he would always come back with everything she asked for. Glenn didn't even need to take money. Good customers ran a tab with Mr. Dewey and paid him off at the end of each month.

One very necessary business was the Cullman Ice and Fuel Company. We just called it the "Icehouse." This was another fun place to visit. The animation was always at a high pitch. Men came and went across the floor in overalls and Hobnob shoes, carrying fifty-pound blocks of ice with large iron tongs. The tongs were constructed so that the heavier the weight of the ice, the harder the tongs gripped. I was fascinated by the thirty-foot aeration tower. Water constantly cascaded down all four sides like a perfect man-made falls.

The tower was constructed of slats that tilted outward. As the water tumbled over these stats, it was aerated and cooled from the original temperature coming from the water storage plant. What happened in the ice house after the water flowed inside was a big mystery. No one could explain just how that water turned into ice. No one seemed to care as long as they could count on being able to have a steady supply of ice.

One of the ice haulers allowed me inside the area where the ice was slid along the sawdust-covered delivery ramp. In the background, I could hear loud whirling noise. I was told the sound was made by compressors. All I could see were large electrical motors pulling very wide leather belts which disappeared into a large box-like apparatus. That peek was all I ever had of the mysterious process of ice-making. By the time I was an adult, ice was being made by large refrigeration units. There was no longer a need for complicated, noisy mechanical compressors and water-cooling towers.

Unlike most small southern towns, the rail line did not impede traffic in the heart of Cullman. The tracks were below street level in a cut made in the 1930s after the town had grown. Bridges arced over the tracks at several street crossings. The bridges were called viaducts. Hardly anything tickled a young boy's fancy more than watching a freight or passenger train come puffing into town. In those days, to a youngster these beasts were "choo-choos." Standing on the viaduct, you had a good view of the trains several hundred yards in both directions. Children have nothing comparable today. Perhaps the closest thing is standing on top of an airport parking lot overlooking a runway and watching jet planes land and take off.

The whistle of the locomotive warned us when a choo-choo was a half mile away, so we could run to look over the concrete wall of the viaduct. As the train slowed down to come into the station on the north side of town, the steam would puff out near the wheels in great clouds. Black smoke billowed from the stack and swirled about. If a person was not careful, the black soot would ruin a white shirt or even turn your flesh a few shades darker.

Often the cinders were more numerous than usual, and you had to watch that no red hot ones landed on your coat, shirt, pants. You had to be especially careful that no small cinder flew into your eye. That was a major pain and happened to me just one time that I can recall. I was much more cautious afterward.

I crossed the railroad tracks twice a day going to and from elementary school. Of course, my journey did not always correspond to the arrival of a train, yet many times I would be able to watch one pull in or pull out. This was the Louisville and Nashville rail line, which was engaged in bringing coal and iron from Birmingham to Nashville, Louisville, and cities further north. Consequently, the line carried significant freight traffic. Of course, in the forties and fifties, passenger trains were relatively frequent as well. The highway system at that time did not permit folks to travel nearly as rapidly by car as they could by train.

When the coal-burning locomotive chugged out of the station, it did so with a loud huff and a big plume of smoke and a hissing of air and steam (thus the onomatopoetic term—*choo-choo*). The train would make a lurch forward and the couplings of the cars would all clang together. The iron wheels of the locomotive would seek traction on the iron rails and would spin and squeal. Then would come the second lurch, moving the train slightly forward, then the next and next and so on until the train began to move evenly and slowly on its way to the next stop.

When I was a child, our family had no reason to ride a train. We were never going far enough north or south. Our visits to friends or relatives was within the county or the adjoining counties, and we traveled by car or truck. I really wanted to take a train ride, so one day when I was five years-old, my mother bought us two round-trip tickets to Decatur (about 35 miles north of Cullman). We boarded the train at the Cullman Depot and rode to Decatur, got off, turned around, and rode the next south-bound train back to Cullman. This took less than three hours. What a delight for me and probably my mother also. I doubt that she had ever ridden a train before that moment. For my dad, this was no big deal. He had not only traveled many times by train, he had been both a fireman and a switchman.

According to the 1940 US Census, the population of the city of Cullman was roughly 5,000. By the time I graduated from high school, that figure had grown to approximately 9,000. Presently the population is close to 17,000. Cullman is the only city in the county of Cullman with a sizable population. Some of the other "towns" are little more than crossroads, but they have delightful names—West Point, Good Hope, Colony, Holly Pond, Garden City, Hanceville, Dodge City, Fairview, Baileyton and Arab (pronounced with a long /a/ and rhyming with Ahab). My all-time favorite place names are *Bug Tussle,* located on Highway 69 about four miles south of Bremen, and the wonderful *Chigger Ridge* to the northwest of Hanceville, now the location of a biking trail.

Other well-named crossroads in Cullman County include Arkadelphia, New Hope, Birdsong, Jones Chapel, Trimble, Gold Ridge, Bremen, Joppa, and Battleground. The latter gets its name from a skirmish between Confederate Cavalry led by Gen. Nathan Bedford Forrest and a Union battalion commanded by Col. Abel Streight. This was the only action the area witnessed during the entire four years of the Civil War.

My wife, La Donna, and I often puzzle over the origin of place names. Some are easy to figure out, but others are very elusive. Take *Bug Tussle*, for example. Did the early settlers in that "neck of the woods" see a tussle between bugs? Or did they run across a bug so big it gave them a tussle? *Chigger Ridge* is self-explanatory. The place is crawling with those little red devils.

"Big Jim" Folsom

Politics is often called the second oldest profession, and it surely bears a striking resemblance to the first.

For a relatively small city, Cullman has the distinction of being home to three governors of the State of Alabama—Jim Folsom Sr. (Big Jim), Jim Folsom Jr., and Guy Hunt. Big Jim and his first wife, Sarah Carnley, moved to Cullman in 1938 when Jim took a job in his brother-in-law's insurance business. Jim served briefly in WWII, but when Sarah died suddenly, he returned to Cullman to care for his two young daughters.

Big Jim began public service by working in two New Deal offices: Civil Works Administration and Works Progress Administration. He was a progressive Democrat who tried throughout his career, both in and out of government, to improve the lot of the working class and the very poor.

Jim was nicknamed BIG because of his height—six feet eight inches. His second wife, Jamelle, was no more than five feet, and standing beside Jim, she appeared exceptionally short. When Big Jim was on the political trail, he kissed a lot of babies, thus acquiring the alternate nickname—"kissing Jim Folsom," although it's doubtful that he kissed any more babies than any other Southern politician.

In his early attempts at election to public office, Big Jim was defeated, twice for Congress and once for governor. Eventually, he turned these losses to his benefit, joking that "No man is a politician until he has been beaten at least twice."

During the forties and fifties, the Folsom's and their children continued to maintain a home in Cullman. Their property had one of only two private tennis courts in town. The other belonged to a local physician and was less than a half mile from our farm. I used to ride my bike by and watch the family playing tennis and swore that one day I would also have a court of my own! Once I was married with two children, the tennis court idea received three vetoes in favor of a swimming pool!

When I was nine years old (1946), Big Jim campaigned a second time for governor of the state of Alabama. He ran on a populist and progressive platform, yet his campaign stops became entertaining events. He hired a country band called the *Strawberry Pickers* (very appropriate since Jim's home county, Cullman, claimed to be the strawberry capital of the world).

Just about every aspect of the campaign was folksy. On the stump, he had a mop made of shucks and a suds bucket as props. He would point out the mop and bucket and then challenge his audience: "You folks provide the suds, and I'll do the scrubbing to get those scheming mills out of the capitol." By scheming mills, I take it he meant the millionaires, or simply the upper crust.

Big Jim's theme song was "*Down Yonder*," a song from the musical "*Waiting for the Robert E. Lee.*" The refrain suggested that folks were waiting on Big Jim to come and save them. "Down yonder someone beckons to me; Down yonder someone reckons on me (is counting on me)." I lived in Cullman during six of his eight years in office.

The phrase "Y'all come" became Folsom's campaign slogan. For Yankee readers, this phrase suggests an open-door policy and a big welcome to everyone. The message was clear: Big Jim was a man for all the people.

Beneath his folksy façade, Big Jim had a solid set of progressive programs in mind. He proposed increasing benefits for the elderly, an improved educational system, a repeal of the infamous poll tax, and an improved infrastructure. Folsom was conscious of the plight of the blacks in the State of Alabama and believed that the state could not become economically healthy until the treatment of blacks was significantly improved.

At Folsom's rallies, buckets were passed around, and folks threw in quarters and half-dollars. This loose change became a major source of revenue for his campaign. The music, the folksiness, the revenue, the progressive platform, all combined to achieve a win for Big Jim. Once in office, he worked diligently to push passage of his various reforms, but the conservative legislature blocked the most controversial aspects.

Big Jim was not able to convince these down-state conservatives (descendants of the plantation owners) that raising the level of blacks would also raise the economic level of the working-class whites. However, he was able to increase spending on education, medical care for the elderly, and for funding for infrastructure, but was unsuccessful in his efforts to extend voting rights to blacks and poor whites through repeal of the infamous poll (or head) tax.

Most farmers in Cullman County were very pleased with Big Jim's governorship. During his administrations, many of the rural dirt roads were paved. Travel became much easier, especially in rainy seasons. In the dry season, you could ride in the back of a pickup truck without continually eating dust.

Governors in Alabama cannot succeed themselves but may run for additional terms after a lapse of four years. In 1954, Big Jim ran again and won by a landslide. However, by this time racial tensions had become so explosive that any social reforms he might have initiated were crushed by the violence and divisiveness of the times.

Politics in Alabama became much more abrasive when George Wallace served as governor. This short fiery demagogue vowed to make his name as the champion of white supremacy. He stood in the door of the University of Alabama to prevent Autherine Lucy from registering. Federal marshals were required to clear the way for her entry. Having made a name for himself in the eyes of the far right, Wallace took his segregation beliefs to a higher level and ran for president on the Dixiecrat Ticket.

During the Wallace years when I was a member of the faculty at Eastern Kentucky University, my wife and I often had black students in our home. One young university student came to "babysit" our two children on occasions. We attempted to explain to our younger daughter about racial epithets. We told her that some folks call blacks the N-word as a put-down. At that time, our daughter was fascinated by *Winnie the Pooh*, *Eeyore*, *Tigger*, and all of *Christopher Robin's* friends. Based on her knowledge that "Tiggers are wonderful" and confusing words, she assured our young babysitter that "Everybody knows Niggers is wonderful things." Isn't childhood innocence a wonderful thing?

Due to its origins as a refuge for political dissent, Cullman was more diversified than many rural towns in the South. Merchants of German descent lived side by side with those of English, Scots-Irish, and Irish ancestry. Catholics worked alongside Lutherans, Methodists, and Baptists. Just down the Bremen Road a few miles from Cullman, a group of Native Americans and blacks had formed *The Colony*, an even more desperate attempt to find a place of welcome.

Nevertheless, much is made of the racist history of Cullman. I knew of only one black maid and her young son living in town in the forties. On my route to the Cullman Elementary School, I passed the house where the maid and her son lived. The little boy used to sit on the porch and watch us white kids on the way to school. He appeared curious and wistful, but the white kids complained that he was the lucky one—not being required to go to school!

In the oft-repeated lore of Cullman, it is said that some citizens once placed signs at the city limits cautioning the blacks: "N—— don't let the sun go down on you." However, I personally never saw these signs at any of the city limits. The folks in Cullman in the '40s and '50s, no doubt, were as biased against racial mixing as any other place in the US, but not likely to have been any more prejudiced.

One current example may offer encouragement that racial biases are slowly fading. In an election in early 2008, the electors in Cullman voted overwhelming for James C. Fields to fill a seat in the State House of Representatives. Mr. Fields is a black and a Democrat in a heavily "red" state.

On the other hand, in the 2008 presidential election, only a small percentage of voters in Cullman chose Barack Obama. Whether this was simply due to faith in Republican social and economic conservatism or whether it was owing to a residue of racial bias is not easily determined. In any case, the city (and the nation at large) has yet to fully realize the dream of Johann Cullmann—the creation of a haven free from political coercion and prejudice.

Reveries of a Barefoot Boy

A boy's will is the wind's will, and the
thoughts of youth are long, long thoughts.

—Henry Wadsworth Longfellow
My Lost Youth

When I was young, no other boys my age
lived closer than a half mile from our
farm. Thus, I spent most of my time
entertaining myself. Being alone is, of course, conducive to reveries, to daydreaming. In solitude, there's
time for meditation on the world's big questions—for
an introvert, perhaps too much time. Many things I
heard in Sunday school and sermons during worship
were taken very seriously: sin, evil, the devil, burning
bushes, angels, and especially heaven. Heaven was
said to be a place where a person lived for eternity, a
place where time did not end.

The notions of *infinity, forever, eternity* were
conundrums for me. I couldn't conceive of these
things. I was unable to imagine "forever" or "eter-

nity." One night when I was seven years old, I lay in bed ruminating about eternity. I couldn't stop obsessing, and I couldn't fall asleep. Often, I had heard Bible-thumping preachers talk of inheriting eternal life if a person ceased sinning, obeyed the commandments, and accepted Jesus.

At first glance, living *forever* seemed like a pretty good thing, especially given the way life in heaven was depicted in the sermons—streets paved with gold, angels playing music on harps. Life in heaven was painted as all peace and joy and pleasure. I imagined having all the candy I could ever eat; having all the toys I wanted; having all the special foods I wanted: Ritz Crackers, chunks of fresh, ripe pineapple, coconut milk, chocolate ice cream, rhubarb pie, and sweet iced tea.

Now, this specific night, I tried to visualize how long eternity would be. I obsessed about "forever." How could anything continue forever? The more I dwelt on the concept, the more agitated I became. Eternity just didn't seem possible. I broke out in a sweat and soon was overcome with an anxiety attack. At that time, I didn't know what I was experiencing, didn't have a name for it, but in retrospect I was having a full-blown panic attack.

I eased out of bed, left my room and tiptoed to my parents' room and woke up my dad.

"How can anybody live forever?" I asked.

In a rather groggy state, my dad was a little befuddled by the question. "Why are you asking me that in the middle of the night," he grumbled.

"I can't figure out how you can go to heaven and live forever," I whispered.

"Well, son, that's just the way it is," was all he could manage as a reply. "Now, go on back to bed and go to sleep. We can talk about it in the morning," he added.

I didn't find much comfort in Dad's reply, but I crawled back in bed, pulled the covers over my head. The only comfort came in knowing that my dad didn't seem worried about eternity. Maybe I shouldn't worry either. Eventually I fell into a fitful sleep.

From that time on, I forced myself to think of other things each time the words *eternity* and *forever* came to mind. In this way, I avoided renewed panic attacks. To this day, I have never again allowed myself to be trapped into dwelling on those conundrums— in regard to heaven or to hell. If I were to do so now, I am sure I would experience the same angst.

At the time, I felt like my experience was unique. No one else seemed a bit concerned about living forever. The expression was tossed about loosely and used in a very trite way. From "I'll love you forever" in the love scenes at the movies to "I'll hate you forever" screamed across the school yard following a boy-girl tiff.

Much later, during my undergraduate days, I found a kindred spirit while reading excerpts by classical French writers. In the *Thoughts* of Blaise Pascal, I learned about the nausea that this scientist and philosopher felt when he first confronted the infinitely large universe made visible by the newly invented telescope. His malaise was equally strong when he observed the tiny world viewed through a primitive microscope.

Pascal was one of the early scientists to view the universe through telescope perfected by Galileo. He also was one of the earliest to use a microscope. Pascal was awed by what he called the *infinitely small* and the *infinitely great*—and the telescopes and microscopes of his day were unable to see one thousandth of what the instruments of the twentieth-first century are capable. One wonders what Pascal would feel in the face of nanotechnology, black holes, and black matter?

The contemplation of an ever-expanding universe that already seems to be boundless is a sobering, if not frightening experience. The complexity of the genetic codes in all living things argues eloquently for an organizing presence in the universe. On this point, William Blake waxed mystically long before the days of nanotechnology:

> To see a world in a grain of sand
> And a heaven in a wildflower,
> Hold infinity in the palm of your hand
> And eternity in an hour.

Beyond the thoughts brought on by talk of infinity and "forever," youthful reveries are fostered by the boring, repetitive actions involved in hoeing corn, chopping or picking cotton and other routine occupations. In these reveries, I took myself away to a far off land and a far off time. I joined with imaginary characters created by novelists like Walter Scott, James Fenimore Cooper, Thomas Costain, Jack London, Conan Doyle, and Robert Louis Stevenson, to name only a few.

For a time, working in the fields under a blazing sun, I became the hero whose prowess dazzled the folks in Camelot and at the Court of Henry II. I was a hero in pioneer America. One moment I was Daniel Boone; in another, I fought alongside Jim Bowie and David Crockett. I discovered new lands and new rivers. I went to the North Pole with Admiral Perry.

As I sweated under the stifling heat, I wove the fanciest of creations. I lived in a virtual world far from the dusty fields of corn and cotton. Sometimes, like the *Connecticut Yankee* of Twain's tale, I imagined myself in a foreign land, in a glorious, heroic age. Other times I lived in a beautiful tree house in the jungles of Africa, surrounding by adoring animals that I had saved from poachers.

Eventually thirst and tiredness would jolt me back to reality. I would look up to see where the sun was located, hoping it would descend more rapidly so I could go home to a cold glass of lemonade. However, with much of the day remaining, my only recourse was to take a swig of water from the glass jug that I had placed in the shade of a sprawling goldenrod plant. My parents thought ice water was quite dangerous to drink if a person was working in the heat of the sun. Consequently, no ice was in the jug from the beginning (not that it would have made much difference). Even though the water was lukewarm, it was refreshing and soothing to a parched throat.

Standing alone in the cotton field, I felt a kinship with *Miniver Cheevy*, the lost soul in the poem by Edwin A. Robinson read in high school English classes. Miniver was "born too late," and—so was I, it seemed.

> Miniver loved the days of old
> When swords were bright
> And steeds were prancing.
> The vision of a warrior bold
> Would set him dancing.

My escapes from the harshness of reality were not always daydreams of faraway lands. I could lose myself in the beauty of nature. I could lie on my back chewing on a blade of grass and gaze at the roiling thunderheads as they morphed from one image to another. Clouds sculpt figures and quickly boil into other fantasy forms—or simply melt away.

Lying on my back, I looked into the sky. On the left and up a few degrees from the horizon, the perfect shape of a fluffy white sheep evolved. Farther back, the silhouette of a wolf appeared moving stealthily toward the sheep.

Turning my head a bit to the right, I saw atop a giant mountain, a charging buffalo, head held low. In less than a minute, all these shapes mutated into vague white puffs. Soon a new set of images evolved.

All that's required for such a theatrical display are clouds, an acute imagination, and a need to escape.

No two skies are alike; no two sunsets. The colors and images change second by second. Ever try to paint a sunset? Sunrises and sunsets are paintings on the canvas of the sky. And unlike paintings by human artists, sky paintings are alive, illuminated, and constantly modulating. The colors and shapes are altered almost from second to second, but the total moving display may remain for ten or fifteen minutes.

Some especially spectacular sunsets may continue even longer and splash yellows, violets, blues, and oranges across a partially cloudy sky, pinking up thunder heads far away on the eastern horizon. In a few moments, a new and silent spectacle will begin as "heat lightning" flashes on and off at irregular intervals within the distant clouds.

Earthly landscapes around Brindley Mountain are rather bland—no spectacular peaks and valleys, just undulating hills. Those of us who grew to adulthood in the area did not have a vista of snowcapped mountains, no major waterways or waterfalls, no windswept prairies, but we had the four seasons. Springtime gave us crocus, redbuds, dogwoods, and forsythia.

Autumn presented us with a changing palette of colored leaves, although the majority of our trees were pines or cedars. In winter, hardly anything is prettier than a Southern ice storm, or more devastating. We had more of those than we had serious snows. In effect, I saw few snowfalls of more than two or three inches in depth during my entire growing up years.

In the spring, we had frequent hard rain showers that often left us with the beauty of a partial or a full rainbow. A clear and full-spectrum rainbow is one of the most awesome sights. It's no wonder it is regarded as a special sign from God. We humans are delighted by every rainbow, and we want others to experience them with us, no matter how often they occur. William Wordsworth captures our awe in these short verses:

> My heart leaps up when I behold
> A rainbow in the sky.
> So was it when my life began;
> So is it now I am a man.

Medieval theologians/astrologers reflected on the imaginary "music of the spheres." They believed the heavens consisted of a series of spheres to which were attached the various stars and planets. These spheres rotated around the earth, causing the stars and planets to move across the sky. The medieval "magi" imagined that this movement produced a heavenly music.

As far as I know, religious fundamentalists no longer espouse this un-scientific notion. However, without the spheres, nature makes music for us if we tune in. With all the electronic gadgets available, fewer folks pay much heed to natural music. Most apparently prefer human-made sounds. Walkers, joggers, and drivers are plugged in, but definitely tuned out.

Wherever I happen to be, I hear nature's sounds even above the sounds of traffic, the roar of airplanes, a gaggle of voices. Both day and night, I am aware of the call notes and songs of birds. I notice the chirp of crickets, the scratchy fiddling of dry flies, the repeating notes of mockingbirds, the gruff, raspy call of the grackles, and the piercing cry of the osprey. Seldom do I miss the far-off chatter of a pileated woodpecker. In the evenings, I catch high-pitched peeps of the martins and swifts, the series of hoots from the barred owl, and the eerie whinny of the little screech owl.

In a traffic-filled town vibrating with the roar of motorcycles, the honk of car horns, the high piercing whine of emergency vehicles, I notice the ubiquitous house sparrows chirping away in their nests in eaves of commercial buildings. When I was a child, the meadows and grasslands were teeming with the noise of killdeers, whip-poor-wills, larks, crows, and quails.

Closer to the perimeter of our little clapboard house, springtime brought the clucking of robins and the warble of eastern bluebirds. The latter were my mother's favorites, and she insisted on having a couple of houses cleaned out and prepared for the returning bluebirds each new season. The brilliant cardinal with its half-dozen calls and songs was my preference.

The fallow fields of our land were alive with wildlife. In urban areas much of that diverse orchestra of sounds is lost. I sometimes miss silence. Many people confuse silence with loneliness. Silence is frightening to them. They seem to relish noise, the louder the better. I am afraid that the modern technical world's constant noise will destroy humanity's ability to contemplate and mediate on life.

I have always been observant of nature's feathered creatures. As a child, I drew them with a pencil and colored them with crayons on the lined pages of a *Bluebook*. I copied all the birds that were familiar to our area of Northern Alabama from a giant *Audubon* book that I found in the school library.

I was never what is called a "birder." That is, I didn't keep count of the species I encountered. I did not go in search of species that I had not yet seen—a few times I enjoyed birding in Central America (Belize, Costa Rica, Guatemala, and the Yucatan.) However, without fanfare, I watched the behavior of the feathered creatures. I can identify many species native to the southeastern US simply by observing their flight pattern. Regardless of what else is happening around me, I am aware of nature—the breeze in the trees, the patterns and lengths of shadows, the various natural sounds, the shapes of the clouds in the sky. For me, communing with nature is a way to stay in contact with both the physical and the spiritual side of life.

I must admit that my spirituality is rather unorthodox. I remember thinking as a child that if I read the Bible, I could gain insight and perhaps even get to know Jesus in the way that many folks in my church seemed to know Him. As a young child, I was more frightened than comforted by thoughts of God. I expect it was because I heard too many fire-and-brimstone sermons. The God I came to know from the pulpit was not awesome in a loving way, but fearfully powerful and arbitrary.

Once I called my brother a "fool" when we were having a sibling quarrel, and he immediately told me I would go to hell for saying that "because it says so in the Bible." He showed me the passage in the *King James Version*. I was about seven years old and very impressionable. I was really frightened. I prayed long and hard to God to forgive me for calling my brother a fool. I didn't want to spend eternity in a lake of fire. However, the more I thought about this, the more I was skeptical that God would care that much about a simple word. I was no longer mad with my brother, and I was in no way trying to offend the Almighty. Would God hold this little word against me forever?

As a teenager, I was active in youth programs at the First Christian Church of Cullman. I was present at services every Sunday morning. My parents attended, and I was expected to do so as well. For two or three years before leaving for college, on many occasions I served communion during Sunday morning worship services. Such an activity would normally be the responsibility of deacons, but the number of men in the congregation was dropping rapidly. A couple of the youth were recruited for duty. In those years, I was encouraged to "make a preacher," to use the South expression. However, this was never something I even remotely considered for myself.

As a teenager, I was interested in philosophy and theology as intellectual pursuits, but not in ministry. I knew that I was too much a skeptic, too cynical, too lacking in grace to study to be a minister of the faith. My idea of a major in college in those days was some form of science—perhaps physics. I was fascinated by what little I had heard of the subatomic world and the ever-expanding universe.

Nevertheless, I continued to search for ways to tap into the divine force in the universe. I was fascinated by the concept of the "Great Spirit" of the Native Americans. The Great Spirit permeated all of life. A spark of the creator was in all people and all animals. I could relate to this concept. It seemed to me, from my limited reading, that some great power pervaded the universe. I did not sense that this power was a "personal savior," to use the language of the evangelicals. For me, the creative force must be much more "mystical." I was unable to express my feelings, but the metaphysical world was as interesting and alluring to me as the physical world. Like most teens, I was searching for my place in the total picture.

I sought refuge in books. I raised more question than answers, and I was becoming more and more a "nerd," to use the modern expression. I convinced myself that learning was much more fun than going to parties with my peers.

One day when I was in my late teens, I saw an ad in a magazine calling for membership in the Secret Society of Rosicrucians. I was intrigued by what I read. The society promised the "Key to Universal

Wisdom." This was very alluring to me. Several past members of the society (according to the ad) caught my eye: da Vinci, Rabelais, Bacon, Descartes, Pascal, Newton, Franklin, Jefferson, and Paine. What a list of great intellectuals! Why had they become members of this secret society?

I sent away for more information and discovered that I was too young to join the society without parental approval. My dad agreed, no questions asked. He was very supportive of anything in the intellectual or artistic arena that I wanted to do. He trusted me to make the right decisions. He always deeply regretted not having gone farther in formal schooling than the eighth grade. His daughter by his first marriage had finished only the eleventh grade, and his son from that marriage had finished only the ninth grade. I was making plans to attend college, and that gave him great pleasure.

In a few weeks, I received the first of the Rosicrucian material by US mail—a couple of book about the "secret" life of Jesus, some incense, some meditative material, some guidance about contacting the Divine Source in the universe. The serious initiate apparently could link up in some way with the power of God. The process was like tuning into radio waves minus the crystal set. The human mind (or soul) was the tuner.

The introductory material spoke of nine Temple Degrees. Apparently, they were similar to Masonic Degrees. In the early degrees, the novice began to master an understanding of space and time and human consciousness in relation to cosmic consciousness. Eventually, with study and practice, using the meditative techniques, the initiate was to reach an ability to communicate by telepathy. This introductory material promised that the diligent and faithful student would eventually understand the nature of the soul.

My skepticism was just too great. Despite all my efforts using incense, music, meditation, and prayer, I was not able to make any contacts with the living or the dead. I decided that I didn't have what it takes to be a mystic. I ceased the meditations and began to study my traditional textbooks in earnest. Never again did I flirt with the occult. I took refuge in rational thought, believing what my brain was able to understand via the powers of reason. If, like Pascal, I someday receive the gift of faith, so much the better. I no longer wished to take time away from the wonders of the natural world to meditate on the metaphysical.

In undergraduate days, one of my favorite authors was Albert Camus. In all his creative works and in his *Essais*, he warned against ignoring the present world in favor of a future one. He felt certain that this was the root of much cruelty and much sin against others. "If there is a sin against life, it consists perhaps not so much in despairing of life as in hoping for another life and in eluding the implacable grandeur of this one." Since reading those lines, I have been ever on the lookout for this natural grandeur and have found that it is always with us. I do very little daydreaming anymore and keep my senses open to the here and now.

Sundays with the Disciples

The *Campbellites* set themselves apart by
rejecting traditional creeds of faith. Their simple
proclamation was—*No creed but the Bible.*

T wo Sundays following my birth, my parents
took me to church. I slept through the entire
service (I am told), lying in the pew beside
my parents. I literally grew up in this pew. Each family
staked out a claim to a particular spot in a particular bench. Attending church on Sunday mornings
seemed the natural thing to do. None of us missed
except for illness.

The church we attended was called the First
Christian Church. This seemed a remarkable name
to me when I was very young. Later I discovered that
the church of my parents was not the "first church"
in town, nor was it the only "Christian" one. The
denomination was better known in close circles as
the *Disciples of Christ.*

The Christian or Disciples congregations grew
out of conflicts with the Presbyterians in the early

nineteenth century. Alexander Campbell and Barton Stone were leaders who opposed much of the formal doctrines and liturgy of the Presbyterians. The result was a new fellowship that prided itself on placing the Bible above all creeds. Consequently, this denomination's mantra became "No Creed but the Bible."

The local First Christian resulted from a split with a Church of Christ in the 1920s. Several professional men were instrumental in the formation of this new congregation and in constructing a building. Two names stand out: Dr. A. P. Martin, a physician, and Mr. George Ponder, a prominent local merchant. Dr. Martin was a very faithful member of First Christian for many years. One Sunday morning in the last 1940s, he appeared to fall asleep in the family pew about two rows back from ours, but in fact he had quietly died. This was a shock and a sad occasion for the congregation.

My parents did not own a car until 1948. Thus, for the first eleven years of my life, we walked the mile and a half every Sunday to the church located at Fourth Avenue and Third Street Southeast. The church building was constructed of a light brown brick and had a large belfry on the southeast corner. I don't know if there were ever bells in that belfry or not. I can say for sure that I never heard any bell sounds coming from it.

On the east side of the building the church had a walk-in basement. At the west end, the basement was totally underground. The sanctuary was in something like a pie shape with three sets of pews on a slanting floor. The length of the pews narrowed as they approached the chancel area. A closed curtain was just behind the pulpit. Behind this curtain was a baptismal basin five by eight feet in length and width and four feet deep. As the congregation faced the pulpit area, the choir was seated behind a low railing to the right of the chancel. A piano and an organ were located at either end of this choir platform.

To the west of the sanctuary, sliding walls opened on another set of pews used only rarely in case of an "overflow" crowd. Classrooms were located on the first and second levels. Additional classrooms and a fellowship hall were in the basement, including a rather large kitchen ruled like a fiefdom by Mrs. George Ponder.

The sanctuary had eight vaulted windows in imitation Gothic style. The main entrance was beneath the belfry and access was up a dozen concrete steps. Consequently, most worshipers entered either through the basement or at a side door facing Third Street. These entryways had many fewer steps.

The entrance to the basement was slightly below ground level. In order to prevent erosion, two concrete walls were constructed on each side of the entrance running eight feet back from the door. The walls were six feet apart. One of the challenges that faced any boy coming to the church was to accept the inevitable challenge to leap from one wall to the other. This long jump was not for the faint of heart. It was a dangerous, and not a few kids were hurt to varying degrees when they failed to make it across and landed on the concrete walk below.

My parents attended church, rain or shine, every Sunday morning, but they never attended evening services because those conflicted with farm chores. (Lord, be praised!) The morning church service was held at 11:00 a.m. Sunday school began at 9:45. Before separating into classes, a hymn-sing lasting about fifteen minutes was held in the sanctuary. The music leader was Mr. Joe Cobb. He had a spectacularly deep bass voice and was usually assisted by Mr. Clyde Glasscock, who was a strong tenor. Clyde's daughter, Josie, by the age of nine or ten was singing solos in a sweet soprano voice. Buell Cobb, son of Joe, was present at the assemblies to sing bass. Afterward, he led the adult males in a Men's Bible Class.

A women's Bible class was led by one of the women. The genders were not mixed in adult classes at this level in those days. Women continued to kept their heads covered in church. They could not serve as deacons or elders. Their roles were limited to teaching the children, the youth, and working in the kitchen.

Youth were placed in classes according to grade level. The teens were grouped in junior high and high school classes. The very young spent most of the time coloring pictures of biblical figures. a verse or two in the Bible and then gave us a drawing to color. That was an easy way to learn about Noah, Sampson, Jonah, Shadrach, Meshach, and Abednego. (These latter three were the "coolest" guys in the Bible despite being in a fiery furnace!) Biblical heroes always managed to do the right thing, with some prodding from their God or from some raving prophet. Our Sunday school teachers at all levels exhorted us to be heroes for God in our lives as well. I suspect we all fell considerably short.

In the summertime, when my family left our house to walk to church, the sun would already be hot. The Bremen road (now old Highway 69) was not yet paved and was very dusty when no rain had fallen for a few days. Sometimes the county road crew came by our house with a truck full of used oil which they sprinkled on the road to hold down the dust. The mixture of dust and old oil gave off the pungent odor of a "filling station." When the weather was bad (rainy or cold), we usually didn't have to walk to church. One of the men of the congregation would drive to the farm and Sunday mornings at our house were unlike any other mornings. We got out of bed, dressed in work clothes, did our various chores, ate breakfast, and then redressed in our Sunday best. We each owned a set of clothes strictly for that day and that day only. I wore a suit and tie from about age nine. My suit was always slightly too small for my gangly arms and legs. The collar of my white shirt always seemed too tight, even though I was what folks described as skinny.

Our Sunday, shoes were polished and brushed before we left for church, in spite of the fact that in clear weather we would be walking the first half mile on a sandy, oily, and unpaved road. On Sundays, our hair received special attention as well. It was wet down good with hair tonic and combed into a nice "roach." Close attention was paid to the cowlick on the crown. With enough oil, the cowlick could be tamed for a few minutes.

Headaches plagued me on Sunday mornings. I swore it was because of the hair oil and the tight collar. Looking back, I recognize that these head-aches were likely due to anxiety. At Sunday school and church, I would be exposed to questions about God and the Bible. I could be asked to sing or quote a Bible verse—or worse, to say a prayer.

The first pastor of our church of whom I have some recollection was a young man named Brother Ralph Saunders. It was the custom in those days in the Disciples Church to refer to the ministers as "brother." Young Brother Saunders was fresh from seminary and didn't yet own a car. He walked the mile and a half to our farm on occasion, always knowing he would be welcomed into the kitchen to have a piece of pie, or if it was near noon, to join in the dinner.

Brother Saunders was succeeded by Brother Tweedy Foster and then by Brother Myron Dick. Several of us in the Christian Church between the ages of nine and eleven were baptized by Brother Dick on Easter Sunday in 1947. By *baptized*, I mean totally immersed. For the Disciples of Christ, that is the preferred method to be washed of one's sins. This was to be a very solemn ceremony but was spoiled a bit because of difficulties with water temperature.

Someone had heated the water way too hot. Some had to be drained and fresh cool water added. This took a lot of time and not a few giggles from the soon-to-be-saved cohort.

The youth in the Disciples Church attended a fellowship called *Chi Rho* (the first two Greek letters in the name Christ). At evening meetings, we played the usual social games of the day: drop the handkerchief, spin the bottle, dodge ball, musical chairs, pin the tail on the donkey, and bob for apples.

Some of the kids' parents had cabins on Guntersville Lake about forty miles northeast of Cullman. The Chi Rho group occasionally held retreats at one of those cabins. Most of the times when they met, I was required to remain on the farm to work. When I did attend these retreats, I felt like the odd man out. I didn't swim, and I sure didn't water ski. Those were activities the city kids had time to learn while I was learning the techniques of plowing and hoeing. Despite the obvious socioeconomic disparity in our lives, I was always accepted in the Chi Rho group. The ministers, the elders, the teachers, and the youth at First Christian all played a role in my early development. All are remembered with fondness.

Brother Gilbert's Bees

The secret to a good sermon is to have a
good beginning and a good ending
and to have the two as close together as possible.

—George Burns

Growing up, my favorite pastor was Brother O. G. Gilbert. I didn't know what names those initials represented; he was always simply "Brother Gilbert" to most of us. (I have recently learned that the *O* is for Oscar.) He had a traditional style of hermeneutics, meaning he read a few verses from the Old or New Testament, told a rather time-worn joke or two, and began the sermon. The latter was divided into three points, with the central message repeated three times. I suppose the repetition was in case we didn't grasp the meaning the first or second time.

Brother Gilbert was not a shouter or a Bible thumper, and this was fine with the congregation, but perhaps they appreciated most his typical sermon length. In the days of long-winded sermons, Brother

Gilbert's was rarely over twenty-five minutes. This meant that those who liked to arrive for the first seating in local restaurants could beat the Baptists and Methodists to the punch.

Brother Gilbert took an interest in me and occasionally invited me to the parsonage (an awe-inspiring, two-story frame house in Victorian style, originally built for the family of George Ponder, owner of the upscale department store in central Cullman). Brother Gilbert and I talked about schoolwork and life's big questions. We didn't speak of religion—why would we? He knew I had heard it all more than once. Besides, it was much more interesting to talk about careers, about the future, or about what books we were currently reading.

We spoke often of the need for a college education. Brother Gilbert had attended Transylvania College in Lexington, Kentucky. He never missed an opportunity to put in a plug for that institution. At that time, Transylvania was partially supported by the Disciples of Christ denomination, and local congregations assisted in this aid.

At first, I laughed at his suggestion. "Transylvania—that sounds like a vampire school," I teased. He brushed aside my comment with a quick story of the institution's early years when it was a rival of Harvard in areas of medicine and science. When I told Brother Gilbert that I was thinking of applying to Harvard, it was his turn to laugh and make a joke. As it turned out, the joke was definitely on me.

When I traveled to Birmingham to be interviewed by a banker who was an alumnus of Harvard and I saw the young men who were also there for interviews, I quickly realized I was out of my league. These young men were poised and articulate, cosmopolitan-looking, well-dressed, while my arms and feet stuck out awkwardly from my outgrown suit. The banker was kind, but he made it clear that Harvard was most interested in an upper socioeconomic class of young men.

Occasionally I helped Brother Gilbert with yard work, and he took me fishing with him several times on the Mulberry River. When we came home, his wife would fry up a "mess" of whatever fish we caught—bluegill, bass, and brim. Mrs. Gilbert was an excellent cook.

Brother Gilbert kept a dozen beehives on property outside the city limits. He was very proud of his knowledge of bees and the quality of his honey. Brother Gilbert decided he would teach me the art of beekeeping. He showed me how to care for the bees and how to gather honey. He taught me to show no fear when around the bees and to avoid swatting at them when they buzzed around. I learned that when I did not show aggression, the bees usually did not sting. Eventually I became comfortable around the hives.

At some point, Brother Gilbert decided that his bees were not as productive as they should be. He had read about a new strain of bee that produced more and better honey. He mailed off an order for a dozen new queens to restock the hives. Now, I must say that restocking was no easy task. The bees remain loyal to the old queen as long as she is present in the hive. Consequently, the old queen had to be found and eliminated before the new queen was placed in the hive.

Finding a queen bee in a hive of thousands of worker bees and drones is not easy. Each section had to be pulled out of the hive and examined meticulously in search of the one large queen. She is surrounded by hundreds of workers who try to protect her. Nevertheless, she stands out fully, due to her size, if you can get through the mass of milling bees.

One fine day Brother Gilbert and I set out to re-queen his dozen hives. We wore long-sleeve denim shirts and blue jeans. We tied down our pant legs, put on hats with netting over our faces, put on heavy gloves that came halfway to our elbows. We had smokers that put out great clouds of smoke. The smoke tended to daze the bees, and they were much less active. The smoke worked as a sedative.

Nevertheless, a goodly number of bees were belligerent because we were threatening the life of the hive. They stung throughout pant legs, climbed up under our gloves and tried to get under the netting over our faces. No matter how diligent we were, we received several stings—mostly through the denim of our pants. These stings were relatively mild, and we just ignored them. Those bees that crawled up the gloves were another matter. They were diligently searching for some bare flesh.

All in all, our efforts were rewarded. We found all the queens except one. The new queens were accepted in the eleven hives where the old queens had been removed. Brother Gilbert was elated by our work. For my assistance, he gave me a quart jar of honey with a large piece of comb and two dollars. It was my turn to be thrilled.

Saints and Sinners

Shy worshippers find comfort with the "frozen chosen." Extroverts enjoy the "holy rollers."

The town of Cullman with its five thousand souls needed quite a few churches to satisfy the desire on the part of the various denominations to set themselves apart from their lesser brethren and sisters who had not yet grasped the true meaning of the Gospel, and thus were still in a state of sin. In this respect, the city is no different from any other town, North or South.

Many southern cities have a Church Street where several denominations built very close to each other on a "main" street. This tendency led to the oft-repeated joke about the man who was walking down Church Street one Sunday morning as various congregations were singing hymns. As he walked past the Methodist Church, they were singing, "*Will there be any stars in my crown?*" As he proceeded to the next block, the Lutherans were singing "*No, not one; No not one.*" As he passed the Baptist church, he clearly heard them belting out, "*And that will be glory for me!*"

That joke wouldn't depict the situation in Cullman. The denominations were scattered around the four corners of the town rather than clustered along one particular street. Nevertheless, the competition for souls remained energetic. The need to distinguish oneself, to set oneself apart, individually or as a body of believers, is a very strong characteristic of human nature.

Some faithful talk of the "primitive church" as though the first-century Christians were immune from the "sin" of hubris. Unfortunately, the facts of history do not bear this out. The early church was wracked with dissent just as twentieth century churches are. In fact, the early church was even more fragmented. The church leaders struggled with profound questions about the nature of Christ. With few exceptions, this issue has long been resolved.

The modern church is racked with squabbles that appear rather petty in comparison: baptism by immersion versus sprinkling; infant baptism versus baptism at the time of conscious acceptance of the faith; instrumental music versus *a cappella* singing; wine or grape juice during the Lord's Supper; a communion of remembrance versus a reenactment of Christ's sacrifice. The list of diversities includes social justice issues: Rock-solid ethical views versus situational ethics. When does human life begin in the womb? When were humans created and how? Did the universe begin with a big bang of energy or was the earth created in seven days? Does the Bible trump science? Can an individual change his or her physiological and psychological constitution? Are women a subset of men?

Cullman was not (and is not currently) spared the human foibles that seem inevitable in matters of faith. When I was young, the town had Methodists, Baptists of several persuasions, Lutherans of two separate synods, Nazarenes, Roman Catholics, and my favorite, Hard Shell Baptists (or Primitive Baptists). This latter group saw themselves as descendants of Old School Baptists. They split off from mainline Baptists over several issues that arose following the Second Great Awakening of the early 1800s when a major fight occurred over the pros and cons of establishing foreign missions.

The term "primitive" Baptist alludes to the belief they hold that their doctrines and forms of worship are more closely related to early (original) Christian worship. Some features of their worship include *a cappella* singing, closed communion, and foot washing. Most hold firm to the doctrine of predestination (election by God for salvation) and efficacious grace. They exhibit considerable anti-intellectualism in their attitude toward Sunday schools, Mission Boards, and theological institutions. To the Primitive Baptist, a spirit-filled man is viewed as a better preacher than an overly educated one. Those folks lucky enough to be elected (chosen for salvation) manifest themselves as "born anew" at some point in their lives. This group is often the butt of jokes for what some deem unreasonableness and hardheadedness. It is natural that they would be jokingly referred to as "Hard Shells."

From the beginning, Roman Catholicism has been a major religious, intellectual, and cultural force in Cullman. The first motherhouse for Roman Catholic nuns in the State of Alabama was founded in Cullman. No other center existed in the state until the second half of the twentieth century. The Community of Benedictine Sisters of Sacred Heart Convent was formed in 1902 just east of the town. The sisters bought one hundred and twenty acres of land from one of the pioneer German families, the Kleins. The religious order built a three-story brick building completed in 1904 using brick manufactured in west Cullman at what used to be called "the brickyard" long after it ceased to function.

Roman Catholics built a small sanctuary in Cullman in 1877, just four years after the town was founded, situated on land donated by the L&N Railroad. This edifice was dedicated to the Sacred Heart of Jesus. A grade school was built next to the sanctuary in 1879 by the Sisters of Notre Dame and is still operating in a new and enlarged structure.

Early in the new century (1916), the earlier structure was replaced with an impressive building in neo-gothic style. This second sanctuary was constructed at Second Avenue and Second Street. It has two bell towers with spires and three large doors representing the Trinity on the west façade as well as a large rose window.

The interior of the church has a barrel vault ceiling and a semicircular apse. The twenty-four beautiful stain glass windows were created in Germany and shipped over to Cullman after WWI. The walls are of russet colored sandstone. This magnificent edifice is a landmark. Its spires, reaching some eighty feet high, can be seen from quite a distance. Driving in from the north on I-65 or US 31, suddenly the roads begin to slope down a slight ridge and off in the distance the west ridge of Brindley Mountain is visible with the first object being the two spires of the Catholic Church. It is one of the most majestic churches in the state of Alabama.

Several Benedictine friars arrived in Cullman in 1888. This led to the founding of the St. Bernard Abbey in 1891 on land just a couple of miles east of town along Eight Mile Creek. The abbey eventually became quite famous for its Ave Maria Grotto created over the years through the dedication of Father Joseph.

Father Joseph was born Michael Zoettl. He came to the US in 1892 as a teenage boy. After several years working with Benedictine houses in several states, he arrived at the Saint Bernard Abbey in 1911. Father Joseph was assigned to the power plant where he soon found the work tedious and boring. He began to make little miniature grottos and figurines which were sold in the abbey gift shop.

By 1932, Father Joseph had made over five thousand miniature grottos. With the encouragement of his superiors, Father Joseph began a much more ambitious project. He started constructing a replica of biblical Jerusalem using concrete, bits of glass, broken pieces of marble and other castaway items. In 1934, Ava Maria Grotto was dedicated. By the early 1940s, the grotto had become a tourist destination. Father Joseph continued constructing miniature basilicas and other religious buildings over the next thirty years.

My parents took out-of-town visitors to the grotto when they came to visit. After all, it was the only attraction of note in the Cullman area at the time other than a covered bridge a few miles to the west. The grotto area was relatively cool in the hot summer because of the number of shade trees. Bushes and flowering plants were interspersed among the various miniature creations.

Unfortunately, during WWII Catholics in Cullman became the object of bias and bigotry. Some folks would avoid meeting a couple of black-robed nuns on the sidewalk. Rumors circulated that Catholics were siding with the Germans. Other innuendoes floated concerning "evil activities" occurring in the rectory between priests and nuns. Most likely some of the accusers were closet sinners.

In the 1970s, my wife served as librarian in a Roman Catholic grade school. Our daughters were enrolled and received an excellent hands-on education from the nuns and lay-teachers. Although Protestant, the girls attended weekly mass with their class. They could not partake of the elements (an exclusivity practiced by several denominations in Christendom).

Our younger daughter, who entered the program in grade five, began to learn the ritual prayers. One day we heard her reciting the Hail Mary: "Holy Mary, Mother of God, blessed art thou among women, and blessed is *the fruit of the loom* Jesus." It was quite natural to confuse fruit of the *womb* with *loom*, seeing as how the TV air waves were saturated at the time by *Fruit of the Loom* commercials, plus she had no idea what a womb was. She had a tendency toward malapropisms in any case. This is the child who ran in from the yard one cold day and proclaimed, "Mommy, Mommy, my chaps are lipped!"

It is not unusual for children to associate words in liturgy and music with expressions they already know. Thus, we hear of children coming home and singing "*Gladly the Cross-eyed Bear*," or bringing home a drawing of an airplane being flown by *Pontius the Pilot*. Over time, I discover more and more evidence that knowledge learned by rote rather than by analysis and a bit of doubting can turn out to be amusingly skewed. In effect, the typical person's biblical knowledge tends to be weak even when he or she is excellent at quoting Scripture. But knowledge seems not to correlate at all with whether a person is a saint or a sinner.

Revivals and Tent Meetings

Come on down folks. The good
Lord's waitin' for YOU—
"Just as I am without one plea, but
that thy blood was shed for me."

Revivals were frequent events in many Southern churches, rural or urban. Preachers in rural churches were often part-time evangelists and visited other congregations to stoke up renewed faith. This was often an avocation for these evangelists. Their major income-producing occupation was often farming, but some were mechanics or store clerks.

These self-styled evangelists, as well as "professional" evangelists, put on a one-man minidrama, pacing back and forth across the elevated floor behind and beside the pulpit, thumping their red-letter leather Bibles. Sometimes they even came down into the "audience" (the congregation of worshippers). After a phrase or two of staccato exhortations from the revivalist, the walls of the tent or building were peppered with shouted *Amen*, *Halleluiah*, and *Praise the Lord*. The worshippers were on the verge of bursting into ecstasy.

The sweaty worshippers kept time with the rhythm of the preacher's intoning words, using their cardboard fans donated by a funeral home. Most of these fans had a picture of Jesus on one side and an advertisement for home on the other.

Few rural churches had ceiling fans, or any electric fan, for that matter. On hot summer days, the windows and doors were open in hopes of getting a breeze. The pungent smell of bodies mingled with the sweet smell of snuff, tobacco juice, cigarette smoke, and heavy-scented bath powder and perfume. These smells mingled with the odor of babies, sour milk, and spit-up.

The cacophony of sounds coming from outside the room was almost as varied. Children left outside the church house played tag or cowboys and Indians. Occasionally, if somebody thought to bring the necessary equipment, a game of horseshoes would break out with its periodic clank as the iron shoes clashed against each other. Mules hitched to nearby rails occasionally cut loose with a mighty bray. The sound of an Indian hen might break through the din with its full-force chatter echoing across the hollow near the church building.

Neither noise nor smell seemed to affect the preacher who had self-mesmerized into a modern-day Jeremiah. His voice would rise to a crescendo and then drop off in soft and dramatic murmurs. The words would be nearly inaudible for a moment and then—*wham*—Jeremiah would slam his fist into his leather Bible, hoping that sinners a mile away would hear and believe.

In the summer, these evangelists held large bandanas in one hand to wipe away the sweat. Most cultivated a singsong method of speaking. I found it fascinating that most could articulate while breathing in through their mouths. This created a sound much like a sobbing child trying to talk, or a person talking while hiccupping. I used to try to emulate that style of oration but was never successful.

From a distance, the exhortations by the evangelist sounded like ranting and raving, but most of the men and women in the church house seemed to be mesmerized. Soon some were rising out of their seats, waving their arms in the air. Their shouts became louder and more personal. "Jesus! Jesus! Save me! Save me!" Soon one would rush down the aisle to the mourners' bench. This would start a flood of sinners into action.

It appeared to me that the bench was called the mourners' bench because the folks who sat there often were crying, but I have since learned that the bench was for those in need of the Lord's saving grace. They were sinners. They were the ones who had missed coming to church for the past several Sundays. They were the ones who had succumbed over and over to the sin of fornication, of making moonshine, dancing or card playing, or just lusting in their hearts.

They were the men who beat their wives or the wives who were beaten by their men folk. They were the "two-timing" men or women and now the preacher had convinced them of their sinning ways and had convinced them that perdition was awaiting them, that hellfire and brimstone would be in their future if they did not break the grip of Satan and come to Jesus. These folks were down on the mourners' bench awaiting the "layin' on of hands."

The preacher was unconvinced that his message had gotten through to all the sinners. He was sure there were many more folks in the congregation in the grasp of the devil, and it was the preacher's duty to flush those folks out, no matter how long it took. He would continue reciting verses from various part of the Bible to illustrate the total depravity of man and his damnation in the eyes of God.

It seemed to me that these preachers had memorized the entire Bible. Now, this was astonishing to me because I had tried various times to read parts of the Bible, but I could never get very far. The words were just too difficult and didn't make sense. What was the meaning of all these *smite* and *smote* and *hath* and *art* and so on. A Bible sat by the radio on the only table in our living room. It was always there inviting me to read. I was unaware that a translation had been done using modern American English (*American Standard*, 1901). Perhaps I could have better understood a translation with more modern vocabulary and syntax than that used in the King James Revised Version (dating from 1885).

One time I decided to begin at the beginning and read the Bible all the way through. Despite all my good will, I never got past the first chapter of *Genesis*. I thought maybe the *New Testament* would be easier reading, so I started with *Matthew* and got hung up on all the *begats* and all those impossible to pronounce names. I decided to leave the Bible to the Sunday school teachers who always seemed to know what a given verse meant.

The First Christian Church also had an annual revival and paid a professional evangelist to come for a week to pep up the congregation, and—if possible—attract some of the un-churched to join. "New" members almost never showed up. Some backsliders might renew for a few Sundays and then fall back on their old ways, and some children might join the church during revival time, but that was all. The congregation seemed like the frozen chosen. No "*Amens*," no "Preach it, brother," no "Thank you, Jesus," and most certainly no screaming or falling on the floor. No matter how many times we sang "*Just as I Am Without One Plea, but that Thy blood was shed for me*," no one came down to profess their faith. I guess those folks who had worked hard all day were "plum tuckered out" and were anxious to get out the door and go home. I know I was.

This annual revival occurred at an inopportune time for my family. It occurred before the crops were laid by. We were the only farm family among the members at First Christian. Revivals ran from Sunday to the following Friday evening. It was hot in the church; the ceiling fans whirled at top speed, and the cardboard Jesus fans were waving. The revivalist would thump the Bible and raise his voice into a crescendo and pace across the raised area next to the pulpit. He was attempting to put the fear of the Lord in the sinners out in the pews. He exhorted us about sin and evil and Satan and needing to get right with God. It seemed to me that most of the listeners were upstanding citizens who were very unlikely to be doing the type of sinning the preacher was describing.

Once Glenn and I were walking back from an evening youth meeting at First Christian, and we had to pass through West Town. We ran across a tent meeting near Seventh Street. We could hear the singing from blocks away. When we got close Glenn wanted to go inside. I was very reluctant, but I was afraid to stay outside the tent by myself.

We entered the door of the tent and peered in. The place was full of folks in folding chairs. The floor was covered with wood shavings. It was stifling hot. The only air came from the front door or from the eight inches of space at the bottom of the tent canvas.

At the opposite end of the entrance, the "preacher" was standing on a makeshift riser. He had his suit coat off, his tie loosened, his collar unbuttoned, and his shirt sleeves rolled up above the elbow. His shirt was dark with sweat underneath his arms. When we were far enough inside to be seen, the preacher motioned for us to come on down front.

"Come on down, young fellars, don't be afraid. Come on down. Have ya been saved? Have ya professed Jesus as your personal savior? Renounce yo sinful flesh and fall down, here and now and profess Jesus as yo Lord." I was embarrassed, but Glenn was elated at a chance to go down and be saved. Not me! I turned and ran back down the aisle and out the tent door. It was only a quarter mile to our farm, and I didn't slow down until I got there. As I ran past the cemetery, I turned my ahead away and prayed no goblins were out that night. After Glenn got saved, he came on home as well. Our dad was not very pleased with him for two reasons. Glenn had already been saved and didn't need to be saved a second time. In addition, he was not ever to leave me to walk home alone again.

Old-Time Radio Shows

The evening is young; the night is long;
Pull up your chair close by the radio.
Sit back, relax, and enjoy the music of
Les Brown and his *Band of Renown.*

T he early console radio doubled as a well-de-
signed piece of furniture. However, by the
1940s, radio sets were being built as table
models, some weighing less than ten pounds. In
those days, radios were simple constructions of vacuum tubes, speaker cones, crystals, and tuning wires
(often string). Kits could be purchased, allowing an
individual to make his or her own set.

When I was five years old, mother's brother,
Captain Cephas Smith, sent us money to purchase
a table-top radio. My dad stretched antenna wire
back and forth across the front porch. Eventually we
were able pick up a Birmingham station broadcasting
some fifty miles away. Programs came in clearly and
without static when the weather was clear.

Acquiring a radio was a life-changing event at our house. In the evenings, we now sat in a semicircle around the radio and enjoyed a variety of musical and comedic programs. In fact, the two genres were often comingled. Comedy shows had orchestras that played opening, closing and interlude music to set the mood. Many comedies featured famous vocalists. Commercials were often little more than musical jingles.

Today advertising on radio and television is ubiquitous. However, in the forties, radio shows had sponsors which "brought" the program to you utilizing a much lower percentage of the total time slot. Promotions by these sponsors were less insidious than today's steady stream of commercials occupying fully one-third of the total time frame.

In the forties, only one product would normally be pitched during a show, often by one or more of the cast members. Shows also had announcers who frequently doubled as a cast member. Commercials were often woven into the plot lines. Cast members both used and promoted the product; consequently, the line between commercial and entertainment was blurred.

The majority of sponsors fell into three groups—soaps, cigarettes, and booze. Fewer ads sponsored food and soft drinks. One memorable new food product was called Jell-O. The product was spelled out in a little jingle—*J-E-L-L-O*. Those early jingles and simple slogans seemed to lock on to some recess of the mind. Ask anyone who grew up in the forties what pops in their mind when they hear the slogan, "Good to the last drop." A high percentage will recall *Maxwell House Coffee*.

Cigarette commercials had insidiousness about them. The ad men must have used psychologists as consultants. Smoking sounded like so much fun. These commercials enticed you want to "*walk a mile for a Camel*" or to "*call for Philip Morrrrisss.*" Health concerns were assuaged by ads that told us that "*nine out of ten doctors smoke Chesterfields.*"

If you tried a cigarette and it burned your tongue, you were just smoking the wrong brand. You needed to switch to *Prince Albert* smoking tobacco because it was specially treated to ensure against "*tongue bite.*" Indeed, Prince Albert was the national "*Joy Smoke.*"

"Does your cigarette irritate you throat?" the pitchman would ask. "Then you need to switch to the only leading cigarette recognized by eminent nose and throat specialists as definitely *less irritating*. No wonder so many of us took up this nasty, unhealthy habit.

Soap ads in the forties and fifties ranged from floor cleaners to dishwashing powders, to laundry detergents, to tooth powder, to shampoo and deodorants. The majority of "soap" commercials were aimed at housewives—promising to help them keep a clean home that they could be proud of. Afternoon dramas for housewives began in the nineteen thirties.

Since major soap companies sponsored these little slices of life, the programs came to be known as "soaps." The first one of these to register in my brain was *Ma Perkins*. I remember playing in our house and hearing out of one ear the background organ music for that "opera." I particularly remember the soothing voice of Ma Perkins giving out her advice for living.

My mother would not miss an episode of *Ma Perkins* if she could possibly avoid doing so. I don't remember what days and times the show was aired, but I know that Mother planned her activities around that time period—making sure she was in the house and not in the vegetable garden or out in the wash house. *Ma Perkins* was sponsored by *Oxydol* soap, touted for its "deep cleaning." Naturally, Mother swore by that product!

Soap companies didn't just sponsor afternoon melodramas. Lever Brothers promoted the "triple action" efficacy of *Rinso White* on at least one evening comedy show. Lever Brothers' ad men also sang the praises of *Lifebuoy* bath soap, which—analogous to saving a drowning person—could save you from very embarrassing moments, occasions when you might otherwise "stink up" the room with BO (body odor or *bad* odor, take your pick).

Products catering to a male audience sponsored sports programs. The majority were tobacco companies, beer makers, and hawkers of shaving products. *Lava Soap* promised to clean the hands of "real" working men. In addition, *Listerine* warned us of the horrors of halitosis. The principal goal at the time was sociability, not sexuality.

These masculine products were instrumental in their efforts to socialize men and boys. We were being taught to keep our bodies clean and our hair neat. By the time I turned thirteen, the most ubiquitous commercial for boys and men was *Brylcreem* ("a little dab 'ill do ya"). That's another slogan that many folks over the age of fifty will remember.

In the forties and early fifties, programming aimed specifically at boys ran few commercials. Unlike today's youth, the boys of that era didn't have much money to spend. What little they managed to get their hands on was quickly dispensed for comic books, marbles, movies, chewing gum and candy. The *Wrigley Company* was one of the first to recognize the power of targeting the young, even those with limited buying power. The *Hershey Company* was not far behind.

Afternoon programming for boys—the Lone Ranger, Hopalong Cassidy, and the Cisco Kid—had few commercial interruptions; some just offered musical interludes between acts. I enjoyed the classical music "teasers" we heard on the Lone Ranger and the Hispanic music encircling the Cisco Kid and his sidekick, Poncho. For many of us, that was our only introduction to music outside the Southern genres of gospel and country.

Rossini's *Overture* to the opera, *William Tell*, is a good example. Most of us knew the general outline of the exciting story of the archer, the son, the apple and the arrow, but we didn't know that William Tell was the subject of an opera. The musical lead-in to the *Lone Ranger* was very stirring. The sound enabled me to picture horses racing along at full gallop. I learned to hum several bars of the melody. I assumed the music had been written specifically for *The Lone Ranger Radio Show*. I was an adult before I heard the complete *William Tell Overture* and realized that I had heard a segment years before as part of *The Lone Ranger Radio Show*. To this day, when I hear Rossini's *Overture*, I see galloping horses and expect any second to hear "Hi ho, Silver, Awaaaay."

Few of us knew anything about operas and *Overtures*, much less the composer Rossini. I was quite ignorant of classical music and pronounced Beethoven's name just as it looked to me—*beet ho vin*—until one of the "city boys" gave me an embarrassing lesson in pronunciation.

The Lone Ranger program always began in identical fashion. As the lead-in music faded, three or four pistol shots rang out. Then an announcer recited with great dramatic flair: *"A fiery horse with the speed of light, a cloud of dust, and a hardy Hi Yo Silver: The Lone Ranger rides again."* Then the music resumed and continued for what seemed like minutes. The announcer then returned to make sure we understood that the Lone Ranger was a "hero." In fact, he was a superhero. *"Nowhere in the pages of history can one find a greater champion of justice,"* we were told.

Dramatic radio programs aimed at young boys were aired in the late afternoons. After riding my bike home from school, I had time to finish the farm chores before the program began. I seldom missed an episode. My imagination was captivated by the honor and dignity of the Lone Ranger—his never-ceasing fight for justice. Even if Tonto spoke "funny," he was equally dedicated to the good and the right. We respected him even while imitating his syntax. "Him plenty bad man, Kemosabe."

We were familiar with this pidgin form of English. All the Native Americans spoke in that manner on the silver screen—so did Tarzan the Ape Man. We knew instinctively that these "poor" speakers of English were not stupid. We also knew somehow that Native Americans were not all murderous barbarians. But we were very ambivalent in our attitudes. We didn't react when the "bad men" called Tonto an "injun" or "redskin," or some other disparaging term.

We always clapped and yelled when the US Cavalry rode over the hills to save a wagon train under attack by Apaches, Comanches, Blackfeet, or Sioux. On the other hand, we had empathy for the heroism of individual warriors like Cochise, Sitting Bull, and Geronimo. The strength and courage of such Native Americans were not lost on us.

Unfortunately, none of us knew that generations of early white settlers had committed genocide and ethnic cleansing—even on the very soil where we lived. No one had spoken to us about the "Trail of Tears." No one told us that the American president whose picture is engraved on the twenty-dollar bill had nearly wipe out all traces of the "civilized" tribes in the Southeast US—indeed that this president had ordered the systematic round-up of women and children and old men of the Cherokee Nation and had them driven to death or to exile in Oklahoma.

If we had little knowledge of the plight of the Native American, we knew even less about the war launched by President Polk to grab the western lands north of the Rio Grande from Mexico. Our history books made the overall Manifest Destiny doctrine seem like an imperative blessed by God. Of course, the Alamo came to symbolize the best of America's heroes.

In view of all this, the popularity of the Cisco Kid seems something of an anomaly in retrospect. Most of us kids loved the dashing style of Cisco and were unfailingly amused by the antics and accent of Poncho. We picked up a little Spanish lingo as a result. Soon we could all say *buenos dias*, *gracias*, *si senor*, *uno momento*, *por favor*, *hombre*, *loco* and a half-dozen or so additional words.

Not all the youth-focused radio programs dealt with cowboys, Indians, and Mexicans. Sky King was a different and exciting radio drama where the struggle between good and evil could scarcely be made clearer. The dialogue and the action would seem full of trite clichés to our cynical ears today, but for a young idealist in the '40s, the drama was a great moral lesson. Characters on the show continually stressed the innate goodness and trustworthiness of Sky King. "He was the most trusted man alive," the local sheriff avowed. As we listened, we imagined that one day we might be considered as equally trustworthy.

King was a rancher and a pilot. He flew a prop plane that he called *Songbird*. Like Trigger, Champion, Silver, and other cowboy horses, King's plane had a personality and played a significant role in the drama. King's niece, Penny, lived at the ranch with him and gave the program a feminine touch. Suspense was heightened by melodramatic organ music. Special effects aided us in creating mental pictures—the sounds of planes, explosions, gunshots, and fisticuffs.

Unlike most Westerns, the Sky King drama had a sponsor. The program was presented by *Peter Pan Peanut Butter*. After a few commercials touting the creamy smoothness and good taste of that wonderful product, you really felt as though you had to have a spoonful on a piece of bread immediately. In those days, a peanut butter sandwich, plain, with jelly, or with banana was a great treat for most kids. I often had a slice of "loaf" bread thoroughly covered with peanut butter while listening raptly beside the radio—my ear only a few inches from the speaker—careful not to drop a crumb on the linoleum floor or smear the doily on the table.

"Loaf" bread was a treat. My mother made a batch of buttermilk biscuits and a pone of corn-bread every day of the year. She never failed to do so even when she was ill. These were the breads we ate with our three meals. She permitted a loaf of "store bought" or "white" bread in her house simply for the purpose of making a bologna, mayonnaise, or peanut butter sandwich for snacks.

The entire family was together for several radio programs. During the noon hour (our dinner meal), we listened to the local farm report which gave the commodity prices (cotton, corn, hog, eggs, and beef). We heard the daily police report, and we learned who had died and where and when their funeral services would be held.

Beginning in 1952, the local news was followed by Paul Harvey and his authoritative *News and Comments* on ABC Radio. A staunchly conservative and super patriotic commentator, Paul Harvey reported news, but he also gave his opinion about various stories. He considered himself a moral compass and spoke to his audience like a Pope delivering an *ex cathedra* address. Harvey added poignant and uplifting life stories meant to inspire us. He read the commercial scripts personally, followed by his famous: "*And now, back to my news, please!*"

Long before the appearance of obnoxious and ubiquitous billboards that mar our view of the countryside in many states of the US, some ad executives tried to catch the public's eye in a more subtle way. I'm thinking of the wonderful little slogans for *Burma Shave* that were staked along many two-lane roads in the forties and fifties. While driving in the countryside, driver and passengers enjoyed the Burma Shave slogans posted at the edge of the road.

Like the barn roofs painted with the ads for *Rock City* and *Cave City* in Chattanooga, Tennessee, the Burma Shave ads have disappeared (except for a recent feeble attempt at a revival). Both visual pitches are things of the past, relics of an art form now replaced by graffiti writers.

Burma Shave signs were placed strategically along the roads about one hundred feet apart. They consisted of six small placards posted a couple of feet above the ground. The slogan, written in doggerel verse, unraveled as the car proceeded along the road. Passengers would stare out the car window, anxious to see the humorous punch line which normally came at the fourth or fifth board. The last board inevitably read BURMA SHAVE. These cute ads began to disappear when four lane roads became popular and when automobiles and drivers traveled with such speed that the signs zoomed by too fast to be read.

The makers of Burma Shave touted brushless shaving cream, which was invented in the 1930s. Before that time, most shavers used a soap cup and a small brush to lather up their face. The pitch was intended to transform the old-style shavers into chic shavers: *Your shaving brush/ Has had its day/ So why not/ Shave the modern way/ With/ Burma Shave.* Another example: *Shaving brushes/ You'll soon/ See 'em/ In some/ Museum/ Burma Shave.* Some of the ads were clever linguistic homonyms: *I proposed/ To Ida/ Ida refused/ Ida won my Ida/ If Ida used/ Burma Shave.*

Safety warnings began to be included in the ads as drivers increased their speed. *Don't lose/ Your head/ To gain a minute/ You need your head/ Your brains are in it/ Burma Shave.* And this one: *If daisies/ Are your/ Favorite flower/ Keep pushin' up those/ Miles per hour/ Burma Shave.*

So popular did these slogans become that contests began to be held each year. The submission chosen as best would be awarded one hundred dollars (wow!). One of my former colleagues submitted a ditty every year, but never won the contest.

Actually, if you get into a groove, writing Burma Shave ditties flows rather easily. The idea is to rhyme the third and fifth billboards and have the last one say Burma Shave. I've put a few together from time to time: *If you keep/ Your eyes/ Upon the ground/ Perhaps you'll miss/ My old red hound/ Burma Shave.* Another quick one: *I have a girl/ Her name is Sue/ I love her like/ The morning dew/ Burma Shave.* The little ditties don't have to make sense. Like limericks, they need to be the proper length, establish a cadence, and have a rhyme.

In the nineteen forties, following the supper hour, we listened faithfully to the national and world news reported by men of the caliber of Edward R. Murrow, Winston Burdett, and Gabriel Heatter. The news hour was followed by primetime evening programs, varying with the day of the week. Such shows as *Edgar Bergen and Charlie McCarthy, Jack Benny, Fibber McGee and Mollie, the Grand Ole Opry, Jimmy Durante, Red Skelton, Our Miss Brooks, the Life of Riley, Baby Snooks, Henry Aldridge, Amos and Andy, George Burns and Gracie Allen*, and a host of others.

My dad had a soft spot for Spike Jones, "the man who killed music," and his madcap band of music makers. Their humorous travesty of serious music provoked side-splitting laughter. They were skilled musicians with traditional instruments, but they also produced all sorts of unusual sounds with non-traditional "instruments": the strum of a wash-board, the weird zing of a hand saw, the whistle of kazoos, the snap of rubber bands, the clang of cow bells, and the toot of car horns. My dad got such a "kick" out of Spike and his band that he would practically fall on the floor. Dad's dentures didn't fit too well, and once some crazy antic by Spike's band caused my dad to laugh so hard that his top denture plate fell out on the floor, producing general mayhem among the rest of us.

One of the evening programs which captivated the entire nation was called *"The Quiz Kids."* Five school children from various grades answered questions mailed to the show by listeners. Joe Kelly was the host. A guest comedian usually made an appearance on the show and generally proved to have much less acumen than the kids. This brainy show is a spiritual ancestor of the present-day *Are You Smarter Than a 5th Grader.*

Sunday morning radio programming was quite different from the morning weekday farm news. On Sunday, we listened to quartets sing gospel tunes (groups like the Blackwood Brothers, the Oak Ridge Boys, the Chuck Wagon Gang, and the local Deep South Quartet in Birmingham).

One of our favorite Sunday morning musical broadcasts hailed from Renfro Valley near Mount Vernon in eastern Kentucky. The theme song of that "down home" mountain group is still etched in some recess of my brain even though I have not been to their Saturday Barn Dances or listened to them on radio in fifty-five years. "*We were born in Renfro Valley, but we drifted far away; now we're back again with home folks in that land we love the best.*" The show was the brain-child of Renfro Valley residents, John Lair and Red Foley. I particularly enjoyed the comedic parodies of country and pop songs by Homer and Jethro, the singing of the Randolph sisters, the antics of Shorty Hobbs and Ella, and the tales of Granny Harper.

Moving from comedic music to comedy and variety, if I remember correctly, the *Jack Benny Show* aired on Sunday evenings. Of all the comedy/variety programs, this was my personal favorite. The show was sponsored in the midforties by *Jell-O* with its lit-tle jingle spelling out this great new, thrillingly and "rich" dessert. According to the announcer, the secret [to the richness] was the "locked-in flavor," whatever that was supposed to mean. My dad was fascinated by this new dessert, which he enjoyed very much (think dentures), and he promptly labeled the stuff "nervous pudding."

The Jello-O commercials were woven into the dialog of the Jack Benny Show. Don Wilson, the announcer/cast member, would belt out praise for the new "locked-in flavor." Apparently the "old" Jell-O lost its favor rapidly and became stale.

Following a musical introduction, Don, in his powerful, deep voice, announced: *The Jack Benny Show* starring Jack Benny, Mary Livingston, Dennis Day, Phil Harris, Rochester, and yours truly, Don

Wilson. Notice that Rochester had only one name while all the other cast members had two names. In addition, most of the white cast members called each other by their first name (except young Dennis who called Jack, *Mister Benny*).

Rochester, on the other hand, was always careful to use Mr. and Miss with all the white cast members. He called Jack, *Mr. Benny* or *Boss*. Despite this subservient role, Rochester had a special appeal with his raspy voice and his good-sense approach to life. As a matter of fact, none of us had our conscience raised enough to be even aware of the inequities and racial overtones.

Following Don Wilson's introduction, Phil Harris, the proverbial drunk, directed his band in a few bars of some commercial jingle. Later in the show, the band played a dance tune, and occasionally Phil would sing a rather comic ditty. But it was Dennis Day, the velvet-throated lyric tenor, who would steal the show by singing an Irish love song. An amazing change came over Dennis when he sang. His chameleon act is exceeded only in later years by the transition that morphed Gomer Pyle, the buffoon with the thick Alabama accent, into Jim Nabors, the rich-voiced crooner. When he was not singing, Dennis played the role of court jester, or village idiot.

To a large extent the humor in the *Jack Benny Show* hinged on Jack's stinginess, his huge money-vault in the dungeon of his house, his antique Maxwell car, and his awful violin playing. When Jack had occasion to play the violin, he made it squawk like a panicked chicken. This was strictly for comic effect. Jack was capable of producing a good sound from his instrument.

For live audiences, Jack had some great physical humor, but when we listened over the radio we were unaware of these gestures. For us, the humor was totally vocal. Jack always got a laugh with his famous line, "*Now, cut that out!*" which he often used in response to some idiotic comment by Dennis Day.

A politically incorrect but very popular comedy in the forties and fifties was titled *Amos 'n' Andy*. The storyline was set in Harlem. All the cast members were ostensibly African Americans played by white actors. The show had evidently evolved from the black-face vaudeville minstrel shows. Although the show was called *Amos 'n' Andy*, the principal character, and the butt of many jokes and *malentendu*, was the ever-scheming *King Fish*.

George Stevens played the role of the King Fish, the leader of the local Fraternal Lodge (in the genre of Elks and Moose). The King Fish spent his energy trying to figure out ways to make a profit without performing any work. He was the archetypical con man, or rather the "would-be con man," since his devious schemes *oft went astray*. In most plots, the would-be deceiver was himself deceived in the end.

The King Fish's wife was Sapphire. She had a good head on her shoulders and tried her best to keep husband George on the straight and narrow. This provoked constant verbal clashes. The language of the Stevens couple, of Amos, Andy and his girlfriend and other bit players was a "gentrified" black English. The vocabulary was basically white, which enabled the audience (mainly white) to follow without difficulty. In order to make the language sound black, the scriptwriters made a few person/number and verb tense changes. The first-person pronoun is always followed by a verb form ending in /s/. For example: I/we *lives* here.

The first- and second-person plural pronouns are followed by the third person singular form of irregular verbs, *you is* and *we is*, for example. The helping verb *will* is omitted from future verb forms: I *be* ready when you *gets* here. Double negatives abound, as well as the ubiquitous *ain't*. All these usages were intended to underline the nature of the subdialect spoken by the characters.

Readers who were alive during WWII will remember the patriotic appeal to housewives to save the grease from their cooking. A few cents per pound for this waste fat was paid by the local butcher. The purpose was to assist in the war effort. Waste fat was used in the manufacture of soap, woolens, tires, and paint, just to name a few items.

This innocent request to the housewife could easily be turned into a linguistic pun for those so inclined. A subtle change in placement of word stress could make a big difference. "Ladies, get your FAT cans down to the butcher" sounded racy when the stress was changed to: "Ladies, get your fat CANS down to the butcher."

The master of puns and plays on words was assuredly Red Skelton. He could take a phrase out of its normal context and create humor. I remember one short skit he had with Beelzebub who comes to Red and says: "*I am Satan.*" Red replies: "*The devil you say!*" He was a real linguistic virtuoso and an amazing ad-libber. Of the various *personas* he assumed, my two favorites were Clem Kadiddlehopper and Junior.

Some just plain "silly" shows were very popular. Everyone loved *Baby Snooks*, the whiney girl who was always outwitting her cosmopolitan and rather supercilious *Daddy*. Then there was the real "dummy," *Charlie McCarthy*, who always got the best of his human handler, Edgar Bergen. As a child, I could hardly wait for *Mortimer Snerd* (another dummy) to make his appearance. This bashful moron stole the show every time.

A few popular programs of the day added permanent expressions to our language. A certain age group still talks about "the life of Reilly" and "Fibber McGee's closet," for example. Few will have forgotten "Good night Mrs. Calabash, wherever you are."

There were also long-lived character types that came out of the comedies of the period. Long before the Fonz of *Happy Days*, there was Walter Denton of *Our Miss Brooks*. We laughed at the antics of Walter and Stretch Snodgrass, the half-wit jock whose counterpart can be found in every high school in the land. Eve Arden, in the role of Miss Brooks, became a standard to measure teachers of English. She was tough, but she was kind and above all, she was fair. My peers and I at Cullman High were lucky enough to have two excellent English teachers in Mrs. Nita Gilbert and Mrs. Mabel Bailey. My permanent love of history was instilled by another Bailey—Miss Alberta Bailey.

A good deal of imagination was required to fully enjoy radio drama and comedy. The listener really was required to participate in order to get the full effect of staging. Television programming does not offer much challenge to our mental prowess. At first, we only had the pictures in black and white, so at least we could imagine the colors.

Once television programming in color became the norm (now high definition), we are allowed be as lazy and uncreative as we wish. We are surrounded with "perfect" color and "perfect" sound, if not perfect material. We, the viewers, are required to contribute nothing. We are no longer challenged. We have become passive observers, rather than participants. Oh, for the good old stimulation of radio! Luckily all the programs are preserved, and if we ever have the time and energy, we can relisten to all our favorites.

"Rotten Potato" Johnson

Education's purpose is to replace an
empty mind with an open one.

—Malcolm Forbes

Cullman City Elementary School was located
at the corner of Seventh Street and Sixth
Avenue, a one-story brick building constructed in the 1930s. The halls and rooms smelled
like paste and mimeograph fluid; otherwise, the
building appeared fresh and new. The structure was
rather impressive to me. The only grade school I had
been inside was the little two-room building at Gum
Pond, which I visited with Cousin Jerry.

At the main entrance to the Cullman
Elementary School, a portico jutted out with four
white columns. The central hall and rooms extended
out from this entryway. At the north and south ends,
two wings ran east at ninety-degree angles.

The first day of public school in the fall tradi-
tionally fell on the first Monday after Labor Day. I

entered the first grade in September of 1944. My family did not own a car, so I walked to school. The way led down a lane from our house onto the Bremen road which was unpaved at the time. When I arrived at Seventh Street, there was not only pavement, but concrete sidewalks. The total walking distance from door to door was equivalent to about sixteen city blocks or roughly a mile and a quarter.

My mother walked to school with me the first day and returned home to her work as soon as class began. She told me not to walk home by myself that first day, but to wait for my brother, Glenn, whose sixth-grade class ended about thirty minutes later than the first grade. As soon as my class was over, I looked for Glenn down the long corridor and then out into the school yard. When I couldn't find him, I panicked and began to run. The mile and a quarter took me just ten minutes. My mother was startled to find me home so early. She thought I must have gotten a ride with a friend's parent.

To begin the school day each morning, we stood to repeat the Pledge of Allegiance to the flag of the United States of America. This was serious business during wartime. Often, we would sing a patriotic song, "*God Bless America*" or "*My Country Tis of Thee.*" Frequently a teacher asked an upper grade class to muddle through the *Star-Spangled Banner.* Since the notes stretch one and a half octaves, the tune can be a "bear" to sing if it is not pitched properly to fit the voices. Francis Scott Key is not to blame for this problem. His poem was set to a British drinking song. I guess if you have enough ale to drink, the vocal range of a song matters little.

I don't remember very much about my elementary grade teachers except two—the third-grade teacher and the-sixth grade teacher. The third-grade teacher was Mrs. Birdie Keyes. (Her name rhymes with *eyes*, not *keys*.) She was also one of my Sunday school teachers. Because Mrs. Keyes made me feel special, I loved being in her class. I spent a lot of time painting posters and drawing long friezes on three-foot wide wrapping paper using colored chalk. Before all the major holidays, it became my "job" to create the appropriate friezes. My favorite season was Thanksgiving. It was such fun to draw Pilgrims and Indians and cornucopias and paint all the loud fall colors.

I had a crush on Hilda Thompson in the second grade, but I pretty much paid no attention to girls after that year. However, in the fifth grade, I was very much attracted to Emma Sue Wenzel. She was a twin. Her sister was Betty Lou (great southern names!). Most kids couldn't tell the two girls apart, but I could. I liked being around Emma Sue. I liked talking to her.

By this time, I was riding my bike to school, and Emma Sue's mother brought her and Betty Lou to school in their car. One day their mother had a conflict and couldn't pick the girls up from school. I walked Emma Sue almost all the way to her house before remembering that I had left my bike at school! I had to walk back to school to retrieve the bike, and then ride home. Naturally I was much later than usual arriving at the farm, and my mother noticed. (She never missed much!) Mother wanted to know what had delayed me. I invented an excuse about helping the teacher with some art project.

My sixth-grade teacher was Miss Syble Brown. She was a beauty and much younger than the other teachers. Miss Brown wore diaphanous low-cut blouses that offered a view guaranteed to catch the eye of a pubescent boy. My fellow peers and I soon learned to come to her desk and stand above her while she sat in her chair. We were often rewarded with titillating views. I am sure she was aware of what we were doing, but she didn't seem to mind.

Miss Brown lived with other unmarried teachers in a boardinghouse two blocks from the school. Unfortunately, one month before the end of the school year, she suddenly married and quit her teaching job. (I say suddenly, but the marriage probably wasn't sudden for her, but the news of it was a surprise to the class.) When Miss Syble departed, a somewhat frumpy and grumpy substitute teacher (in comparison) named Mrs. Yarborough became our teacher for the remaining month.

The principal of the Cullman Elementary School was Mr. R. P. Johnson, a giant of a man. We thought he was at least eight feet tall. It took a very brave soul (or a very stupid one) to risk being sent to Mr. Johnson's office. But behind his back, we called him names to our hearts' content. Our favorite thing to call him (when he was *not* in earshot) was Rotten Potato Johnson.

I was sent to Principal Johnson's office only once in my six years in elementary school. I was in the second grade at the time. During recess on the school grounds, all the kids ran around like banshees. I tended to hang out by myself or else have a good wrestling match with Robert Herring, a neighbor kid.

I had not yet learned many social skills and certainly had not learned how to avoid conflict. My dad had told me in no uncertain terms that he expected me to take care of myself and not to allow myself to be bullied in school. He did not expect me to come home "whining." That word came to my mind when a third-grade boy started to hassle me about my homemade flour-sack shirt.

Without thinking of eventual consequences, I gave the kid a roundhouse poke in the nose. Blood gushed out, and a crowd gathered. The kid was sobbing and wiping his nose on his sleeve. Somebody called one of the teachers over. She took me and the bleeding kid to Principal Johnson's office. I was deathly afraid. We were asked to tell our stories of what happened. I could not talk because I was crying full force out of fear for the punishment I was sure I was about to receive from old Rotten Potato, but also out of fear for what would happen to me when I got home and my dad learned that I had been taken to the principal's office.

Mr. Johnson was a bit confused. He wanted to know why I was the one crying when the other kid had the bloody nose. I finally was able to blurt out that the kid had been making fun of me. For some unknown reason, I was not punished by Mr. Johnson, nor by my dad. Nevertheless, I was careful in the future not to punch another kid without a very good cause. In Cullman Elementary, we were graded on something called "Deportment." Punching someone in the nose lowered the grade in this area significantly.

Having had almost no social interaction before attending school, I was apparently forgiven occasional *faux pas* relative to decorum and deportment. I will give just one example. One day my second-grade teacher asked me to find Hilda Thompson. It was recess, and many of the kids were milling about in the hallway. I asked one of the girls in my class if she had seen Hilda. She replied that Hilda was in the girl's restroom. Being faithful to my obligation to find Hilda, I barged right in. Such screaming you never heard! I couldn't figure what the fuss was about, but I beat a hasty exit. The teacher immediately informed me that under no circumstances was I ever to go into the girl's restroom again, no matter what errand I was told to perform. I may have been naïve, but I was a fast learner.

As kids, we dreamed of our future positions in the world of work. What we projected for ourselves in the nineteen forties was quite different from that of children in the twenty-first century. Small boys in my youth were fascinated with mechanics and occupations that made noise, the bigger and the noisier the better. For that reason, little boys at various stages talked of becoming locomotive engineers—never brakemen or firemen or switchmen—just engineers. That desire often changed if they had an opportunity to see up close, or ride on, a fire engine. What a great sound! What a thrill to drive at top speed down the city streets, horn blaring. How great to put out fires—to save people's lives.

If a kid lived on a road that was being graded for paving or widening, he spent hours watching and listening to the huge bulldozers and earth movers. Again, what a great and powerful sound! How fun it would be to make huge piles of dirt and ride over the top of the piles with a tractor. I imagined how much fun it would be to load a dump truck with dirt.

The play of little boys was often in imitation of the forms of work they saw in real life situations. Boys wanted dump trucks for Christmas and birthdays—earthmoving equipment, graders, fire trucks, and tractors. If the child was lucky enough to come from an affluent family with a large play area, the boy might ask for a big Lionel electric train set. Then he would be the envy of everyone for blocks around.

Another career that excited boys in the forties was that of airplane pilot. It was great fun to have a toy airplane or to make planes from kits. Youngsters living during WWII were fascinated with fighter planes and bombers. We learned their names— Mustangs, Hellcats, Messerschmitts, Zeros, B-17s (the flying fortress) and B-29s (the super fortress)— and we learned their various uses.

About the time the war ended, we learned about the development of German V-2 rockets that could travel over hundreds of miles. Space travel was no longer just the science fiction of comic strips. We were hungry to learn more about space exploration, and we had one of the greatest German scientists, Wernher von Braun, only forty-five minutes away at the Huntsville, Alabama Arsenal. Soon the jet plane arrived, followed by the breaking of the sound barrier. Many of us were avid followers of all these new technologies but hadn't yet really believed we would soon go to the moon.

In the third grade, I made my first attempt at writing poetry. Mrs. Keyes asked each of us to write a poem in celebration of the beginning of spring. Naturally, my poem was entitled "Spring." I didn't exactly keep the same rhyme scheme in every stanza. Nevertheless, the teachers liked my effort, and the poem was mimeographed and reproduced as part of the weekly school handout.

Spring

Spring! Spring! Spring!
Spring is like a new and beautiful gate
Where big red sun never pauses to wait.
No! He just shines his rays right through
And softly touches the new morn dew.
Yes! He shines o'er trees and flowers too,
When spring arrives for me and you.

Spring! Spring! Spring!
Leaving behind the nights full of gloom
Lilies and tulips are leaving their tombs.
Readying themselves for early March blooms.
Hark! Hear the chanting of the bluebird clear?
Spring is here! It's not just near!
Spring is here for all children dear.

Spring! Spring! Spring!
It's the time when flowers open each bud
And frogs and snakes awaken from sleep
And crawl their way from out of the mud.
Birds seek a mate that they may keep
They hop about and sing in merry rhyme!
'Tis spring, the world's resurrection time!

Spring! Spring! Spring!
Spring's the time when Easter comes
And Bunny, for all his pals and chums,
Brings colored eggs and coated gum.
Remember Easter's the Lord's special day.
So let us praise Him with singing so gay,
Then all little children may go out and play.

For my ninth birthday in 1946, my parents bought me a twenty-four-inch maroon single-speed bicycle. I mention "single-speed" only for younger readers. In that era, none of us kids had bikes with more than one gear. I think I saw my first three-speed bike when I was in high school.

My dad took it on himself to teach me to ride the bike. I don't know if he had ever owned one, but he could ride. Unfortunately, he rode my bike a bit too fast down the hill from our house toward the main road. About halfway down that lane, Dad hit a loose, sandy area and the bike skidded out from under him. He fell on the end of a handlebar and bruised his side. From that point on, I sat on the seat and pedaled, and he pushed.

As soon as I mastered my new maroon bike, I began to ride it to school. No more walking. The bike trip was relatively easy except for a couple of hills. With only one gear, you had to really pump to make it up a steep grade, unless you could get up a lot of speed beforehand.

Biking to school was fun (except for rain, ice storms, and extreme heat), but the ride could also be hazardous for another reason—one you might not think about. The hazard was not caused by car traffic. Most days I wouldn't see more than two or three cars the entire way to school. No, the danger came from a grade school compatriot named Loretta Tankersley. She lived up the hill about a quarter of a mile from our farm.

It was impossible to get to school from my house without passing Loretta's house, and she loved to tease all the boys. She got a thrill out of swooping down on an unsuspecting boy and giving him a kiss. Loretta could ride faster than many of the boys. If they jumped off their bikes, she would pursue them on foot. It was very embarrassing to be caught and kissed by Loretta. It was not that she was unattractive; it was a matter of maintaining our masculine honor.

By the beginning of the nineteen fifties, middle-class families in Cullman (as in any other American town) were striving to keep up with, or get ahead of, their neighbors, the proverbial Joneses—to have the biggest black-and-white television, the latest wringer washing machine, the newest clothes dryer, the car with the brightest chrome and the widest white sidewall tires. While it was not the case in Cullman, many whites in the suburbs of major northern cities began to fear an encroachment of well-to-do blacks into their neighborhoods.

Airplanes were still a novelty when I was a child. When one flew close enough to be heard, we would run out in the yard. Of course, these were all prop planes. We very rarely saw a large cargo or passenger plane, mostly single engine, single-wing or biplanes came our way. But on the news reels at the movie houses we saw footage of US, British, and German fighter planes and bombers.

When I was nine years old, one incident occurred that is forever burned into my memory set. One of my Uncle T. A. Smith's sons was roughly my age—William Burnham, called Babe. The family lived in a big white house on Main Street in Cullman. Uncle T. A. (the postmaster in Cullman for almost thirty years) had a free-standing garage for his car built some thirty feet south and west of his residence. The driveway to the garage was concrete.

One fine day Babe and I were playing together, and Babe got the urge to play with matches. He came out to the driveway with a box of wooden kitchen matches. We started playing in front of the open garage door. We struck a few matches in the classic sort of way, but this was not very exciting. We began to try to launch the matches into the air while they were lit.

The process was fairly simple. The match was held with the head down on the concrete. The index finger of the left hand held the match steady while, with the right hand you flicked the match with thumb and finger. If done properly, the match would soar off in an arc and land some fifteen or more feet away, blazing as it went. This was really an exciting game. We used up the entire box of matches over the next twenty minutes or so. Babe tossed the empty box in the trash can in the garage, and we rode our bikes off down to a nearby park.

A few minutes later, we heard the shrill whine of a fire truck siren. We decided to follow it and see where it went. Unfortunately the fire engine stopped in the driveway of Uncle T. A.'s house. We quickly noticed that the garage was a roaring blaze of fire. We quickly sped off back to the park. After about thirty minutes, we rode back to the house and ran in to ask nonchalantly what in the world had happened to the garage, which by now had burned to the ground. The firefighters had explained to Babe's mother, Aunt Sara, that apparently some old gas soaked rags in the loft of the garage had caught fire due to heat—

some sort of automatic combustion. We were two very relieved boys. This meant we were spared some major punishment. I never told anyone about the game with matches, and I bet Babe didn't either.

During my fourth-grade year, I barely escaped a serious automobile accident. One early spring day when the weather was especially rainy, Mr. Roberson, the grave digger for the city cemetery, offered me a ride home from school in his old pickup truck. His son sat in the middle of the seat, and I sat on the end, leaning against the passenger-side door. I was not aware that the rickety old pickup truck had a loose latch on the right-side door.

As we left the school, Mr. Roberson made a left turn a bit fast, and the passenger door flew open. I went tumbling out onto the wet pavement. As I hit the ground, I rolled quickly to my right, barely avoiding the back wheel of the pickup. My body was not injured at all, but my coat was torn by the rough pavement, and I had a hole in my pants leg. That was all.

However, poor Mr. Roberson was a total basket case. He had stopped the truck and run back to me as I was getting up. He was shaking, and his deep, sun-tanned face had turned ashen. He felt my arms and legs for broken bones. He was so frightened of what could have happened that he hardly paid attention to my assurances that I was okay.

Mr. Roberson drove me home in the pickup, steering with one hand, never turning loose of my shoulder the entire trip, except to shift gears. He went inside our house with me and, shaking all the while, told my parents what had happened, apologizing profusely. My dad could see that I was no worse for the wear and tried to reassure Mr. Roberson. He finally calmed the man down and sent him home. This was well before the days of constant litigation. My parents would never have tried to make life difficult for the hard-working Mr. Roberson.

The cemetery was close enough to our farm for me to watch Mr. Roberson as he dug graves. With nothing but a shovel and a pick, he could complete a grave in half a day. It amazed me to see Mr. Roberson work. When he began a grave, I could see his entire body. In a few minutes, I saw only above his knees. Soon I saw him only from waist up. A big pile of red dirt was growing. Eventually only Mr. Roberson's head was visible along with his shovel, making constant arcs above the dirt pile. Finally, only the shovel appeared above ground-level. In the afternoon, following an interment, Mr. Roberson had to reverse the process and refill the grave. Watching him convinced me that Mr. Roberson had a job I never wanted. We could not foresee that the backhoe would be invented in short order enabling a grave to be dug in just a few minutes simply by maneuvering a few levers.

When I reached the fifth grade, the school population had increased beyond the capacity of the building, even though the first cohort of "baby boomers" was still three years away from entering the first grade. One class would be obliged to meet in an old residential structure that sat on the campus.

My name appeared on that list. The old frame building was heated with a pot-bellied stove that sat in the middle of the room. On cold days the stove was either too hot or too cold. Students were constantly moving their desks closer or farther from the stove.

During the fifth grade, I was told by some fellow classmates how babies come into being. For quite a while I refused to believe the story. It seemed so implausible. But neither did I dare to ask my parents for verification or denial.

This was also the year my dad bought a 1949 Ford, a two-door sedan. This model came on the showrooms in the summer of 1948, and Dad bought his in August. This new Ford cost slightly over 1,700 dollars, including tax and tag. My parents had been scrimping and saving for years, so the car was paid for outright. A major financial boost occurred when Mother received a small inheritance from her parents' estate.

This was the first time my dad was willing to purchase a car since the ending of the war. He refused to jump ahead of the list of people waiting for a car. It was possible to move up the list by paying a "black market" price. At age fifty-two, my dad now owned his first car. He traded that '49 Ford in for a Ford Falcon in the nineteen sixties and drove it until his death in 1983. Since the Falcon was barely broken in, Tom Smith, T. A.'s oldest son, and a lawyer in Cullman, drove that old Falcon around for another five or six years.

After buying the car, Dad came home with a joke about the color of the car. When he asked the salesman the name of the color, the fellow said "sea mist green."

Now, due to the failure in Southern dialects to release final consonants—in this case the /t/—Dad thought he heard "See Miss Green."

His reply was, "Why do I have to see Miss Green to find out the color of my new car?"

"Hell, sea mist *is* the color," the salesman replied.

Dad used that joke many times afterward until he practically wore it out.

I received a big box of tinker toys for my twelfth Christmas in 1949. The boll weevil had been especially devastating on the cotton crop that fall and my parents had no money (especially after the car purchase). Except for the traditional candy canes and oranges, the sum total of my presents consisted of one sweat shirt and the box of tinker toys. I was embarrassed when I returned to the fifth grade class that January. We had show-and-tell about our Christmas gifts. It seemed to me that everyone had received great gifts. I wasn't about to be left out of the fun. I made up a story about the "cool" things I had received.

In the sixth grade, I was back in the main school building. The teacher, Miss Syble Brown, didn't particularly care for us boys, and for good reason. Part of the problem was our ages. We loved to be ornery and aggravate teachers. Bud Bottcher, George Ragsdale, and I formed a modern-age "three musketeers" group—all for one, and one for all. If one got into trouble, we all three did. The trio spent a lot of time writing on the blackboard fifty times or more: "I will do better in class from now on," or "I will not disturb the class by talking," or "I will not throw spitballs in class."

I would like to claim that I was a leader in this group, but that would not be true. I was strictly a follower. I was afraid to instigate trouble, but felt duty bound to get involved in whatever trouble Bud and George might invent.

One thing that compounded our devilishness was Miss Syble. As I noted earlier, she was a full-bosomed woman in her mid to late twenties and had a very alluring smell—a combination of perfume and bath powder mix, apparently.

The greatest trauma of my elementary school years occurred during this year. A commencement ceremony was planned for sixth-grade graduation. Bud Bottcher and I were asked to prepare a little skit. We decided to do a take-off on the "*Poor Scholar's Soliloquy*," written a few years earlier by Stephen Cory as part of a longer essay called "Childhood Education."

The piece was mainly a condemnation of the educational system of the day. The poor student in the essay is capable of doing manual activities, but can't perform well in the school system, which is not geared to his needs. The young fellow is not good in history, he's not good in geography, he's not good in grammar. He knows a lot about cars and machines.

The whole soliloquy is similar in many ways to a later popular tune by Sam Cooke titled "*Wonderful World*": *"Don't know much about history/ Don't know much biology/ Don't know much about a science book/ Don't know much about the French I took…"*

Bud and I reworked the soliloquy into a dialog skit. Bud was the actor, a born comic with loads of personality. We practiced the skit for Miss Syble several times. She seemed to appreciate what we had done. However, one day she said that because my voice had such a nasal twang, she planned to ask Gene Glasscock to assume my role. I was devastated. However, magnanimously, she allowed me to introduce the skit during the commencement ceremonies.

Miss Syble did not stay around for the graduation, having married a month before. The substitute teacher, Mrs. Yarborough, wrote on my final report card: "You did excellent work toward the commencement program." Some compensation! I never completely forgot this slight, even though I almost passed out from anxiety while announcing the skit. The last word I tried to utter stuck in my throat. Even so, I was not ready to admit that because of my "shyness" or "backwardness" I would probably have messed up the skit had I been allowed to do it.

The sixth grade was the only time in elementary school when I received a paddling on the hand. The paddling was by Mrs. Yarbrough. A "field day" was given to the sixth graders just before the end of the term. We were allowed to come to school dressed in shorts and T-shirts. (The girls came to school with blouses and skirts over the top of their short and T-shirts and took them off while playing outdoors.) We spent most of the day in field events: softball, kick ball, and basketball. Near the end of the school day, we returned to the classroom, and the girls put their skirts back on over the top of their shorts.

At some point, Janice Johnson sashayed past my desk. Without thinking at all, I flipped up her skirt, exposing the shorts she was still wearing. The teacher saw my action and quickly gave me a tongue lashing and paddled my hand with a ruler until it was red and burning. She was not interested in my explanation of innocent intent, nor the fact that the girls had just been outside all day in their shorts. My classmates thought the whole thing was very funny, especially Janice—who did not come to my defense at all.

Four sixth-grade classes totaling 141 students graduated on May 25, 1950. We processed into the gym to the music of "*The War March of the Priest*" by Felix Mendelssohn. I have no idea who came up with that choice nor why. It is true that war drums were rolling, and the US would be engaged in the Korean conflict before we returned to school in the fall.

The sixth-grade choral group sang "*For the Beauty of the Earth*." A well-dressed and poised Warren St. John welcomed parents and friends to the ceremony. Warren was the son of a noted lawyer in town. After this, Warren apparently attended a prep school in the North because he no longer attended school in Cullman. Warren had told us he planned to attend law school. Strangely, when I was a teaching assistant at the University of Kentucky in the summer of 1962, I walked into a class of intermediate French language students and there sat Warren.

I never had the chance to ask him what he was doing at UK enrolled in a French course because he dropped the class during the first week. No doubt he remembered his socially awkward grade-school classmate and doubted that any such rawboned farm kid would be capable of teaching intermediate French.

The whole incident was rather weird. Warren had drawn my name at Christmas season when we were in fourth grade. He gave me one of the "neatest" presents I ever received as a child—a paisley silk tie and handkerchief set. I wore them on special occasions for several years.

During the elementary graduation service, each homeroom class was responsible for a performance of some kind. One class sang "*Down by the Old Mill Stream*"; another put on a little skit called *Let's Make the World of Tomorrow Today*. Another performed a skit entitled "Goodbye to the Sixth Grade" with music by the class and words written by Jimmy Kilpatrick.

My classroom performed a skit called "Six Years of Education." The words were spoken by the class, and the music was written by Nancy Dunlap and Lady Claire Davidson. Nancy was showing signs of becoming an excellent musician. She would soon be playing first trumpet in the high school band. She eventually married the band director. Lady Claire

Davidson was not a real "lady;" she just had an aristocratic-sounding name, and she could play a "mean" clarinet.

Despite all the pomp and circumstance, all of us were glad to be finished with elementary school. We felt that we were definitely growing up. We were ready to face the junior high years at the "big" school located in the north end of the town. I personally was looking forward to being able to ride the county school bus when the weather was bad, something I was not able to do during my elementary years.

Less than one month after our graduation, the US was engaged in a civil war in Korea. Only five years after the end of WWII the US was back in a deadly shooting war. The combat in Korea was part of a larger Cold War that had developed between the US and its allies on the one hand, and the USSR and China on the other. North and South Korea were the proxies in this struggle. During Saturday matinees at the movie theater, we were again exposed to footage of combat in the black and white newsreel segment.

We were soon returned to practicing for bombing, this time with the deadly serious atomic bomb as a threat. Some of the exercises we carried out seemed somewhat silly to us, knowing as we did what had happened to Hiroshima and Nagasaki, Japan. These were very unnerving times, even for young teens with boundless energy and optimism. To quote Dickens, "It was the best of times; it was the worst of times."

Hardscrabble Farming

I am a farmer singing at the plow.

—Jesse Stuart
Boy with the Bull-tongue Plow

When I was young, living on a farm seemed very pleasant. I loved to climb on the seat of the one-horse wagon and ride to town with my dad. I sat tall and proud. Sometimes my dad would hand me the reins, and I would "drive" the horse. This was a better thrill, by far, than playing with my little toy tractor.

The wagon was constructed of wood except for iron rims around the wheels and metal springs. In lieu of a tongue (used with multiple animals), this wagon had shafts. The horse or mule was hitched in between the two shafts. I'm not sure what age I was when Dad began allowing me to help with the hitching, but I stood on a crate to reach the neck of the mule to attach the collar and hames. Iron traces (chains) hooked to rings on the hames allowed the animal to pull a load using its shoulder muscles.

Of course, when hitching a horse or mule, the first item of harness placed on the animal is the halter and bit. Sometimes a mule can be quite stubborn about taking the bit, especially if the mule senses uncertainty or fear in the harnesser. I soon learned that you show the animal who is in charge.

The reins (of half-inch rope) hooked onto the rings of the halter at the level of the bit. This allows the animal to be "steered." If "gee" and "haw" are not sufficient instructions, a light (or heavy) tug on the reins causes the bit to pull left or right against the tender part of the animal's mouth. The remainder of the leather harness circles the girth of the animal, and a belt goes behind its haunches allowing the animal to back the wagon. The shaves are supported by this harness.

Our wagon bed had removable sides about fifteen inches high. The sides could also be increased in height by adding additional boards. The rear wheels were larger in diameter than the front wheels of the wagon for more torque. The breaking mechanism was extremely simple. A lever, when pulled back, forced a wooded slab against the rear wheels. This created the friction needed to slow a wagon down when descending a hill. The turning radius was rather wide for this type of wagon. The driver had to be careful not to turn too abruptly; the wagon could be turned over rather easily.

The wooden seat in the front section of the wagon bed was removable. This seat had iron strips underneath to form a primitive spring to take some of the jolt out of the ride. The same type of spring was also located between the axles and the bed. Nevertheless, the ride was anything but smooth except on soft level ground.

While riding in the wagon was thrilling, not everything about farm life was enjoyable. By the age of six, I was expected to do a few simple chores. Feeding corn to the Rhode Island Red free-range chickens began as a fun activity, but as an everyday routine, it soon became just a boring chore. Combining snack time with chores was a way to make them more palatable. I filled my pockets with parched or raw peanuts and ate them as I went about my duties. When in season, a stalk of sorghum cane or a raw sweet potato made nice treats as well.

As I grew older, the duties a young boy was expected to perform became less amusing and more onerous and time-consuming. At some point, my jobs began to include the shelling of dried corn from the cob so that the kernels could be scattered around on the ground for the chickens. We had a corn crib inside the barn where this shelling took place.

First, the ears of corn had to be shucked. After shucking a few dozen, the ears were placed one by one in the corn-sheller. Holding the ear with the left hand and turning the crank with the right sent the kernels flying into a wooden hopper. The empty cob was then tossed aside. These cobs had uses, which will be mentioned later.

I often played a mental game with the corn-sheller to see how many cobs I could separate from their kernels in a minute or in five minutes. The speed thus developed gave me an edge when the occasion arose for me to shell two or three bushels at one time, readying the corn for milling.

In those days, we didn't spray corn crops in an effort to ward off weevils. Thus, many kernels had weevil larvae in them. When Dad returned home from the mill with ground cornmeal, it always contained a significant number of dark specks. These specks were ground-up weevils, which couldn't be totally sifted out before being baked into bread. We used to say jokingly that our protein came from these weevils.

In addition to eating the kernels thrown about in the yard, the chickens were fed and watered in the hen house. The store-bought processed feed was poured into a narrow trough. In order to ensure strong eggshells, farmers often fed laying hens ground-up oyster shells as a supplement to the other feed.

Every evening a few eggs were gathered from the nests in the hen house. This was an easy task unless a hen decided to "set" on a batch. In that case, she would fight to keep a young boy's hand from "stealing" her eggs. An irritated hen can peck rather ferociously, and her claws and spurs are sharp and wicked. The expression "mean as a wet hen" should be changed to "*mean as a setting hen.*" Such a fighting denizen had to be "quarantined" for a time in a separate coop until she came back to her "senses."

As a young lad, I performed many odd jobs in and around our house and for our neighbors. One of the oddest was the job of washing hen eggs for our nearest neighbor, Woodrow Graham. Woodrow had four large henhouses filled with white leghorns. Egg farms were not mechanized at this time. Fresh laid eggs did not drop into a trough and roll down a belt and into a washing area where the cleaned eggs were crated.

On his farm, Woodrow Graham gathered the eggs by hand and culled out the ones needing washing. By the time I was twelve, I often helped him with this project on Saturday mornings. During a couple of hours, I probably washed four hundred eggs. If I remember correctly, Woodrow paid me a penny per egg. This was excellent money for that era—two dollars per hour of work when the minimum wage was seventy-five cents an hour.

Eventually I was old enough to climb up the vertical ladder leading to our barn loft. My job was to throw down hay and fodder at feeding time. I always remembered our old neighbor, Mr. Bill Lessman, each time I climbed down that ladder. He had fallen from his barn loft and broken his back when I was four years old. The opening in our barn loft was approximately three feet by three feet. The ladder, which was just a series of hand and foot rails, descended straight down the wall.

Consequently, to descend from the loft, you had to turn your back to the opening and grab onto the rails of the ladder and start down backward. After a short amount of time, I could do this with great agility, but at first it was a bit scary. However, I was too proud to show any fear. My dad didn't seem to be afraid, so I didn't want him to think that I was.

The more I grew, the more farm chores I was asked to perform. By far and away, my least favorite tasks came at hog-butchering time. (This event occurred in late fall on a day when the morning temperature began near or below freezing to limit any spoilage.) Hogs were killed quickly, usually with a shot to the head with a rifle. My dad owned a twelve-gauge shotgun, but this was not appropriate for such duty. Instead, Dad asked one of the neighbors to come over with a twenty-two rifle. In exchange for this, the neighbor received a small portion of the meat. Immediately after the gunshot, the hog was bled. Our German neighbors enjoyed receiving this blood, which they used to make blood sausage. The head of the hog was a prized item for making "head cheese." (The neighbors called it *Sülze*.) Of course, pig knuckles and pig feet were prized as well. As one of my French cousins likes to say, *"Tout est bon, comme dans le cochon."* (Everything is good, like in a pig.) Some of the poorest kids found a good use for the stomach. They would tie off one end, blow it up, tie off the other end, and use it for a football, but it was good for only a short time.

It is very true that every part of a pig had some value whether it was cooked immediately or pickled, salted, smoked, or dried for later use. Tripe was made from stomach and intestines. Chitterlings were deep-fried tripe. Pigs' feet were pickled, as were other "less savory" parts. Mother would have no part of the "lights" (lungs), however. Those organs were given away. She did keep the brains, however, and for breakfast the day after hog-killing, we had brains scrambled with eggs.

Hog butchering was a real craft. One had to know how and where to make the cuts for the hams, the ribs, the sections that were to be made into bacon, the parts that were to be ground into sausage, the back bone, which would be cooked with greens. All this "carving art" was my dad's job and remained a mystery to me.

In preparation for butchering, several gallons of water were drawn from the well to fill a large metal drum that was positioned over a fire. When the water was near boiling temperature, the carcass was dipped into the barrel using a pulley and wench. The scalding water softened the skin and loosened the hair, making it easier to scrape away with large sharp knives. At about age ten, I was "invited" to join in the hog-butchering ritual. I quickly discovered that the task was far from easy—not only was it hard work, it was rather unpleasant, to put it mildly.

For the next few days following butchering, we ate those parts of the hog that were not going to be preserved. The day after butchering, we ate liver cooked with plenty of onions, which was surprisingly good. My favorite meal, however, was fried pork tenderloin—finger-licking and lip-smacking good! For at least a week following the day of butchering, we ate freshly ground sausage seasoned with sage at breakfast.

The entire hog carcass was fully cut into portions by late afternoon of the first day. The parts that needed to be salted down were placed in the saltbox. The bits and pieces to be made into sausage were in the kitchen. After supper that evening, we all worked at grinding up the meat into sausage, adding the salt and sage to it, and forming the meat into patties, which were then packed in large urns.

Hog-butchering day was always the longest day of my life. I was bone tired when the final pieces of meat were ground into sausage about nine or ten o'clock at night. For mother, the next day was a hot one. She spent the entire day over the stove, cooking the sausage patties and packing them into quart jars. These jars were sealed shut and stored. This allowed us to have sausage from time to time throughout much of the year.

Once the meat in the salt box had cured, Dad hung up the hams and bacon slabs in the smoke house. He gathered hickory wood from the forest nearby and used it to build a fire under the hanging meat. The fire was kept smoldering and smoking for many days. Blue smoke seeped out of all the cracks in the smoke house. The constant smoke and heat finished the curing process and gave the meat a good "hickory-cured" flavor.

Another by-product of hog butchering was soapmaking. In the early forties when store-bought soap was scarce, mother made soap to use in washing clothes. This soap was made in a black kettle over a wood fire. Several pounds of meat scraps were boiled in water to which a can of Red Devil Lye was added. For hours, this "material" was stirred frequently with a wide wooden paddle. The lye broke down the meat into the consistency of gelatin. When the water was boiled off, the gelatin was cooled and cut into cakes of soap. For softer soap, more grease was used. For tougher soap, more lye was added.

While the processes involved in hog butchering were long and hard, at least it came only once a year. Learning to plow was a challenge that seemed more agreeable and much manlier. We used only a one-horse turning plow. A singletree was attached at the clevis of the plow tongue. Two chains attached to the hames were then attached to the singletree.

When I was eleven, my dad gave me a few lessons using the one-horse turning plow. It took some time to get the "feel" for the plow, how to keep it running straight and at an even depth. The technique involved very subtle movements of the plow handles, up and down, and left and right.

The same kind of subtle technique is used with an electric floor buffer. Any quick jerk can cause the buffer to spin out of control. In my three years at Transylvania College, I became the "buffer-in-chief" at the library during the weeks between terms, so my experience with the plow proved useful.

When plowing, the reins are draped loosely around the plowman's neck or wrapped loosely around each hand while gripping the plow handles. The horse or mule was controlled by voice. This was a bit of a problem for me at first because my voice had not yet changed, and it didn't sound very commanding to the animal. I had to work at giving commands as loudly and as gruffly as possible so that authority could be heard in my voice.

With a novice at the plow, an irascible mule is likely to just take off across the field rather than follow the row. A one-hundred-thirty-pound kid pulling on the reins is not likely to impress a twelve-hundred-pound mule that has its eye on some nice green sprigs of grass.

To stop the mule, you have to sink the plow point into the ground so that it works like an anchor. If the plow point goes deep enough, the mule will be stopped dead in its tracks. At that point, there must be a show of force. In such a situation, my dad would just walk up to the mule and give it a good right-cross with his fist. However, at that young age, I lacked the power to impress a mule in that fashion. My option was to give the mule a strong whack on the rump with the reins.

After a few episodes, the master/mule relationship was established to my satisfaction, and I could concentrate on maneuvering the plow in the proper manner to turn the soil for planting. It would be another year before my dad would trust me to use the other types of plows, scratchers, sweeps, distributors, and planters.

The next step for me was learning to lay off terraces and rows. Finally, I developed enough skill to distribute fertilizer and plant seeds. The amount of fertilizer that goes into each row is controlled by a lever on the distributor that changes the size of the aperture. When planting, the number of seed and the space between seeds is controlled by a disk fitted inside the planter. Once I could handle this part of farming, I felt I had accomplished something very worthwhile.

Once the plants were up and growing, the real work began in the old "subsistence" style of farming. The plants, corn or cotton, had to be thinned because more seed were dropped than could be sustained as full-sized plants in the poor soil of northern Alabama. This thinning out of the plants, once they were out of the ground an inch or two, was done by hand with a hoe—the most primitive of farm implements.

The thinning (or chopping) was only the first round of activity with the hoe. All the weeds and grass needed to be hoed out at least twice in the early growing season; otherwise, the weeds sucked away the nourishment intended for the cotton or corn plants. The grass and weeds between two rows were controlled by running either a sweep or a scratcher through. Maneuvering the scratcher was fairly easy, but one bad bobble with the sweep and you could wipe out several yards of young cotton or corn.

A very delicate hand was required on the shaves of the plow and a good command of the mule. None of this activity is presently a part of cotton or corn growing. Today, the land is turned by a tractor pulling a wide set of disks so that in one turn around a field the tractor accomplishes what the old turning plow took ten turns to do. Now the distribu-tor-planter that follows the tractor lays down many rows at a time and close together. Enough fertilizer is used so that the plants can be very close together, eliminating any need to chop out plants. Once this planting is done, the farmer can wait for the crop to grow and mature. No need for hoeing or plowing anymore. This makes the old farming method seem not only quaint, but rather futile.

Work on a farm was not limited to working with the crops, hoeing, and plowing. Trees sometimes needed to be trimmed or cut, and the logs would then be sawed with a crosscut saw. Although a stren-uous activity, two-person cross-cut sawing can be fun and competitive. Much coordination is required and much stamina as well.

Fences were frequently in need of mending; holes for new posts had to be sunk or new barbed wire needed to be strung (or the existing wire required tightening). Large rocks had to be hauled out of the newly turned fields in the spring. A fresh batch of rocks worked their way to the surface each year. Some of these rocks would weigh over twenty pounds, although most were in the five to ten pound range.

My dad built a slide to use for rock-hauling, made entirely of wood with wood runners. A mule or horse pulled the slide around the field, and the rocks were piled on, but not to the point that the mule would no longer be able to drag the slide. The rocks were taken to a "rock pile" where they awaited use.

A farmer had to constantly fight noxious weeds and grasses, especially those growing in the pasture or within reach of a stretched neck through the fence. Raw milk retains the flavors of the weeds and grasses a cow eats. One weed in particular, the bitterweed, wreaked havoc with the taste of milk. Bitter weed was prolific and grew to about a foot high with tiny leaves on the stem and a daisy-like, yellow bloom at the head.

A mowing machine had been invented which attached to a tractor. With this device, hay could be easily mowed or bitter weed could be cut down. However, we did not own either a tractor or the mechanized mower. As a consequence, the bitter weed had to be attack by a human and a good, sharp sling blade (a slinger). The sling blade has a three-foot handle and is swung directly in front of the person using it. It is made to be used with a one or two-handed grip. The idea is to develop a pendulum swing and keep the tempo steady. When there was no pressing work, my dad loved to send me down to the pasture with the sling blade to do away with as many bitter weeds as possible. I could get a rhythm going with the slinger and cut large swaths. I made a game of it, and the time would go faster.

Other noxious weeds and grasses include Johnson grass cockleburs, goldenrod, and dock weed. These plants are too tough for the lightweight slinger. They called for the use of a scythe. (Think of the image of the Grim Reaper.) The scythe has a five-foot curved handle with two adjustable handgrips. The long and narrow blade is also curved in the shape of a new moon.

In the days before mechanized mowers, the scythe was the standard tool to cut (reap) hay, wheat, and other grains. The proper technique of the scythe requires a long sweeping motion, bending over slightly to put the blade near and parallel to the ground. I could use a slinger for hours at a time, but I tired of the scythe in a very few minutes.

One noxious plant could hardly be controlled. I'm thinking of the plant imported from Japan to help with erosion—the infamous kudzu plant. The various tendrils of kudzu can grow from eight inches to a foot in one twenty-four-hour period. In one season of growth, kudzu can destroy a small tree by choking out the sunlight. The root of a kudzu plant grows deep into the ground so that uprooting it is next to impossible. Sprays have been developed to kill the vines, which die back in winter anyway. But killing the vines is a temporary measure. The plant grows out swiftly again from the roots. Containing kudzu is a permanent and ongoing battle.

A break from work occurred around ten o'clock each morning. This was the occasion for a midmorning snack of some kind. In the fall, cotton picking, fodder pulling, or corn gathering was stopped long enough to eat a watermelon. We grew our own every year. When melons were judged ripe enough, they were stored in the cellar. The temperature in the cellar, even in summer, probably never exceeded 65 degrees. For our midmorning break for rest, we carried one of the watermelons out under a shade tree and sat on the grass to eat it. Mother would never tolerate a cut watermelon inside the house.

A juicy twenty- pound watermelon was cut in half. Mother and Dad had a few pieces, and Glenn and I finished the rest—he ate one half, and I ate the other. We mostly just ate the "heart" of the watermelon. The remainder of the meat and rind was given to the animals. To a pig, a watermelon was the closest thing to heaven—perhaps also for a ten-year-old boy!

One year, we grew some large and very delicious watermelons called "all-heart." Dad decided we should save the seeds from one of the larger and better-tasting melons. The next spring, he gave me the task of growing the watermelons from those seed. I picked a sandy location and planted a couple of dozen hills. Something about that growing season was special. The right amount of sun and rain and soil quality all came together. The melons grew to exceptional sizes, many weighing from fifty to ninety pounds. No lie! Only a few folks who live around Sand Mountain will be easily convinced. That year, we cut a watermelon which we weighted beforehand on the cotton scale. It was ninety-two pounds. It fed the whole Gum Pond clan with baskets of scraps left over for the hogs and mules. Never again was I quite as successful, even with the seed saved from those large melons.

One of the mules adored watermelon, but her favorite treat was cobs left from cutting fresh ears to make a dish of creamed corn. (We called this corn *rosnears*. I was a late teen before I realized the words were *roasting ears*. We had to be careful how many fresh cobs we gave this mule because the fermentation of the left-over corn and cobs in her stomach would bloat the poor devil something fierce.

On a farm, there are several critters to keep an eye on. You could call them nature's "meanies." In the hot summer, the meanest of all were the almost invisible red chiggers. What an unpleasant itch they created, and they managed to attach themselves in the most inconvenient places on the body. For many people, poisonous plants were the greatest hazard to living near wooded or weedy areas. I'm thinking of poison ivy, poison oak, cow itch, and poison sumac (pronounced *shoo-mate* in the dialect of lower Appalachia).

Some allergic people claimed they needed only to come near (but not touch) one of the poisonous plants to suffer a skin reaction. In my case, I had no reaction to any of the poison plants, and that was a very good thing. All four of these noxious weeds grew on our farm or in the nearby woods where I often played.

With luck, I also avoided snake bites during my carefree early childhood. Three of the four poisonous snakes in the United States lived on or near our farm: cottonmouth water moccasins, rattlesnakes, and copperheads. We also had plenty of "friendly" snakes: black racers, king snakes, puffing adders. Other critters to watch out for were rabid raccoons, possums, rabbits, and the occasional hydrophobic "mad" dog that roamed the fields from time to time.

My parents believed completely in planting crops and vegetables according to the phases of the moon and the signs of the zodiac. They referred frequently to the *Farmers' Almanac* and had a calendar in the kitchen that indicated the phases and signs for each day of each month. Even as a little kid, I was somewhat skeptical of these signs. I couldn't figure out how any of them could make a difference in how a plant grew. But my parents had faith that all life was affected by the moon and the zodiac, and I didn't question them.

I never paid much attention to the ritual, but I did learn that the waxing and waning of the moon was part of the key to the system. To oversimplify a bit, crops whose edible material grows above ground are planted while the moon is waxing (going from new to full). Plants whose edible material grows underground are planted when the moon is waning (going from full back to new). You might ask what about those plants in which the edible parts are both under and above ground. In that case, the underground takes precedent.

The moon has four phases. The new moon is the beginning of phase one. From a half moon to a full moon is phase two (or second quarter). From full moon back to a half moon is phase three (third quarter). The fourth phase (and quarter) takes the moon from half to a tiny sliver (new moon).

The twelve signs of the zodiac are divided into four groups of three, each representing the four basic elements: earth, water, fire, and air. Cancer, Pisces, and Scorpio are water signs. Taurus, Virgo and Capricorn are earth signs. My mother was convinced that vegetable crops had the best yields when planted while the signs were in earth or water. Fire and air were considered to be barren times.

Weeding and pruning were best done during those signs. Fire signs are Leo, Aries, and Sagittarius. Air signs are Gemini, Aquarius, and Libra. If someone said his Irish potato yield was very small, Mother would explain that this was because they were planted in the wrong phase, causing the above ground plants to grow hardily, but the roots to be skimpy in providing the tubers.

At least when working a vegetable garden, one can see quick results; however, looking down row after row of cotton or corn needing to be chopped or hoed was a sobering if not depressing experience. One wondered if it would be possible to cover so much ground. Chopping and hoeing were such monotonous tasks. I decided early on that the best thing was to make a game out of the hoeing. For example, I tried to see how many times I could chop just the right amount of excess plants with one strike of the hoe.

In those days of labor-intensive farming—so different from the mechanized methods of the twenty-first century—the corn and cotton were planted in rows about two feet apart. The seeds were dropped from the planter in such a way as to guarantee a good "stand." This meant that one or more little plants sprouted every inch or two. The typical light-weight hoe was roughly five inches in width. When chopping cotton or thinning corn, the idea was to cut out the excess plants, leaving five-inch spaces between each stalk. Thus, the remaining ones had enough nourishment to grow to maturity.

The soil on Brindley Mountain was not rich enough to sustain a heavily planted field of corn or cotton, and it was much too expensive to fertilize the entire field. Before the planter was run through the rows, a distributor went ahead dropping a fixed quantity of guana (pronounced "*gyou-aner*"). This was a natural fertilizer harvested in the South American country of Guiana. It was essentially just ground up bird droppings. The only other fertilizer we ever used was the manure from the barn stalls, which was distributed on the soil in the early spring before the ground was broken.

Before leaving the subject of hoeing, I must tell the anecdote about the little boy who was sent into the field to bring fresh water to a group of women who were busy chopping cotton. Trying his best to be friendly, the young boy greeted the women by asking, "How are all you *hoers*, this morning?" One of the women, with little sense of humor, didn't take kindly to his *faux pas*, and took out after the kid with her hoe handle. The young boy learned the nature of his error and never made it again.

When we were out in the fields, we always took a jug of cool water—never ice water. Ice water was considered dangerous—too cold. It could cause unknown health problems. Of course, in 95- to 100-degree heat, a cool jug of water will not stay that way long. We tried to find a shady spot for the jug, but this was often almost impossible. Usually the most shade we could find was a bush or big weed.

When we happened to be working near the creek, we had a good spot to place the water jug away from the heat of the sun. If we were near Richard's Woods, we could set the jug of water in the shade of a tree. However, regardless of the amount of shade, the water was lukewarm or even hot within a few minutes. We learned to drink it like that. When thirsty, one can't be too picky. We drank our R. C. Colas at room temperature until we owned a refrigerator. Even then, we drank refrigerated sodas without ice. One or two ice trays did not make a lot of ice, and that quantity was needed for the noon iced tea. If we made lemonade, we would put two cubes of ice in each glass. (No automatic icemakers existed at the time.)

As travelers to Europe will know, folks there do not use much ice. They grew accustomed to very little at a time when they had very small refrigerators, even in the bars and cafes. A couple of cubes of ice were the maximum distributed and remains so even today when ice is relatively plentiful.

I never had a problem with this lack of ice when traveling in Europe or elsewhere outside the

US because of my years on the farm, but when I was accompanied by student groups, they were constantly complaining. However, when they returned to the States, they began to complain that they got only ice and very little soda in their glasses. Go figure!

Although it sounds a bit corny and folkloric, most rural women chose Monday as the day to do the family "wash" (laundry). The reason was simple: Monday morning the family dressed in clean work clothes and the past week's dirty clothes needed washing. So why was the change into clean clothes done on Monday? Again, the adage about a Saturday night bath was quite true in many cases. New underwear and pj's were put on after those Saturday night baths. Of course, since the next day was Sunday, no self-respecting woman would wash on that day—the day of rest and the time for going to church and for visiting in the afternoon.

On our farm, as was the case with most rural Southern families (and rural folk in general anywhere in the country), "wash day" was a major project before the advent of washing machines and dryers. On our farm, we had a washhouse, which was a small add-on room to the smokehouse and woodshed. This washhouse was about six feet by twelve feet. Two large zinc wash tubs were placed on a work bench. A large cast iron kettle sat just outside the door of the washhouse.

In preparation for washing clothes, several things had to be done. First, water had to be drawn from the well and carried to the kettle. About five buckets were enough, if I recall. A bucket held between two and three gallons. Once the kettle was sufficiently filled with water, a wood fire was lit under it.

When the water eventually reached near boiling temperature, chunks of homemade lye soap were added. The lye soap cut the grease, grime, and sweat from the dirtiest of overalls. The clothes in the kettle were stirred with a large wooden paddle. After this process, the overalls were put in one of the number ten tubs and scrubbed with a scrub board (now seen in antique shops and Cracker Barrel Stores).

Finer clothes were not put through such harsh treatment. Bed linen, however, was placed in the kettle for a few minutes. Since the sheets and pillowcases were homemade from *guano* sacks, the rough treatment in the kettle served to "soften" them up a bit. Then the sheets were well-scrubbed on the scrubboard. After a few times, they became significantly softer.

More buckets of water had to be carried to the washhouse to fill up the tubs for the second phase of washing. One tub held rinse water, and the other held a combination of cool well water added to the hot water from the kettle (before the soap and overalls were added).

While the work clothes and bedding were boiling in the kettle, Mother scrubbed other clothes on a rub board in the warm water tub in which she had put some store-bought soap (*Oxydol*, for example). The washed clothes were then shifted over to the rinse tub. Even the clothes boiled in the kettle were then brought into the warm tub to be washed some more. The hot clothes were brought in by picking them up with a paddle. In the rinse water, a product called "bluing" was added. This was to make the clothes "whiter." Fancy that! It all seemed puzzling to me.

After the rinsing, the clothes were wrung out by hand as best possible. The hard part was ringing out full-size sheets. The wrung-out clothes were placed in an empty tub and hauled out to the wash line. The line was made of several strands of twisted wire or a heavy gauge single strand. The wire was attached to poles at each end and propped up at intervals with a pole with a notch in the top end to push up under the wire.

The damp clothes were hung on this line with the aid of clothespins. These pins were of two kinds, those with simple notches and those with spring action. I was never sure which were used for what clothes.

As you might expect, this procedure was an all-day affair with the housewife taking time out to do the other household chores and to prepare the noon meal. All this turned out okay except on cold and rainy Mondays. Disasters were never far away. A sudden rain or windstorm could wreak havoc, and the clothes could be lying in the mud.

When the clothes were finally dry, they were semifolded and placed in a basket. The next day was ironing day, and everything had to be ironed. No permanent-press garments available! Until the house was wired for electricity, Mother ironed using two irons, which she heated on the cookstove or the pot-belly stove.

If Monday was washday and Tuesday was ironing day, the day for visitation was Sunday. In those days, guests came unannounced—we had no telephone. This visiting on Sundays was something of a ritual. Guests came to chitchat. Something cold to drink in summer and hot to drink in the winter was available along with a piece of cake or pie.

We kept a lookout down the driveway to see if we were going to have visitors. If it was warm enough, visitors joined my parents on the porch. This allowed those who chewed tobacco to spit off the porch onto the ground. Smokers could light up downwind and not cause too much grief to nonsmokers.

All the porch furniture was handcrafted by my dad. This required considerable skill. Dad had no power tools. He used a handsaw, a couple of sizes of wood planes, rasps, sandpaper, hammer and nails. With those simple tools, he made benches with backs and arms, sloping wooden "easy" chairs, swings, and so on. After he retired from farming and we moved to the city, one night someone (or ones) came by the house and stole all the porch furniture.

This did not deter Dad for long. He simply went to Buettner's Lumber Company and bought the wood to build new chairs and benches. The one positive outcome of subsistence farming is that the farmer learned to be almost totally self-sufficient. My dad believed there were few tasks he couldn't accomplish. He passed this belief on to me. I still have many of his hand-tools, which often serve me well.

Oh, Them Cotton Fields

Five cent cotton and forty cent meat!
How in the world can a poor man eat?

—Lament from the Great Depression

Raising cotton on a small farm in the forties was about as labor-intensive as one can imagine. First, the land had to be "turned" in the early spring. Once the soil was well tilled, terraces and "beds" were "laid off." The fertilizer was distributed; then the seeds were dropped into narrow furrows with a horse-drawn planter using a disk that allowed one seed to drop every half inch to insure a good "stand" of plants.

Once the plants sprouted the chopping process was critical. Only one or two plants were left separated by the width of the hoe. This allowed each plant enough nourishment and given good weather conditions, the plants will grow rather rapidly. As cotton stalks develop, they grow "squares." These so-called squares are not square at all but pyramidal. A bloom forms inside the square in late June and early July. The bloom is white the first day, then a pinkish color the next day. On the third day, it turns purple, dries up and falls to the ground.

Assuming the bloom has been pollinated by bees, wasps, flies, or some other insect, a small round "bole" begins to grow inside the square. The bole grows larger and larger until it is the size of a large walnut. When the bole opens, the cotton appears.

To those who have not picked cotton, the activity looks like a breeze, even fun. However, anyone who has picked for a day or more can tell you that the task was very hard on several parts of the body. First, a cotton-picker had to spend hours in a stooped position, unless he or she chose to pick while "walking" on their knees. The back soon tired from the stooped position, and the knees were easily bruised by small rocks unless heavy pads were strapped on. Without pads, walking on the knees, even on sandy soil, was not very pleasant after a few hours. A better technique was to alternate, bending for a while and then kneeling.

Cotton, of course, is soft and fluffy, even with the seeds inside. However, what is not soft are the burrs that pop open to expose the cotton fibers. A bole has five sections that split open in the shape of a starfish or a star fruit. The end of each section has a thorn-like point. This thorn becomes harder and sharper as it dries. It's difficult to pick cotton without scraping your hands against these thorny points. As the weather gets cooler, the points of the burrs seem to scratch even more. Some pickers wore soft cotton gloves with the fingers and thumb cut out. This gave some protection to the hands, if not the fingers.

Cotton boles ripen in a continuum over several weeks. In early September, the first boles open. Some do not open until early November. In the old-style intensive farming when the picking was done by hand, this labor was repeated three four or even five times during those two months. Presently, with the huge expense of mechanical harvesting, the picking machine is driven through a field late in the season. After this pass-through, more boles will continue to open. This is the reason you will see a field in the late fall or early winter with a significant amount of white fluff. It appears the field has not yet been picked. In addition, genetic engineering has produced a much smaller plant with a shorter opening season.

On our farm, cotton was picked by hand. The picker wore a long cotton sack with a strap which passed over one shoulder (left if the picker was right-handed, right if the picker was left-handed). A good picker's hands flew through the plants drawing the fibers from several boles with both hands before pushing the fibers into the open sack dragging behind. This process was repeated many times over until the sack was full or so heavy that the picker's shoulder hurt so much that the sack had to be weighed and emptied.

Somewhere in the middle of the field, a wagon was stationed in which the sacks of cotton were emptied. First, the sack of cotton was weighed with a P

Scale (for *pois*, as in *avoirdupois*). This scale was in the form of an iron bar or shaft with numbers marked along it and grooves on the top. This bar had a hook on the top and one on the bottom. The top was hooked to a wooden pole extending out from the top of the wagon. The sack of cotton was draped over the bottom hook. The weight of the sack caused the bar to rise straight up.

To measure the number of pounds of cotton, the P (an iron weight with a curved hook) was hung from one of the grooves on top of the bar. The weight could be moved left or right depending on the position of the bar. The true weight was determined when the bar was level. There were light P's and heavy P's, to make the weighing easier.

The average sack was weighed when it contained about forty pounds. A fast picker could pick between 200 and 275 pounds in a day by working from sunup to sundown. The amount varied depending on the number of open boles per plant and the speed and strength of the picker. The more boles that were open on the plants, the faster the picker could fill the sack.

The rate per pound paid to pickers in the late '40s and early '50s was three to four cents per pound. I remember mostly getting three cents when I picked for some of the neighbors. As a young teenager, I was unable to pick more than about 125 pounds in a day, no matter how hard I tried. I guess I was too much of a daydreamer. Anyway, after a ten-hour day, I managed to earn a little over three dollars. This wasn't so bad when the price of a movie was generally less than fifteen cents, a bag of popcorn dripping with butter was ten cents and a bottle of soda was an additional five or six cents.

I began to pick cotton at the age six using a sack that my mother sewed especially for me out of a "flour bag." This was a colorful cotton bag in which twenty-five pounds of flour was sold. I didn't pick for very long at a time at that early age. Other things kept catching my attention—a frog, a doodle bug—an arrowhead—an unusual weed or flower. I could easily hide among the cotton stalks believing that no one knew where I was. Luckily, I wasn't expected to pick much. It was a matter of having "fun" with the adults.

With my little sack, I would pick awhile, play awhile, perhaps take a little nap in the shade of the plants. At the end of a couple of hours, I would be all washed up, in the figurative sense (and needing a literal wash). I probably picked ten or twelve pounds over a period of a couple of hours. My dad paid me one penny per pound. When I was older, he no longer paid me. This was part of my responsibility to the family. My dad did, however, allow me to plant a small plot of cotton that was my own. I received the price per pound that he received at the gin for that particular wagon load.

About twelve hundred pounds of raw cotton was required to make a bale of ginned cotton; the leaves, parts of boles, seed, sand, gravel, and the occasional rock were ginned out. The cotton was then pressed tightly into an oblong bale, partially covered with burlap and bound with steel straps. The amount of money earned per bale was determined by buyers. They considered several factors: the projected year's harvest, government price supports, and the quality of the cotton fiber. A buyer would pull a handful of lint from the bale to determine its elasticity and length. The price was then offered.

Each year, my dad hoped to average about $200 per bale. The critical question was how many bales would be produced per acre. To give a concept of the size of an acre, it can best be considered as slightly smaller than an American football field. Technically an acre is 264 square rods. A rod is sixteen and a half feet, so this equals 43,560 square feet. As a comparison, a football field is exactly 45,000 square feet. On the Sand Mountain range (and on Brindley Mountain) where the soil contained minimum nutrients, the cost of fertilizer had to be considered. This was Dad's job, and he kept a little notebook and a stubby little pencil. All his calculations went into this book. He could determine how much he had spent on fertilizer per acre, how much each acre produced, and how much the gross return was. A farmer's life is so very different today with computers and programs to help with such calculations.

By the early 1940s, International Harvester and John Deere companies were working on the design for a mechanized cotton picker. By the late '40s both had two-row pickers on the market. By the 1960s, these mechanized pickers could pick six rows at a time and travel at about five miles an hour. This meant that a machine could pick close to 200,000 pounds of cotton in one day, using a crew of three or four. It would require eight hundred to one thousand humans to pick the same amount of cotton in one day. This marked the end of small cotton farmers unless they were able to ban together and pay for the services of a mechanical picker. Growing cotton became feasible only when planted in large fields of several hundred acres. My dad was wise to sell the farm in 1954.

The boll weevil came into the US from Mexico in the 1930s. By the mid-1940s, the nasty little bug was ruining a third or more of each crop in northern Alabama. The devastation became especially pronounced in the fall of 1948. Large farms were beginning to use tractors to spray DDT on the fields, creating a fog of dust. At first, since we didn't own a tractor, we foolishly tried to pick the weevils off the young "squares" and pinch them to death or drop them into a can of kerosene. Years later, I penned this "ode" to the Boll Weevil, the nemesis of King Cotton.

Boll Weevil

What hardy bug attacks a king?
Boll weevil with its mighty snout,
Dethrones the anxious growers, too.
"Another year they'll put us under.
In the poor house, if you please!"

Son, git out 'n' gather up them squares.
We'll burn them critters all to hell!

A mighty seesaw battle raged!
Doomsday seemed a losing year away.
Yet salvation came in chalk white dust
Its name was DDT—"piez'n" to most folks
Tough job it was to spray with hand-held pump.
Sometimes we'd wear a mask, but mostly not.

Son, be sure'n put a hanky over yer nose
That powder's mighty bad to breathe.

Now some new farmer down the road
Acquired a tractor rigged to spray
Four rows of cotton at a time
And raise gigantic clouds of dust
Like autumn fog upon the breeze.
A fog that killed a slew of birds and bees
And fish and prob'ly even trees.

But saved our crops, and thus our livelihood
To drive again to town with wagons,
Loaded down with cotton for the gin.
We made enough to pay off the banks
And just like fools we rushed ahead, come spring,
To start the cycle over once again!

Nothing we did made much of a dent in the number of weevils, and many of the bolls were severely damaged. This greatly reduced the per-acre yield of cotton staple. The futility of our struggle against the boll weevil serves as a great illustration of the dead-end nature of intensive farming. By the age of ten, I was promising myself a better life when I became an adult.

Queenie, Maud, Mama Cat, and Rex

Animals are such agreeable friends—they
ask no questions, they pass no criticism.

—George Eliot

I have a snapshot in my memory bank of
being awakened on a snowy winter morning
to the sound of banging. The noise was caused
by our young mule that, in a dreadful snit, was
kicking the walls of her stable. The little filly was
named Queenie, aptly named because she acted as
though she had special privileges and was ruler of
the barn lot.

Queenie loved to bite. She bit anything she
came near—her mother, the feed trough, the cow,
the hand that fed her. In fact, Queenie was down-
right mean. She chased the cats and the chickens that
ran loose in the barn lot and tried to stomp them
to death. Queenie was afraid of only one thing—my
dad. One time he gave the little colt a roundhouse
blow to the side of her head when she threatened to

bite him. After that brain-scrambling lick, she gave him a wide berth.

Queenie's mother, Maud, was normally a rather placid mare. She tolerated a lot of foolishness from her little offspring. However, when she finally had enough, she would take a good nip out of the hide on Queenie's rump. After that Queenie would slink off to a corner of the lot and lie down and go to sleep.

One day, my ten-year-old brother, Glenn, was feeding the chickens in the barn lot. While Glenn had his back turned, Queenie came trotting nonchalantly by and suddenly gave Glenn a swift kick in the leg. His leg wasn't broken, but badly bruised. Glenn came limping out of the lot squealing like a stuck pig. That incident was the last straw for Dad. The next day, he took Queenie to Kinney's Mule Barn. She was sold at auction for fifty dollars and good riddance. My dad didn't know the man who bought Queenie. Given her temperament, he was glad he didn't. He would have hated to pass her off on a friendly neighbor.

As I noted, Maud, the mare, was generally a calm animal. To me, she appeared enormous. My dad would sometimes set me on Maud's wide back, but I couldn't stay on she had such a wide girth. My legs were too short to reach her sides. I was never very comfortable around that old mare, but I did love to ride in the wagon when Dad hitched her up to go into town. "Make her run, Daddy," I would always say. He usually would comply for a few hundred yards before we got too near town and the paved roads.

Most of the time, I could count on a ride to town with Maud; however, one day Mother sent me and Glenn out in the orchard to pick cherries at the time Dad was planning to go into town. Dad hitched up Maud to the wagon and was about to leave. I came out of the cherry tree and ran toward the wagon. Unfortunately, Mother saw me. She gave me strict orders to get back to my job. I pitched a fit and put on a good cry. My mother was not moved in the least. She threatened to use a switch from the cherry tree on my hide if I didn't dry my face, stop my whimpering, and get back to work.

There was nothing to do but acquiesce. It turned out to be a good thing Mother didn't give in to my fit. Her stern discipline paid off that day. While Dad was passing through the narrow main street that ran through West Town, a loud car horn spooked Maud. She began to run with Dad tugging back on the reins with all his might. Despite his strength, he couldn't get Maud back under control. As she tore down the street, the right front wheel of the wagon struck the bumper of a large pickup truck.

The wagon began to tip. Dad realized that the bed was going to turn completely over. He reacted quickly and jumped as far to his left as he could. He almost cleared the wagon bed, which caught him on his right knee. He turned loose of the reins and Maud kept dragging the overturned wagon for another block. She veered left into Willow Creek, and the wagon caught on a wooden bridge. Before

Maud could hurt herself too badly, Mr. Ervin Tucker cut her loose from her harness and calmed her down.

In the meantime, Dad crawled out of the street and onto the sidewalk. His knee was in bad shape. One of the clerks in the West Cullman Grocery offered to drive Dad to the emergency room at the Cullman hospital. My dad refused to go directly to the hospital. He wanted to be driven to our house to tell Mother that he was okay. He didn't want her to worry when he didn't return home after a reasonable amount of time.

One of the sharper images that I carry with me is the sight of Dad limping into the house. He pulled up his pant leg and showed us his mangled and bloody knee. I almost threw up at the sight. Then Dad calmly got back in the car and was driven to the hospital. His knee was not broken, but the wound took several weeks to completely heal.

My mother used the incident as a teaching tool. It became one of those "I told you so" moments. She pointed out that a young boy should always obey his mother without throwing a fit because mothers always knew what was best. If I had gone with my dad, I would not have been able to jump, and I would have been killed. I was a bit skeptical of Mother's reasoning. Perhaps if I had gone with Dad, we would not have been in the same spot at the exact time when the horn sounded. Perhaps Maud would not have been spooked that day. Nevertheless, I was sufficiently chastised.

The trauma Maud had undergone was so severe that Dad doubted that she could ever be trusted in town again. It was her turn to be taken to Kenny's barn and sold at auction. Dad looked over the stock in the barn and found a four-year-old female mule who seemed well-mannered. It turned out that this medium-size mule indeed had a sweet disposition. We named her Nell. Since her back was not nearly as wide as Maud's, I could soon stay on her, and loved to ride her to the fields. Four years later, Nell was the mule I learned to plow with.

When I was in the second grade, a cat belonging to one of my classmates gave birth to thirteen kittens. Obviously, this presented a big problem for the mother cat and for the owners. How could all these little squirming creatures be properly fed? When I heard about the litter, I agreed to take one. We had lots of cats on our farm who hung out in the barn where the hunting was good and there was always milk.

The little female kitten that I chose to bring home was jet black and barely had her eyes open. I naturally named the cat *Blackie*. Not much was expected of Blackie. I took good care of her, making a nice bed in the corn crib. I made sure she had her share of the milk morning and night. (Dad would spray out a few streams into a bowl for the cats when he was milking.)

To everyone's surprise, Blackie, who was a short-haired Persian mix, gradually grew into a big and beautiful animal. She was larger than most cats and had powerful neck muscles. Blackie loved to sit on a ledge in the corn crib or stable and watch for gopher rats. Now some barn gophers can weight three or four pounds and be six to eight inches long, not counting the tail. They have a mean set of teeth and are not something to tangle with. Most of our other cats contented themselves with field mice, but Blackie loved the challenge of the gophers. She learned to pounce on the back of a gopher and break its neck before it could sink its teeth into her. It was an amazing feat.

That's not all. Blackie could catch birds, often while they were in the air. You may find that hard to believe. However, mockingbirds and blue jays seem to enjoy aggravating cats, even when the cat is not near a nest. These contentious birds like to dive bomb cats—to fly by their heads and give them a peck. Most cats are intimidated. However, some will try slapping at the birds. Blackie had other ideas. She would pretend to cower and let the mockingbird, or the jay, get quite close. On the second or third fly-by Blackie would leap high in the air and grab the surprised bird in her claws. I witnessed that operation on several occasions.

Blackie liked to be petted and would always come to my call. But like all cats, she was independent and wary of most humans. She had a mind of her own and could get along without human attention. She would go out hunting in the fields for hours and bring back all sorts of creatures for her children or as gifts to leave on our doorstep.

Most of our cats would use up their nine lives in a few years. A wild dog might be the final cause, or a snake bite, or a car flying by on the Bremen Road. However, Blackie seemed to avoid disaster year after year. She had several litters of kittens and outlived most of them. After a while we started calling her *Mama Cat*, rather than Blackie. She was still going strong at age eight when my Dad sold the farm. Naturally she was not cut out for city living, so she remained on the farm.

Mama Cat never had an offspring with the same powerful build or the prowess that she had. She was like some super athlete that comes along only rarely. I thought of her later when I read T. S. Eliot's *Book of Practical Cats* and even later delighted in the musical *Cats*, which Weber based on Eliot's work. One of the poems describes Old Deuteronomy *who had nine lives, [and] whose numerous progeny prospers and thrives.* Blackie seemed to combine the mystique of Mr. Macavity and ingenuity of Mr. Mistoffelees.

Every farm boy needs a dog to keep him company. Cats are not good companions if a boy is traveling across the fields looking for rabbit tobacco or quail eggs, or when hunting "big game" in the woods. When I was ten years old, another classmate gave me a little mixed breed puppy. He weighed about ten pounds at the time and grew into a thirty pounder. He was mostly black with some russet color around his nose. I called him Rex. Why I chose that name is lost in the fog of the past. Most likely I had heard other dogs with that name. I had no idea I was giving this little mutt the name *King*.

Rex and I enjoyed some good times together prowling about the countryside. When I arrived home from school, Rex never left my side when I was outdoors. He was my constant companion as I went about my chores. Rex was not allowed in the house. In my mother's opinion, a dog in the house was a serious no-no. She was not an animal lover. Consequently, Rex had his little doghouse near the barn door. That was not the only place he could take shelter. He could go under our house, or when the barn door was open, he could find a batch of hay to lie on. He never seemed to mind that he could not come into our house.

Rex did all the things a normal dog does. He fetched sticks and balls and chased his tail like an absolute fool. He could catch peanuts and popcorn tossed into the air for him. He could mangle a large bone in short order. Rex loved to spook rabbits and chase after them, but he never caught one as far as I know. For him, it was the chase that counted.

One day Rex followed me to the RFD mailbox across the Bremen road. He had done this many times in the past, but this time he was hit by a motorist and killed. In a split second, I had lost a good friend. I buried Rex in a grave below the barn lot where he had played so often chasing chickens. I carved the name Rex on a sandstone rock that stood as a tombstone. I cried, but I could not express my pain. All I said to my mother was, "I didn't want him to die." If that wasn't a classical understatement, I don't know what is. However, it was consistent with my nature to guard my emotions closely. I had strong feelings, but it may not have appeared that way to others.

Farm Neighbors

Eh vat now! A gut morgan to ye.

—Herr Richards

The neighbors on the east and west sides of our farm were brothers, Wilhelm Adolph Lessman and Frederick Lessman. They emigrated from Germany around the turn of the century and maintained much of the cultural and culinary traditions of their native land. They brewed their own beer and made their own wine. One type of wine was rather unusual as it was made from the berries of the poke plant, which some folks said was poisonous. Once when Dad complained of rheumatism, Wilhelm gave him a bottle of poke berry wine and assured Dad, "Eet vill do you mooch gut." According to Wilhelm, the wine had great medicinal properties. Dad took a couple of sips, made a face, and recapped the bottle and kept it in the cellar for the next fifteen years.

Wilhelm (who changed his name to Bill during WWI) and his wife, Klara, and son, William, lived west of us across the Bremen Road. Klara was noted for her homemade blood sausage and head cheese. From time to time, she offered a portion of one or the other to my mother who took some to be polite, but quickly threw it away as soon as she returned home. The Smith-Creel clan didn't eat the "likes of that." I never knew Klara because she died at the age of fifty-seven when I was only one year old.

The eastside of our land bordered on Frederick Lessman's property. Both Fred and Bill contracted with sharecroppers who worked a portion of their land, yet they personally tilled much of their acreage. Each year, Bill Lessman planted crops of corn, hay, peanuts, and potatoes. He planted some cotton, but with only himself and one teenage son, raising cotton required more effort than they could afford. Occasionally my dad would give Bill a hand with some large-scale task.

The tillable land on the western side of Bill Lessman's property was farmed by the Nix family. He was the stoutest man I can remember seeing in my youth, "stout" meaning very strong, with great endurance. The only other man close to the power of Mr. Nix was Mr. Roberson, the local gravedigger. He had protruding biceps and forearms usually only seen on a weightlifter. These came from digging graves with a pick and shovel.

The Lessmans had a dog named Prince, a big collie. I was afraid of Prince, but Mr. Lessman liked to set me on Prince's back so the dog could give me a ride. One of my earliest traumas involved Prince. Someone poisoned him (or he accidentally ate poison). He searched for water and drank in our creek under a wooden bridge. Glenn and I found him a day later, dead, lying in the water. I dreamed about Prince for weeks. That poor animal was my introduction to death.

Misfortune continued for the Lessman family. During the summer of 1943, Mr. Lessman died following a fall from his barn loft while hauling up bales of hay from his wagon. Dad happened to be helping with this task and was present to see the fall. I remember hearing the siren as an ambulance came to take Mr. Lessman to the hospital. Living in the country as we did, I think that was my first experience with a siren. Despite hospital attendance, Mr. Lessmann died the next day. His back had been broken. He was sixty-eight years old.

My dad became young William's surrogate father. At age eighteen, William was called for a physical by the local draft board. Dad encouraged him to seek an exemption to military service because he was the only member of his family remaining to work the farmland. But William wanted to defend his country and went off to boot camp.

Before William left for basic training and later to the war in Europe, Dad convinced him to marry his sweetheart, Doris Nix, and make her the beneficiary of all the land and property. When we next heard from him, William was a private in Company G of the Ninth Army. The Ninth fought in the Battle of the Bulge and in late February of 1945, crossed the Rhine and was sweeping around the northern edge of the Ruhr Valley in Operation Grenade. William was killed in a battle near the Weser River a few miles north of Osnabrück.

When word came that William had been killed, one of Doris's relatives shouted the news across the Bremen Road to my dad who was working in our orchard. I happened to be standing close by Dad at the time, which was usual for me. The incident is quite clear. I can still see the pain on my dad's face. He pulled out his handkerchief to wipe his eyes. This was the first and last time I ever saw my dad cry.

William's remains were returned to Cullman, and he is buried alongside his mother and father in Cullman City Cemetery. Doris never remarried, as far as I know. For many years, she lived alone in a sandstone house she had built on some of her property located across the Bremen Road from the cemetery and William's grave.

Other neighbors of German descent, Mr. Richards and his wife, lived on forested land just to the northeast of our farm. Mr. Richards was quite a character. He was the person called upon by the local farmers when they needed a young shoat neutered. Mr. Richards would show up with his razor-sharp pocketknife and a small Irish potato. "Eh vat, now? A gut morgan to ya," was his normal greeting. Apparently he did not distinguish between English "morning" and German "morgan."

I never saw Mr. Richards wearing anything but a pair of dirty blue denim overalls. Most of the time, he had a cigarette butt hanging from the corner of his mouth. He rolled his own using Prince Albert tobacco from a can. He struck his match on the side of his pant leg. I tried that several times with no success. I guess your pants need to be stiff with dirt for that process to work effectively. Since I was not allowed to get that dirty, I had no chance of success. He was an interesting fellow, Mr. Richards, to say the least.

Shortly after the end of the war, Woodrow and Gladys Ruehl Graham moved onto twenty acres south of our farm, which was part of the land Dad had originally cleared of trees in 1931. Woodrow and Gladys were in their thirties and had no children at the time; a girl named Nancy was born in 1953.

At first, Woodrow grew cotton, but after a few years of losing a third of his crop to the boll weevil, he decided that staple crop had no future. He built chicken houses, stocked them with white leghorns and began to produce eggs. Gladys had an administrative job with the local electric cooperative which furnished income while Woodrow established the "egg business."

Both my brother and I took on many odd jobs for Woodrow. We chopped cotton and hoed corn. We picked cotton for him for three cents a pound. I thought I was a pretty fast cotton picker, but after nine or ten hours of back-breaking work, I would weigh in at about a hundred and thirty pounds. For that effort, I would earn three dollars and seventy-five cents. At the time, the minimum wage was forty cents an hour, if I remember correctly.

Woodrow was like a big brother to me. He frequently told me risqué jokes that he knew I would not fully understand. He no doubt enjoyed seeing me blush. When he went rabbit hunting, he liked to have me tag along even though I didn't have a rifle or shotgun. He would let me shoot his .22 rifle, which I found easy to do. I never killed any living thing with it, but I did bust up a few tin cans. Woodrow also liked to give me a shot or two with his ten-gauge shotgun. I think it was mainly because he liked to see me fall backward when the gun recoiled.

Woodrow liked to go fishing, and he especially liked to gig for frogs. When we went gigging, we would go out around an hour after dark to a nearby creek teeming with bullfrogs. I normally held the lantern when we were close enough to gig. Woodrow was fairly accurate, but I was awful. To me the frog appeared in one place and was actually somewhat to the side. The distortion of the water depth and my astigmatism created this illusion. I did much better as the lantern-holder.

By the time Glenn left for Flint, Michigan, in the summer of 1950 to make his fortune, Woodrow was basically raising laying hens and gathering eggs. Any time he and Gladys wanted to leave for a few days of vacation, I took over the care and feeding of the hens for him. I was only twelve years old the first time he asked me. One day a year or so later, I was remiss in closing the door to one of the hen houses, and one of the hens escaped. I chased that "biddie" around the house a couple of times and tried to corner her, but to no avail.

Eventually frustration boiled over, and I reached down and picked up a smooth rock about the size of a silver dollar. I threw the rock at the hen with the motion of a shortstop throwing to first base. The rock hit her in the neck and almost broke it off. She staggered around for another twenty seconds and then succumbed. I was embarrassed that I had killed one of Woodrow's prize-laying hens, but my anger had gotten the best of me. I buried the old biddy in Lessman's Woods and never told Woodrow what I had done. He never missed one out of two thousand chickens.

When it was time to vaccinate the white leghorn chickens (at about twelve weeks), I was always the "catcher." This work was usually done with three people—a catcher, a holder, and a vaccinator. A man of African American descent who lived on the Kinney farm about a mile south of our farm was the holder. His name was Hazel. His wife was the cook and housekeeper for Mr. and Mrs. Kinney (of the Kinney Mule Barn), and Hazel did odd jobs for them and for other farmers in the area.

Hazel was fun-loving and a great kidder. He gave me the nickname *June bug*. No doubt this was because I was small and agile. Hazel had no other name that I ever heard spoken. This seemed rather peculiar to me. Hazel always called adults Mr. or Mrs. When he was comfortable enough with folks, he would call them by their first name—preceding the name with *mister*. There was Mister Forrest, Mister Woodrow, Mister Bill, and so forth. With the women, Hazel always used *missus*, plus the woman's married surname. Never under any circumstance did Hazel use a white woman's "given" name. This deference was taken for granted. Hazel never seemed bitter or resentful. Since I had no contact with any other blacks (none were on the streets of Cullman when I was growing up), I was in my midteens before I began to understand the social and moral implications of Jim Crow Laws and the deference that blacks were obligated to show to whites.

I have no idea how old Hazel was when we were working together. He was probably in his late fifties or early sixties. He died a few years after I left the area to attend college. The end of an era came when Woodrow Graham died in January of 1997. He was the last person to know me as *June bug*, the cotton-chopping, egg-washing, pimple-faced, frog-gigging teen. A big part of my past died with him—much of it was "good riddance!"

Family Tales

Full many a gem of purest ray serene, the
dark, unfathomed caves of oceans bear: Full
many a flower is born to blush unseen and
waste its sweetness on the desert air.

—Thomas Gray
Elegy Written in a Country Churchyard

C an you trace your ancestors back to Noah?
A distant cousin believed she could. She
assured us our Scruggs line could be traced
back to Noah's descendant, Serug. Now this seemed
crazy to me until one day in Paris when I telephoned
the *Tour d'Argent* restaurant for dinner reservations. I
gave my last name to the reservation desk and spelled
it carefully, using French pronunciation. When I
arrived that evening, the maître d' asked for my name.

"Scruggs," I said and spelled it for him.

He looked up and down his guest list. "*Alors,
zat name, eet does not appeer on zee leest,*" he said,
rather haughtily.

I figured it was time to switch to French. "*Eh
bien, Monsieur, j'ai bien* téléphoné ce matin pour

réserver," I insisted. Well, sir, I called this morning for a reservation. "*Veuillez regarder encore.*" Please look again.

He perused the list majestically. Suddenly a light came on in his head. "*Aha,*" he said. "*Eer eet eez—SERUG!*"

The place where our parents lived when we were born was not determined solely by them. A long series of causalities were involved in the creation of any given community. Another long string of causes and effects brought our parents to that specific community. Indeed, everything was put in motion in the earliest stages of human history. Yet where our parents were living when we were born determines much about our early world view.

Both my mother and my father were born and raised in the southeast corner of Morgan County, Alabama, only a few miles apart. My mother, Ora Mae Smith, was the eighth child born to William Thomas and Martha Jane Creel Smith. My father, Forrest Puryear Scruggs, was the fourth child born to James Carl and Margaret Ann Baker Scruggs.

In the early 1880s, my great grandfather Judson Scruggs left South Carolina with his family in a covered wagon in search of a better life. He established a homestead in Morgan County, Alabama. This occurred very shortly after the creation of the town and county of Cullman.

On my maternal side, the Creels arrived in the area a generation earlier, moving west from Carroll County, Georgia. The Smiths came to Morgan

County two generations earlier. The Bakers (my dad's mother's line) appear to have come to the area from Tennessee around the middle of the nineteenth century. When the other four great grandparents are added, the list includes Ryan, Petty, Andrews, and Qualls.

When I search back seven generations, I find that my sixty-four ancestors were all in America at the time of the Revolution. In this mix are names like Hicks, Dobbins, Puryear, Camp, Wilkins, Quinn, Leake, Marshall, and Cocke—all English, Scottish, or Irish names.

One ancestor of German heritage, Johann Ulrich Swope, arrived in the American colonies sometime in the first half of the eighteenth century. Johann is a fifth-generation grandparent. I have to extend my search back to the ninth generation to find an ancestor who possibly arrived from France. That ancestor is Gilly Grosmarin. Of course, thanks to the Norman conquest in 1066, this could be a French family name that arrived in England in the eleventh or twelfth centuries.

It appears that most of my ancestors arrived at some point in the British Isles and finally migrated to the New World by the mid to late seventeenth century. This migration to the American colonies began early, and for the most part, these ancestors came into the colonies through southern ports.

Most of my ancestors passed through Virginia. Their descendants then followed the migration routes down the Appalachian Mountain Range into North Carolina, South Carolina, Georgia, Tennessee, and eventually into Alabama. You would have to say that given any slight turn of events at any time or place by one or more of these ancestors and I would have been born somewhere other than Cullman County, Alabama.

DNA testing of some dozen males with the Scruggs family name shows a common ancestor back to the tenth generation. Three Scruggs were living in the vicinity of Jamestown, Virginia, by the second half of the seventeenth century. Apparently, they left England at the time of the civil war in that country. During the sixteenth century, the Scruggs/Scroggs appear to have lived in the Midlands or in the city of London. Further testing reveals the likelihood that the Scruggs line came into England by way of the Danish invaders, either by direct invasion in the eighth or ninth centuries or with the Normans in the eleventh century.

But Scruggs or Scrogges is only one of 1,012 ancestral names if one researches back only to the tenth generation of grandparents! In actuality, there are considerably fewer names due to marriages by couples with a common surname. But in any case, the possible locations where I could have been born seem staggering. In actuality, my dad bought land in Cullman County, just outside the city limits of Cullman in 1930.

The land was previously owned by Jerry Morgan, Dad's father-in-law, a stern redhead with a long handlebar moustache. He died in 1943 and was the first person I ever saw laid out in a casket. He was not buried until his sons who were in the military had received passes to come home for the funeral. During the war, this took some time. Mr. Morgan was laid out in the living room of his house. The odor of carnations and other flowers and the smell of death made me squeamish. I was reluctant to go to funerals after that, but there was no skipping those of close family members.

I grew up hearing stories about family members who lived through the US Civil War, or the *War Between the States*, as some Southerners continue to call that conflict. Such stories are the core of "Southern-ness" and Southern literature. Vague memories of that internecine struggle lay behind many deeply held opinions and passions. Tales passed from generation to generation. These stories live like restless ghosts in the attics of the mind.

My mother had a great uncle who was born during the Civil War. His father died in the battle of Vicksburg and left a widow and three children. Uncle Bud Anders was the oldest of these children. He lived to be one hundred years old and was a special link to times past. I visited Uncle Bud on several occasions with my mother when I was a preteen. Uncle Bud was straight as an arrow, slim, with gray hair. He wore glasses with round black frames and resembled a photo of some nineteenth-century scholar.

For the first nine years of his life, my dad sat at the knees of his paternal grandfather who spent three years in the infantry of Holcombe Legion, South

Carolina Volunteers. Grandpa Judson Scruggs was a great storyteller and dazzled young Forrest with tales of exploits against the wily Yankees. Jud's stories were never about the horrors of that conflict, although he had witnessed more than his share of blood baths at Second Manassas, Kinston, Charleston, Vicksburg and the death camp at Elmira, New York. Jud's stories were about comic incidents or about hair-raising escapes or near escapes.

Most of the tales about Jud's war years that made a permanent imprint on my dad were full of comic relief, of tricks played on comrades, of foot races in camp, of unexpected snow falls, of escape through tree tops, of hard-cider drinking "Dutch" in Pennsylvania. My dad would retell such tales with a smile and a chuckle. He enjoyed repeating them, and I enjoyed hearing them.

Many of these stories were passed on to me, revised and embellished with my dad's own imagination. The tales were as exciting and heroic as any stories found in historical novels I read in subsequent years. Later in life, researching the Legion's battles in state and federal archives for a book I was writing, I discovered that the major storyline that I had heard as a child was basically correct.

My dad told other stories about Jud building a log cabin, damming up a creek, building a grist mill and sawmill, and growing tobacco. Dad told of Jud blacksmithing and tanning leather. Jud had been a teamster during part of his military service, and he was quite skillful with a rawhide whip. My dad said

Jud could cut off a man's coat buttons with a whip and not tear the cloth. Apparently, there were few trades at the time that Jud could not do. This trait was passed on to his grandson, Forrest.

Much family lore was repeated at wakes and funerals when folks reminisced about the deceased person's life. When I was very young, I attended "viewings," church services, and graveside services for Grandpa Jerry Morgan, Mama Smith, and Aunt Flossie Cobb. I missed the funeral for our close neighbor, Bill Lessman, because I had a case of whooping cough. I also missed the funeral for Grandpa Scruggs due to a case of scarlet fever. When I was nine years old, I attended the funeral for Grandma Scruggs. This was the first time I remember paying attention to any sermon. The text was from 1 Corinthians, chapter thirteen about faith, hope, and love. The Pauline poetry in these passages made a real impression on me. To this day that sermon is the only one for which I remember the Scripture reading verbatim: "*Now abideth faith, hope and love, but the greatest of these is love.*"

These funerals were always open-casket affairs with considerable singing, crying, fanning, and preaching. I was too young to remember anything about Mama Smith's funeral, except that the weather was cold and very rainy. About my aunt Flossie's funeral, I only remember her husband, Uncle Clyde, with his head stuck in our car window crying and promising to take good care of their only son, Avery, who was four years old.

These early funerals were not antiseptic as are the memorial services of today. Death was in the room and in the sanctuary. The pain of death was palpable. The smell of death was potent. Folks showed no shame in displaying emotions in public. Of course standing around the open casket, some of the talk was trivial and insipid: *"Don't she look nice? She looks just like herself! Ain't that a purty dress?"*

After the church service, everybody piled into their vehicles and formed a long cortege and drove off to the grave site. All other traffic pulled off the road to show respect. After a short graveside service, the casket was lowered into the ground while the mourners stood around. This was closure. This was dust to dust and ashes to ashes.

Gum Pond and Fairview Clans

Call it a clan, call it a network. Call it a
tribe; call it a family. Whatever you call
it, whoever you are, you need one.

—Jane Howard
Families

S outhern families in rural areas tended to be
quite numerous in the nineteenth and early
twentieth centuries. These large and extended
families were very clannish. The kinfolk often lived
in close proximity to one another until the search for
jobs in the North in the 1930s broke up many families. Members of a clan took care of each other. They
visited one another. They held reunions. They paid
periodic visits to the graves of ancestors and kept the
sites well-groomed.

The matriarchal clan to which I belonged as a
child was the Smith family. The yard at the Smith "old
home place" in Gum Pond was totally flat and had not
a sprig of grass or weed. The yard was swept with a

brush broom and carefully manicured. This created a huge area for games of marble or croquet. I have never seen another yard so well-groomed and grassless.

Grass lawns were viewed as nuisances. There was already more work to do on a farm than time to accomplish it all. No one wanted to add mowing a lawn to the total. This was a totally nonproductive activity. Vegetable gardens and flower gardens were another matter, work usually left to the womenfolk.

The kitchen in the old home place was rather large. It needed to be in order to accommodate such a numerous family (fifteen children, twelve living into adulthood). A long wooden dining table occupied the middle of the room. It had long benches on both sides. This kitchen seemed very inviting to me with its large cookstove and china cabinets.

The odor of pies cooking in the great wood-fired oven permeated the house. Only a few feet from the back porch, just off the kitchen, stood the old log smokehouse. This facilitated the procurement of meat for the breakfast table. Will Smith and sons butchered their meat. This included hogs and beef cattle. The hog meat was salted and smoked in this old log building, which outdated the living quarters.

Many houses in the rural South were unpainted, but the Smith house was always impeccably white. Mama Smith and her mother (Grandma Creel) were both believers that cleanliness is next to Godliness, a trait my mother inherited to the fullest degree. These women were quite obsessive about dirt and dust—in the house or on clothes.

There were plenty of fun things to do at the "old home place." My uncle Herman ran the little grocery store on the property near the house. The store had been started late in the nineteenth century by great grandfather Sherrill Smith. When he died, his son, and my grandpa, Will Smith (William Thomas), continued to operate the store and supply the needs of farmers in that area of Morgan and Cullman Counties. Will also made sorghum syrup for himself and for other farmers who furnished their cane.

When Grandpa Will died of skin cancer in January of 1932, Mr. Rayburn Miller took over operation of the sorghum mill. Power was generated by a mule hitched to a long pole. As the mule walked around and around, the mill crushed the cane to produce the raw juice. The juice was heated in a large flat metal pan. As the juice cooked, foam appeared on the top of the thickening juice. This was my mother's favorite way to eat sorghum. I preferred a spoon of sorghum on a hot buttered biscuit. A word of caution to Yankees, sorghum must be eaten rather sparingly. Too much is a guarantee of heartburn.

The supplies for Grandpa Will's little store were bought in Cullman. The round trip from Gum Pond to Cullman and back took the better part of a day by horse-drawn wagon. When automobiles became available, Grandpa Will bought one, a Ford Model T that he ordered from Sears and Roebuck. With the Model T, Grandpa Will could make the trip to Cullman and back in a couple of hours, assuming the road was not impassible due to heavy rain or ice.

Grandpa Will accepted cash from the farmers for the store goods, if cash was available. However, he would also barter with farmers, trading canned goods, flour, meal, and other staples for fresh vegetables, beef, and pork.

As other farmers in the area acquired automobiles, Will had a gas pump installed in front of his store. I remember the old pump that was supplied by Gulf Oil Company. The upper part of the pump had a glass tube with markings to show gallons. A hand pump was cranked until the desired amount of gasoline appeared in the upper tube. A hose was then placed in the opening to the automobile tank and gravity did the rest.

In the early 1940s, the grocery store was little changed from what it had been in earlier years. The store was stocked with nonperishable items: canned and boxed goods, and such items as soda crackers which came in a large barrel. Cheese came in a large hoop, flour and sugar in large bags. Sometimes large stalks of bananas were brought back from Cullman.

When in season, oranges and tangerines were bought in Cullman and hauled to Gum Pond. Local fruit (apples, peaches, pears) were sold in season. Potatoes were available in fifty-pound bags and were weighed as needed. Rolls of cloth were measured to order for rural women who sewed most of the clothes for their family. Overalls, Levi's, work shoes and leather goods were also available in the store. Mother made a little money when she was a young girl by selling lemonade, pound cake, and grape pies at the store.

In later years, with electrification, it became possible to sell items that had to be kept cool (soft drinks such as Coca-Cola [pronounced co-cola], RC Cola, Orange Crush, Root Beer, and Grape Soda). Before electricity, only a limited number of bottles could be kept cold for a time with ice brought from the Cullman Ice House. The staples most in demand by local farm families were flour, sugar, crackers, canned salmon, tuna, and sardines. Jars of Vienna sausages and pickles were frequent sellers as well.

Tobacco products were in high demand. Grandpa Will and later Uncle Herman stocked all the major brands of snuff, chewing tobacco and smoking tobacco (Old Gold, Mail Pouch, Seven Seas, Pike, and Prince Albert). As a kid, I found empty Prince Albert tobacco tins very useful as places to carry all manner of personal items: crayons, marbles, buttons, candy, and money.

It was not unusual in those days for older women to dip snuff, and there were very few farmers who didn't chew a plug of tobacco when out in the fields. Indeed, the only vice the country preachers steered clear of in their exhortations was the vice of dipping and chewing. If one crossed the line, some of the elders would call him aside: *"Brother, you done stopped preaching and gone to meddling."*

The Gum Pond store had a unique smell that is hard to describe. Various odors mingled together: coal oil, gasoline, leather, waxed floors, aging wood, dust, snuff, crackers, cheese, and fruit. Any little kid who hung around the store long enough would eventually be given something to eat and drink. Everybody's favorites were RC Colas and Moon Pies. Kids liked to shake up the cola and squirt it down their throats or pour salted peanuts in the bottle with the cola and then drink and eat simultaneously. Plenty of choices of penny candy and gum were kept in a glass case. Strings of black licorice candy and peppermint sticks were real hits.

When I was quite young, Mother would make frequent visits back to her childhood home to spend a few days and nights with her elderly mother, whom all the grandkids called Mama Smith. I say elderly, but she was not old by today's standards. She died at age seventy-two.

Mama Smith's hair was plaited and wound about the top of her head. She wore high-neck dresses, usually with large white collars. She almost always wore an apron. She had no teeth, but she did own a pair of wire-rimmed glasses. (Apparently seeing was more important than chewing.)

Mama Smith seemed the epitome of the elderly matriarch. As I recall her, she sat placidly in an armchair as though on a throne. She was always neatly dressed. I found her presence quite intimidating. She already had several grandchildren, so my arrival was nothing special. I don't remember her having much to say to me or holding me on her lap. If she did, it was when I was very young.

As a child, I never spent a night with my other grandmother and grandfather, my dad's parents. They lived in Fairview, which was even closer to our farm than Gum Pond. When we visited Grandma and Grandpa Scruggs, it was usually on a Sunday afternoon. Kinfolks of all sizes and ages were often at that "old home place." In the summer, the men sat on the front porch and spun yarns. In the winter, they sat around the fireplace in the living room keeping the fire sizzling with the juice from their snuff or tobacco.

Several uncles on that side of the family chewed tobacco. The champion was my uncle Fred. He was as skillful with a squirt as Private Tussie in Jesse Stuart's novel (*Taps for Private Tussie*). Uncle Fred would sit in a rocking chair about five feet from the fire and pick out an ember and snuff it out with a big juicy squirt. However, it was a greater feat when he chose to hit the brass spittoon. The *plinking* noise as the juice made contact with the metal was unlike any other sound. Uncle Fred kept a bandana in his hand to wipe his chin. Despite his accuracy with the squirt, he couldn't keep a bit of juice from dripping down his chin. If Uncle Fred was outside, he would pick out something on the ground for a target. He particularly liked to disturb a carefully constructed anthill and send the critters scattering.

Uncle Fred and Aunt Norma had four girls and two boys. The oldest boy, James Robert, was in the US Navy during the war. The younger boy, Frank, was several years older than I. When we were out in the barn lot, we invariably got into corn cob fights. Frank was the champion at this bit of warfare. He was one powerful thrower! When he hit you with a corncob, it took a piece of skin off where it hit. When two teams were assembled to have a corncob war, it was very prudent to have Frank on your side.

Corncobs weren't the only thing Frank was good at throwing. He had a good accurate throw with rocks as well. One of his favorite targets was the outhouse behind the old home place. He especially liked bombarding the privy while Grandma Scruggs was in it. This would piss Grandma off royally (no pun intended). Frank got more whippings for this than any other crazy stunt he pulled in his teenage years. Grandpa claimed that Frank was just naturally mule-headed like his father, Fred. As a teenager Fred and Grandpa Jim had more than a few serious run-ins, which culminated with Fred leaving home at age sixteen.

For many years Grandma Scruggs wove cloth on a homemade loom that Grandpa Jim had built for her. She also made her own thread. First, she took a handful of wool and used a carder to separate and straighten the fibers. (A carder was something like a brush with stiff heavy bristles.) Once the wool was carded, Grandma would spin the loose wool into thread with her spinning wheel.

The thread was dyed and then woven into a blanket, shawl, socks, sweaters, and other apparel on her loom. If this sounds like an arduous process, it was. When the family was still together, the children helped with the carding. The girls were taught to spin thread, but the weaving was Grandma's thing.

In the nineteen forties, after Grandpa Jim died, Grandma came to our farm to visit on several occasions. She would stay for a week or more at a time. Preparations had to be made before her arrival. Grandma dipped snuff constantly, thus she had to have a homemade spittoon and a black gum twig to swirl the snuff around between her cheek and gums. My job was to cut a twig from our black gum tree and trim one end into a brush, which Grandma could use to push the snuff around in her mouth. Glenn located an old tin can and put a few hands full of dirt in it. This became Grandma's spittoon.

Grandma Scruggs lived with her youngest daughter, Aunt Jewel, after the death of Grandpa. Aunt Jewel was married to Ernest Elrod and lived in Gadsden, Alabama. Uncle Ernest worked in the Goodyear Plant. They had four children: a girl named Cewilla and a boy named Jimmy Dan were older than I. Two other girls, Glenda Sue and Annie Jo, were a bit younger.

Jimmy Dan was slight of build and worked hard to become bigger and stronger. He had a set of barbells in the basement and spent a lot of time lifting weights. In his late teens, he managed to buy an old model A car. This model had not been retrofitted with an electric starter, so the motor had to be set in motion with a hand crank. One day Jimmy Dan was not holding the crank properly, and he broke his thumb when the crank kicked back. He had his hand in a cast for weeks.

Normally Glenn and Jimmy Dan would take off in the Model A. That left me to play with Glenda Sue and Annie Jo. This meant sissy stuff like jump rope and hop scotch. Lucky for me, we never stayed very long. We had to be back on the farm before dark to take care of the animals.

Progenitors

As long as you have the blessing of your parents, it doesn't matter even if you live in the mountains.

—Greek proverb

I think that Forrest, my dad, was Grandma Scruggs's favorite son. She often told the same story about his enlistment in the US Navy in 1917. She said that Dad packed a small duffel bag and said goodbye to the family and walked out the front door. He walked a hundred feet or so down the dusty road on his way to hitch a ride to the train station in Decatur. Suddenly he paused, turned around, and went back into the house. Dad sat down at the pump organ and played and sang *Crossing the Bar,* the poem by Alfred Tennyson which had been set to music.

Sunset and evening star,
And one clear call for me!
And may there be no moaning of the bar
When I put out to sea.

For though from out our bourne
of time and place
The flood may bear me far,
I hope to see my Pilot face to face
When I have crossed the bar.

After basic training in Norfolk, Virginia, Dad was assigned to the mine sweeper *Chattanooga*, which steamed up and down the northeast coast from Boston to New York City. Having an itch to see something of the world, Dad had asked for overseas duty. Unfortunately for Dad, an administrative *snafu* occurred, and his orders went to Cherbourg, France, but he remained on the *Chattanooga*.

During the bitterly cold winter of 1917–18, while standing watch, Dad's feet were severely frost-bitten. For the remainder of his life, he experienced numbness and coldness in his feet in winter, caused—he swore—by this incident. Dad also contracted the Asian flu, which killed some thirty million people worldwide. He lay sick in a large hospital ward with several dozen other sick men. He remembered seeing men covered in a blanket and taken out for burial. In his delirium, he thought he would be next. Ironically, my mother had a case of influenza in the same time frame back in Gum Pond.

One of my earliest memories of Dad was watching him shave. This occurred late every Saturday afternoon in preparation for Sunday worship. He would also shave during the week if there was some special event he needed to attend, but just working on the farm all day, he saw no reason to be clean shaven every day.

In those early years, when he shaved, Dad used a straight razor honed to a fine edge with a leather strop (which, by the way, he threatened to use on me if I misbehaved—but that was an empty threat). We had no indoor plumbing at the time, so Dad shaved in a corner of the dining room near a window where he had plenty of light. He had a small mirror which he hung on the wall or sat on the window ledge.

The shaving lather came from soap in a cup. He had a brush which he wet in hot water and twirled around in the cup to make the lather. First, though, he placed a steaming hot washcloth on his face and held it there for what seemed like a minute. Then he held the straight razor in what seemed a strange angle and began to shave off his whiskers. He seldom cut himself, which was amazing to me. The entire process was a remarkable exercise, and I could hardly wait to be able to do the same myself.

Before WWII began, Dad was engaged in construction work in Huntsville, Alabama, at the Redstone Arsenal. But his strength began to fail, and he was obliged to resign. He was diagnosed with pernicious anemia. This meant that he needed heavy doses of iron and vitamin B12. To obtain enough iron, Mother fried calf liver once a week. For the B12, she gave Dad a shot in liquid form in his hip, also once a week. He was declared to have a disability by the Veterans' Administration and began to receive a small pension.

Despite the disease, Dad found new part-time work at the local cotton seed oil mill while keeping up the farm work. The oil mill whistle was the time-keeper for the town of Cullman and the surrounding area. The mill whistle called the men to work at 7:00 a.m. It blew again at 12:00 noon for the lunch break. The whistle blew again to remind the men that it was time to return to work at 12:30. The workers were always glad to hear the "quitting time" whistle which blew at 6:00 p.m.

Dad ceased to work at the oil mill in 1942 and only farmed after that time. Despite his health issues, he could plow all day with short breaks at midmorning, noon, and midafternoon.

> My father worked with a horse-plough,
> His shoulders globed like a full sail strung
> Between the shafts and furrows.
> The horses strained at his clicking tongue.
> An expert, he would set the wing
> And fit the bright steel-pointed sock.
>
> The sod rolled over without breaking,
> At [rows end], with a single pluck
> Of reins, the sweating team turned round
> And back into the land. His eye
> Narrowed and angled at the ground,
> Mapping the furrows exactly.
>
> —Seamus Heaney
> Follower

Most farmers rolled their own cigarettes rather than pay the higher price for prepackaged cigarettes. A lot of smoking tobacco was sold in small pouches along with a small book of cigarette paper. Most men wore overalls with a pocket in the bib which seemed to have been made intentionally for the tobacco pouch and the small book of papers. This made for handy rolling during work activities.

My dad began to smoke at age twelve and continued until my birth. This meant he smoked for some thirty-two years. He always rolled his own cigarettes. The story is told that Dad could roll a cigarette while plowing a field and never have to stop the mules. This sounded a bit like a tall tale to me. However, he said the reins were tied together and placed behind his back. He steadied the plow with his left hand while reaching into his bib overall pocket and retrieving the paper with his right hand. He put the paper between his thumb and index finger of his left hand while gently guiding the plow with the remaining fingers and palm.

Dad then reached into his pocket and retrieved the tobacco pouch and opened the pull-string with his teeth. Then he poured the necessary quantity of tobacco onto the paper and returned the pouch to his pocket. He then rolled the paper into a cigarette and licked the edges of the paper with his tongue. He placed the cigarette in his mouth, still guiding the plow with his left hand.

Dad then reached into another pocket of his bib overalls and retrieved a kitchen match which he struck on his pant leg or on one of the metal buttons of his overalls, never stopping the plow. It seemed to me that a person would need a smoke very badly to go through such gyrations, but my dad assured me that after a time this process could be done automatically. My thought was, why not just stop the mule long enough to build the smoke and then start up again?

My parents were both raised with strict discipline. Their parents and grandparents believed firmly that if you spared the rod, you spoiled the child. They would never question the traditions handed down by their ancestors, so they also believed that corporal punishment was the surest way to bring up a child in the way of the Lord (and society). Now, in the forties and fifties in the South, and I expect, the rural areas in most of the US, corporal punishment of children in the home and in school was widely practiced.

A small child was spanked with the hand or with a paddle of some sort, but when a child reached the age of five or six, the hand was no longer feasible. There was too much likelihood of bruising the hand or breaking a blood vessel. At this point, what was called for was a *switch*. By switch, I am talking about a small limb from a tree, where the thickest part would be about the diameter of a man's little finger.

The best switches were limber, and the best tree for switches was the peach tree. Now, in my case and that of my brother, we were sent to the tree to cut the switch to be used on us. One was tempted, of course, to cut off a very tiny switch. However, if the switch was too small, we were sent back for a thicker one.

Usually the switching was done through our blue jeans or overalls, but it still stung quite a bit. A fine line existed between what was acceptable discipline and what was cruelty. Luckily for me and my brother, my dad never crossed that line. He was careful not to give us more than we could bear, and I never had welts that lasted more than a day.

During the punishment, if we began to cry, Dad would say, "All right, that's enough. Stop the sniveling and dry your face." If we kept up the "sniveling," he would say, "Stop it right now, or I'll give you something to cry about." I never could understand that comment, since we were already crying because of what he had done.

My mother, Ora Mae Smith, was raised by thrifty parents. In her family, nothing was ever wasted. Mother's natural thriftiness was compounded by the Great Depression. Thriftiness became frugality. This frugality ultimately became something of a joke. Not only could Mother pinch a penny until it screamed, she could take a fivepound slice of ham and feed six people at dinner for five days running. She would cut off six small chunks of ham and put them on a platter and place them on the table. The rest of the ham stayed on the kitchen counter, out of reach. Now five pounds of ham equals eighty ounces. The math is simple. If you have six people eating a small piece of ham for five days, that means thirty pieces of ham. This equals 2.66 ounces of meat per serving. Yet no one ever left the table hungry—even those who were accustomed to having a dinner meal containing a ten ounce steak, or two pork chops, or a half-pound hamburger patty. How could my mother accomplish this? We all decided it was a miracle!

We began comparing Mother's exploits with ham to the stories of Jesus feeding the four thousand or was it the five thousand?! Jesus was able to convince his entire listening audience to share. Mother's secret was less spectacular; she included five or six additional side dishes of vegetables. If the season permitted, these dishes always included fried okra, stewed squash, well-cooked green beans, creamed corn, speckled butterbeans, tomato slices, cornbread, and plenty of iced tea. With all these other items on our plate, who needed a big portion of ham? Indeed, a little bit of everything was put on the plate at once. The veggies ran together, and this was all right. The various combinations were what made the distinctive Southern taste.

As a non-Southerner, my wife was unaccustomed to vegetables being "overcooked," and especially all dishes being either fried or stewed. The vegetables seemed rather bland to her. My mother only seasoned with salt and a bit of pepper, plus a chunk of salt pork in the beans or greens, called "fatback" by the homefolks.

However, a greater culinary surprise for my dear wife was the way Mother cooked only one dish at a time. When one vegetable was fully cooked, it was put in a bowl and set aside. Preparation for the noon meal began around nine or ten in the morning. As a consequence, by noon some of the dishes had been sitting and cooling for as much as two hours. By the time every dish reached the table all the food was cool or cold. No part of the meal was hot.

Now, the habit of beginning to cook the noon meal in the early morning hours was a leftover from the days of no air-conditioning when a stove that burned wood gave off a great deal of heat. Mother had to work in a hot kitchen in the summers, and like all Southern rural cooks, she began her dinner preparation early in the morning before the day-time temperature reached ninety degrees or more. When the farm workers came to the house for the noon meal, they had been in the scorching heat for as long as five hours. Most preferred food that was not very hot.

Even in the days when Mother had an electric stove that gave off little heat and when she had a window air-conditioner in the dining room that also helped to keep the kitchen from becoming severely hot, she continued her old method of cooking early and serving food cool.

Another peculiar Southern trait shocked my wife. When the plates, glasses, and flatware were cleared from the table after the noon meal, the bowls and plates containing the remaining uneaten food were left on the table. A cotton cloth was placed over these bowls. These dishes sat on the table until it was time for the evening meal. The vegetables were then warmed and placed back on the table.

No new dishes were prepared for the evening meal. We ate leftovers. This was the old-fashioned rural way of doing things, and my mother was loath to consider changing. My wife and daughters simply picked at the supper food. They were sure they were going to "come down" with ptomaine poisoning!

My mother was obsessive about cleanliness. She did not have much in the way of worldly goods, and her furniture was inexpensive. The wooden floors and linoleum was well-scuffed, but she swept and mopped every day. The beds were carefully made, clothes were hung up, the oil cloth on the dining room table was wiped to a shine, the dishes were washed and dried by hand and put away. The entire house was as spotless as a farmhouse could be. We all wiped our shoes thoroughly when we came into the house. If not, we immediately heard about it, and we had to spring into action to clean up anything tracked in.

Now life on a farm is very conducive to tracking in "stuff." We tried our best not to get our overalls too dirty. If we did, we brushed them off before coming into the house. Mother could tolerate dirt stains, but she could not tolerate grass stains. I guess they were hard to scrub out on the washboard. If she saw stains on my clothes, it was a sure signal that I had been in the grass, playing ball, wrestling, or doing some other fun activity.

Mother had an unusually keen eye, not only for dirt. She could walk across the lawn and suddenly reach down and pick a four-leaf clover—in a spot where I had spent the last fifteen minutes trying to find one. When Mother walked across a sandy area, she could spot a doodlebug trap from twenty feet away. When she saw one, she would stoop down and call to it: "Doodlebug, doodlebug, come out, come out." As far as I know, none ever accepted her invitation.

Mother considered anything that was "unclean" to be "nasty." This could be anything from mud on a person's clothes to the nature of a person's personality. "That's nasty!" she would often say. Smoking was a "nasty" habit, so she would not tolerate it in her house. In the days when a majority of men smoked, she had many fewer guests. If a smoker came, you can be sure they didn't stay long. Without asking them not to smoke, Mother had a way of making them aware that she was disgusted by their behavior.

When I started that nasty habit while in college, it was quite a bone of contention between my mother and me. I never smoked inside her house, but of course. she could smell the odor on my clothes. She did not hesitate to make her disapproval known. But as you might guess, very few smokers ever kicked the habit due to nagging alone, even the smoker's own personal self-nagging. My mother's constant innuendos about nasty smokers did not stop me either. But for her sake (and mine), I am glad that she lived long enough to see me become a reformed smoker.

Other habits that were "nasty" include tobacco chewing (hard to disagree with her on that one) and dipping snuff. The intolerance for those tobacco products put Mother a foul of her in-laws. Dad's father chewed, and his mother dipped. His one brother who lived relatively near us chewed mightily. I don't remember Uncle Fred ever visiting us, but we went several times a year to his farm when Dad's parents were living with Fred and his wife, Norma. Fred chewed and Norma dipped.

Despite this "nasty" habit, they were "good" people who frequently helped their neighbors without recompense. They were good-natured and loved to sing around the old pump organ in their living room. Aunt Norma was an excellent cook. She always had a tableful of food available when anyone came by to visit. It seemed she always had a fried chicken leg or two, and she was far and away the best "chicken fryer" who ever placed a floured and seasoned piece of chicken in hot grease. Actually, a daughter, Frances Harris, was a close second.

Aunt Norma baked the best pies you could ever imagine. However, all this was lost on my mother, who could only see that Aunt Norma's apron was stained and that she sometimes had a dab of snuff juice in the corner of her mouth.

When Mother eloped with my dad in 1934, using a Ford Model A borrowed from Mr. Bill Lessman, I bet she didn't know Dad smoked and chewed. He was a handsome man who dressed neatly and was clean shaven when he went visiting. He had begun to chew tobacco when he was a small tike. His grandfather, Jud, was a heavy chewer and grew his own tobacco. As a young boy, when my dad complained of pain in his arms and legs, the country physician, Ole Doc Evans, diagnosed him with rheumatism. The Doc told my grandfather to give my dad tobacco to chew. "That'll purge the bad fluids," he told Grandpa Jud.

I don't think Dad took too well to tobacco as a child, but later in the Navy, and while working in a Chevrolet parts factory in southern Ohio, he was around chewers and began to take a plug from time to time. Dad said he smoked as many as two dozen cigarettes in a day while he worked. He was smoking when he married my mother. However, by the time I was born (three years later), he had quit. His story is that he felt sick one morning when he lit the first cigarette of the day while preparing a fire in the cookstove. He says he threw the cigarette into the fire and never rolled another smoke. Now, Dad had a tremendous amount of willpower, so the second part of the story is likely correct. His reason for quitting (feeling sick) is a little harder to accept. Most likely he had been reminded each day from the beginning of their marriage just how nasty his habit was. But then, who can be sure? My mother claimed that Dad had more morning sickness than she did when she was pregnant with me.

Bad words (four-letter words or cuss words) were nasty in my mother's estimation. Because they were nasty, she was always threatening to wash my mouth out with soap. Now, to have one's mouth washed out with today's mild and perfumed soap would not be pleasant, but to have one's mouth washed out with homemade lye soap would be a serious punishment indeed. I was always very careful not to go too far with nasty words and avoided ever having this terrifying soap purge.

Drinking "likker" (hard booze, wine, and beer) was a nasty habit. For a few years, West Town had a saloon and sold alcoholic beverages. This meant there were some unpleasant people hanging around West Town. When Mother walked to the center of the main town of Cullman, she avoided walking past the saloon. She skirted well to the far side of the street.

Drinking was a very serious issue for both my parents. When my sister began dating her future husband, Richard Schnur, my dad and my mother were immediately opposed. Rumor was that Richard's father was a hard drinker. Whether this was true or not made little difference. In my parents' view, if Richard's father was ever a drinker, then Richard would eventually become one as well. Richard had a second strike against him, as if "likker" was not enough; his family was Roman Catholic, anathema to folks who were dyed-in-the-wool Baptists. Although my parents attended the Disciples of Christ Church, they were essentially unreconstructed Baptists.

Mother was so opposed to drinking that her relatives who partook of a social cocktail or a beer from time to time kept this a secret from her. One of my favorite uncles, one of mother's brothers, was a social drinker. But Mother never knew this. One of her favorite nieces also had an occasion cocktail.

Mother never suspected this either. She would have been appalled.

After our marriage, I felt that my wife, La Donna, and I should tell Mother that we drank socially. It didn't seem appropriate to deceive my own mother. I would have a glass of wine or a cocktail in my house when she and Dad were present on a visit. We did not hide the bottles. She kept quiet except for an occasional innuendo (and a not too subtle one at that). One day while visiting us, she looked in the bathroom mirror and remarked that her nose was red. "And I never touched a drop of alcohol in my life!" she proclaimed proudly.

Brother to a Horsefly

Like a horsefly, he was never still, always
flitting about; a bit of a pest.

My brother, Glenn, had a couple of nick-
names. To some of his peers, he was
"possum" because he was so small for
his age. In a school yard brawl, he tended to "play
possum." Others gave him the nickname "Squirt" or
"Banny" Rooster, due to his diminutive size. I passed
him in height and weight when I was eleven and he
was seventeen. But I never had his energy or stamina.

As a teenager, Glenn was always as busy as a
horsefly. For this reason, Woodrow Graham began
to call him "horsefly." Constantly in movement,
Glenn didn't always keep his mind fully on the task
at hand. One spring, Dad planted several hills of
pumpkin seed near our bottom land. More seeds
were planted in each hill than would be needed.
Afterward, when the plants were up an inch or two,
they needed to be thinned.

On this occasion, Dad sent Glenn to thin the
beds and eliminate any weeds and grass. A few days
later, Dad checked on the pumpkin hills. To his

surprise, not a single pumpkin plant was visible. However, each hill had a nice stand of cockleburs. Glenn had mistaken cocklebur plants for pumpkin plants! He left a nice stand of cockleburs and eliminated all the pumpkins. Dad was not pleased. The whole process had to be started over. In Glenn's defense, the two plants are very similar when they are an inch or two out of the ground.

In addition to working on our farm, Glenn chopped cotton and hoed corn for farm neighbors. Such hard work was enough to cause him to think up various get-rich-quick schemes. For a while Glenn raised hamsters in the hope of selling the young ones at a good profit. This project wasn't successful for two main reasons. First, Glenn didn't know that male hamsters eat their young. Newborns must be kept separate from adult males. Not knowing this fact cost Glenn the first batch of young. Second, there was little market for pet hamsters in Cullman, and the cost of feeding the hungry rodents soon outweighed what little profit Glenn made from selling a few of the little creatures.

Next, Glenn tried his hand at selling Blair and Watkins products—pie mixes, cake mixes, spices, and canned products. He ordered these items direct from the company and had to pay up front. Then he had to figure a way to sell and deliver them. Since we had no phone at our house, this meant that Glenn had to ride his bike around looking for customers. When he found a person who would purchase a product, he then had to deliver that item or items to them on his bike in all types of weather—hot, cold, or rainy.

Despite his energy and determination, Glenn could have the most rotten luck. One day he was robbed in broad daylight east of town on an infrequently traveled dirt road. He lost forty-eight hard-earned dollars, a small fortune for him.

In those early teen years, Glenn weighed no more than a hundred pounds. His mother had been severely asthmatic and died within hours after giving birth to Glenn. He inherited the asthmatic condition, but he could ride his bike for hours at a time. He kept up his efforts to sell Blair and Watkins products and probably made enough money to buy himself a few new clothes. However, failing to make serious money was a major disappointment to him.

One day while riding his bike in city traffic, Glenn was jostled by a car. He fell over and drove the bike handle into his side. At that point, Glenn decided to forget a career selling products on his bike. He found a safer occupation as soda jerk at the Peoples Drugstore. That was his best job ever, as far as I was concerned. I could come into the drugstore, and Glenn would make a root beer float or a cherry Coke for me. He was equally kind and generous to several of his friends. Eventually he had to leave this job because he was spending more money on treats than he was making in wages.

Glenn's next project was lawn care. In this job, his stamina and energy served him very well. He was extremely reliable and would never shirk a job, no matter how large or small. However, the competition in the mowing business was a little too much for Glenn. He was not well-known in town, and the town boys seemed to get all the good mowing jobs. Glenn got the dirty, cleanup tasks.

Glenn spent a good deal of time with his mother's family, the Morgans. One of his young uncles, Junior Morgan, suffered a freak accident and was killed when struck on the forehead by a piece of broken bat handle while playing a game of baseball. Glenn was present and saw the accident. He never forgot it. This was, I believe, the greatest trauma in his entire life. He mentioned it often and told the story in dramatic and gory details.

Junior was the youngest son of the second marriage of Jerry Morgan. The first wife, Glenn's grandmother, had died. Sometime later Jerry married a woman whose first name was Nola. Glenn always called her "Miss Nolly." He loved to visit her house because Miss Nolly always gave him treats, often ice cream. Glenn had an aunt on the Morgan side whom he called Aunt Keneely. I suspect that her name was Cornelia. His pronunciation of the name "Cornelia" was in imitation of adults. It was consistent with the pronunciation of words in lower Appalachians (indeed, the deep South in general) which usually limited words to three syllables. Some examples are pneumonia or /new mon nee/ and rheumatism or /ru ma tiz/. Sometimes a four syllable word would have a simpler substitute. For example, a person with diabetes was said to have "the sugar."

Glenn was always on the move, but unfortunately, his business work ethic did not extend to schoolwork. He had undiagnosed learning disabilities and tended to give up on the tasks that teachers gave him as homework. Dad would try to work with Glenn, but Dad had only completed the fourth grade and part of the fifth. As a consequence, he was not able to help with the more advanced math and science problems that Glenn brought home.

At age eighteen, having just completed the ninth grade, Glenn left home to travel to Flint, Michigan, to make his fortune in the Chevrolet plant where one of his uncles, Carlton Scruggs, was employed. Glenn was employed in the plant less than a year when he was drafted for duty during the Korean War. He was sent to Fort Bliss in El Paso, Texas. After basic training he worked as a chef in the base kitchen. When his military service was completed, Glenn returned to Flint and resumed his job in the Chevrolet Plant. After a few years, he left that job and was hired by Coca-Cola in its bottling plant in Flint. He remained with that company until his retirement. He currently lives in an assisted living facility near Flint.

I have very few memories of my half sister, Edna Margaret, while she was living at home. There is, however, one very vivid image. I was sitting in a potato field playing in the dirt and listening to Dad and Edna's boyfriend, Richard Schnur, in a heated argument over the issue of marriage. Dad gave an emphatic *no* to Richard's request for Edna's hand.

During their argument, I was very agitated because it seemed to me they were going to fight at any moment. Richard worked as a welder at Apel's Machine Shop in Cullman. He was very muscular and rough-looking and outweighed my dad by at least fifty pounds. I worried without cause. My dad was not easily intimidated and was able to take care of himself. He, too, like Glenn, had been called a "banny" rooster when he was young, but Dad never hesitated to stand up to men larger than himself. He lost one job that I am aware of after knocking a coworker off a scaffold in the midst of an argument over tools.

Edna and Richard eventually eloped after he was drafted into the army. When Richard left for boot camp, Edna and one of her cousins, Kate Eleanor (pronounced *Elner*) went to Texas to study nursing. Kate was the daughter of Dad's older brother, Fred, who owned a farm in Fairview not far from the old Scruggs homestead.

One day when I was nine years old, Richard came by the house with a big cigar, announcing that a baby was born. They named him Richard Jr. and called him Richie. At age nine, I was an uncle! That seemed quite weird. Edna and Richard had four more children. Richie died at a young age from epileptic seizures. Three of the children live in Cullman. After Richard retired from Apel's, he had the terrible misfortune to suffer a broken back when a tree he was cutting down fell on him. He courageously struggled with this disability, and eventually died of a heart attack. With so much misfortune in her life, Edna has long struggled with emotional disorders. Currently she is living with her daughter, Mary Glenn Posey, and enjoying her grandchildren and great grandchildren.

The nuclear family of the little clapboard house was split first by my dad's death in 1983 and by my mother's in 1998. Due to her "good clean living," Mother lived to the age ninety-five. She was visually impaired but was mentally alert and could tell you the birthdays of all her eleven siblings and most of her nephews and nieces and her grandchildren.

All-Day Singings

Shall we gather at the river, the beautiful, the beautiful river, gather with the Saints at the river that flows by the throne of God.

—Gospel hymn

Two Southern rituals were guaranteed to please all ages. One was the all-day singing with dinner-on-the-grounds which so many rural churches sponsored. Never was there so much food in one place at one time. At the Primitive Baptist Church at Gum Pond, all-day singings occurred during the summer. Women began cooking for this event very early in the morning. By ten o'clock, the long wooden, rickety tables that stretched the length of the churchyard would be bowing under the weight of hundreds of dishes of food.

The featured food for any dinner-on-the-ground was fried chicken (all home cooked—KFC was years in the future). You could pass up and down the sides of the tables in the church yard and see a variety of styles: the pale chicken with the skin removed, the dark brown chicken fried with skin intact, the crusty batter-dipped chicken. Milk gravy made with flour and the grease remaining in the frying pan. This was the ever-present "country sauce."

Country ham, hickory smoked by local farmers, was the second most popular meat dish. This was followed by meatloaf in various styles. Fresh vegetables by the scores lined the tables. One vegetable was featured during the heat of summer: fried okra, stewed okra, okra and tomatoes, and pickled okra. Add to this all styles of green bean, string bean, flat bean, and every imaginable variety of field pea. In the legume family, my all-time favorite was the humble speckled butterbean steeped in its own juice, having been slow cooked for a couple of hours with a slice of salt cured bacon. Nothing is better with cornbread crumbled in the juice! Turnip greens and stewed turnips were far from favorites, but I must admit that cornbread crumbled into the "pot likker" (juice from the cooked greens) was mighty tasty.

Corn dishes also showed the imagination of the Southern cook. You had your choice of whole kernel, creamed, on the cob, stewed with tomatoes, mixed with green beans or limas, and various corn puddings. Add to this all the raw fruits and veggies: cantaloupes, watermelons, tomatoes, onions, and radishes.

The lowly Irish potato was well represented: in the jacket, mashed, buttered, fried, and boiled. The yam or sweet potato was not far behind: in the jacket, mashed, cooked with a topping of pecans, syrup, brown sugar and butter. Other tubers included beets pickled and floating in vinegar with slices of onion.

Breads were not lacking; cornbread in pone or muffins, and fat, fluffy (homemade) biscuits filled bread baskets. From time to time, a stray loaf of white bread found its way to the table intended for some picky kid who wanted a slice smeared with jelly and peanut butter.

However, despite all these piles of healthy food, the desserts were the crowd favorites. Here, the sky was the limit: sweet potato pies, pecan pies, coconut pies, custard pies, apple pies, peach pies, cobblers made from grapes, blackberries, dewberries, strawberries, and peaches. A choice of cakes and puddings of all kinds was there for the taking. For many kids, the all-time favorite was banana pudding.

All this food was washed down with sweet tea that had sat around in jugs with lids or wax paper over the openings to keep flies and bees from drowning in the sweet amber mixture. No beverage will quench the thirst like sweet tea. Nothing is more refreshing on a hot day even if the ice has long since melted. A few folks chose to drink a bottle of *co-cola* (Coke), Grape Soda, or Orange Crush.

Those who wanted water went to the artesian well in front of the church and drew a bucket of relatively cool water. A lone tin dipper hung by the well and was used by most folks who took a drink of water, unless they had remembered to bring a glass or cup of their own. The dipper could be wiped off with the sleeve or the tail of a shirt, but it continued to smell of snuff and tobacco. At least half the folks who partook of the well water were chewers or dippers. I guess it was lucky that most of us were either indifferent to or ignorant about germs; otherwise, no one would have ever taken a drink of that well water.

During the morning hours, adults spent most of their time in the church house singing or listening to a hell-bent-for-leather sermon. The younger kids spent the day playing hide-and-seek, tag, horseshoes, or jump rope. The teenagers usually disappeared off into the woods. By eleven-thirty both children and adults were chomping at the bit to have at the food. But everyone was required to wait for the preacher to calm down and end his sermon. No one could eat until a long and profound blessing was given by one of the elders. As soon as the *amen* was heard, we all dug in with gusto. Once the coverings came off the food, the fight to keep the flies and bees away began in earnest. Nevertheless, the flies and bees always had their fair share.

After gorging with food, the children resumed their play. The men lay around in the grass nodding off to sleep. The women busied themselves tidying up and putting the leftovers in baskets to take home for the evening fare. By two o'clock in the afternoon, the adults were back in the sweltering church, rocking back and forth in the pews, fanning themselves with cardboard fans or hankies and singing with gusto to the Lord's glory.

If the Hard Shell Baptists had permitted a piano in the room, it would have rolled from side to side.

As it was, the little wooden church house vibrated with the sheer joy of the occasion. For a farm family, there was little to equal the pleasure of these all-day singings. One could observe or one could participate. There is no communal activity today that can be compared to these gatherings.

Decoration Day

Mother's not dead, she's only a-sleeping.
—Traditional Gospel song

Another major celebration occurred in May when all the rural churches hold Decoration Day services. This is a special Sunday when all the ancestors buried in the church cemeteries are honored. This celebration was an outgrowth of the Civil War, the time to honor the dead of the Confederacy. Decoration Day remains a significant event in many rural cemeteries in the twenty-first century.

A custodian for a small cemetery was a rare thing in the nineteen forties and fifties. On Decoration Day everyone pitched in to clean the grave sites, repair the tomb stones, plant flowers, or add vases of flowers. The ancestors of the various clans in my family were buried primarily in two cemeteries: Etha and Lawrence Cove. At Etha Baptist Church, Decoration Day occurs on the second Sunday in May, conveniently coinciding with Mother's Day. On that day, we all gravitated to the cemetery. We were all decked out in new spring clothes. The colors were bright and cheery. All the gray and black woolens had been returned to the cedar chest to wait for the return of the first cool days of late fall. Cousins from all around the area met over graves and reminisced. The worship of souls long passed was palpable.

In the forties, no grass was permitted to grow in Etha Cemetery. Every little miscreant sprig was yanked up. Fresh flowers were laid on the graves and on the stones. Everyone wore a rose on their breast, white if their mother was dead, and red if their mother was alive.

People stood and prayed and cried over the newer of the graves. All the while, the breathless exhortations of the week-end preacher and the gospel hymns of the congregation escaped out the windows of the little wooden church. Worshippers constantly entered and exited the front door. No matter the external weather, the sanctuary was warm. The smell of sweat, snuff, cheap perfume, and aftershave permeated the stale air.

The preacher was soon down to shirtsleeves, tie loosened. He seldom stood behind the little wooden pulpit, but rather paced across the upraised floor waving his arms and thumping a well-worn Bible. He didn't need a lectern to hold sermon notes because he had no notes. It was amazing to me how many verses of Scripture that semiliterate man could quote verbatim. The whole process was a spectacle worth at least a ten-minute visit. If the weather was cool, which was often the case because of what folks called blackberry winter, a longer stay inside the church house was a pleasant way to warm up.

After a couple of hours at the cemetery, the various clans retired to their respective "old home places" (if one still existed) for a big meal. By the time I was seven years old, the families were retiring to Eva to the farmhouse of the eldest of the Smith clan, Frances, who had married the tough and wiry Walter Murphree. Walter was a "special" guy—a Republican in a sea of New Deal Democrats. For some unknown reason, he detested President Roosevelt. While everyone else pronounced the name *Rosyvelt*, Uncle Walter called him disparaging *Roooozevelt*. Uncle Walter also spoke an unusual Appalachian dialect. One phrase struck me as particularly funny. He would always ask, "Kin I holp ye?" And expressions like: "This here rain ain't holpen the crops none a-tall." Later, to my surprise, I discovered that this form for the verb *help* was in use as far back as the eighth century in England.

Uncle Walter enjoyed teasing and aggravating kids—young boys, in particular. He would invite whoever might be at his farm, dressed in their Sunday best, to come out to the pasture to see his prized bull or into the cornfield to see the big rattlesnake or copperhead he had killed with a hoe the day before. At a hundred and thirty pounds soaking wet, Uncle Walter could outeat any man weighing three-hundred pounds. However, ten minutes after a meal, he was fast asleep, sitting straight up in his chair.

I have no specific memories of Sunday dinners at the Murphree place. However, I remember distinctly the smell of a bush growing in the front yard of their house. The shrub was about three feet in diameter and about the same in height. It had blooms that looked a lot like fuzzy strawberries, only a darker and richer red, bordering on purple.

The blooms smelled like overripe strawberries. The bush was delightful. Even the twigs and bark had that great smell. The name of the plant was simple—*Sweet Shrub*. The Latin name is considerably more pompous: *Calycanthus Floridus*. In different regions of the South, this bush has other names—*Carolina Allspice* and *Hairy Strawberry Shrub*, for example. The plant grows from Pennsylvania to Florida and west to Mississippi. However, I have never smelled another bush as sweet as the one on the Murphree farm in Eva, Alabama.

By 1950, the clan no longer met at the Murphrees for Mother's Day. (Frances and Walter sold their farm and moved to Cullman in that year, if I recall correctly.) The new Murphree house in town was not large enough to accommodate the entire clan, so the Decoration/Mother's Day reunions began to be held at T. A. Smith's house on Main Street in Cullman.

Uncle T. A. (Thomas Albert) was the second child of Will and Mattie Smith. As I noted in a previous vignette, T. A. was the postmaster in Cullman for thirty years and had a large yard and an impressive two-story frame house with a wide wrap-around porch. His wife, Aunt Sara, was a fantastic cook, and between what she prepared and what the other women of the clan brought, we always had a feast to compare quite well with the dinners-on-the-ground at Gum Pond. The thing I remember most about T. A. and Sara's house was the *parfum*—the word *smell* does not do justice. The admixture of kitchen odors, waxed floors and polished furniture, the richness of the carpets and drapes—all combined to create an aroma that I will never forget.

To have some semblance of equity, my parents always left the Smith clan in midafternoon for a quick stop at the Scruggs's clan which was meeting at Uncle Fred's place (the "old home place"). There we spent time with the yarn-telling, tobacco-chewing side of my family. In the kitchen, Aunt Norma always had batches of leftover food setting out for anyone who cared to indulge. I always went straight for her fried chicken. Even after the pieces of chicken had sat uncovered on a platter on the table for at least eight hours, the taste was still wonderful. There was plenty of leftover bread and desserts, but it was a drumstick and a biscuit that I made a dash for.

I feel sorry for those who have not experienced the sheer joy of a Southern Decoration Day and the exquisite tastes of the simple foods prepared by the calloused hands of farm women. No gourmet dinner at the *Tour d'Argent* in Paris can surpass the number of taste buds enlivened by those meals.

The World of Books

There is no frigate like a book
To take us lands away,
Nor any coursers like a page
Of prancing poetry.
—Emily Dickinson

I have no memory of ever having a book read to me, only newspaper comics. My parents could not afford to buy children's books, and I don't recall picture books lying around the house. Glenn was unable to read even the lessons required at his grade level. Dad did not have time to read any material other than the paper and his *Woodmen of the World* magazine. When Mother sat down, it was to darn, knit, or crochet. In my parents' defense, neither had gone past the eighth grade in a one-room rural schoolhouse.

The first book I ever read to myself was *Bambi*. I sat in the dining area of our house in my highchair (minus the tray) and read while Mother prepared a meal. What a fantastic new world of pictures and words opened up to me. I could scarce believe it. With a book one could escape into a completely new realm far from the confines of the little clap-board house.

At first, I couldn't figure out all the words, but with the aid of the pictures, I could follow the action fairly well. From that moment on, I have been hooked on reading. More complicated books like *My Friend Flicka* and *Lassie Come Home* followed as soon as I had sufficient vocabulary.

It wasn't long before I discovered comic books. I was a bit too stingy to use my hard-earned dimes to buy my own copies, but I really didn't need to. Several of my friends were constantly lending me their copies. The two friends who supplied me with the most comics were the neighborhood twins, Donald and David Styles, my opponents in the game of marbles. Their house was in West Cullman about a quarter of a mile from our farm. They had stacks and stacks of great comic books. My favorites were the *Superman* and *Batman and Robin* series.

In grade school we received copies of the *Weekly Reader*, and *Boys Life* which were always fun to peruse. The little library in the school had a set of the *Hardy Boys*. In the early days, whatever I could find that I was capable of reading was okay with me. I wasn't picky.

As soon as I could ride my bike to the Public Library in Cullman, I began to delight in what seemed to be a vast selection of books. Reading adventures would be endless, it seemed. Thinking back on this period of time, after years of work in international education, I am reminded of the little poem by Janice James:

> I've traveled the world twice over,
> Met the famous: saints, and sinners,
> Poets and artists, kings and queens,
> Old stars and hopeful beginners,
> I've been where no one's been before,
> Learned secrets from writers and cooks
> All with one *library ticket*
> To the wonderful world of books.

In the nineteen forties, the Cullman Library was housed in the basement of the Fuller building. The librarian was very helpful and willingly gave me suggestions for reading. She often proposed Conrad's *Lord Jim*, but for some reason, I never selected it. However, I read many books about exotic lands and romantic times.

I eventually discovered most of the authors a young boy in those days would be likely to read. At first, I was reading versions edited for young people. That's how I read Robert Louis Stevenson's *Treasure Island* and Daniel Defoe's *Robinson Crusoe*, the *Swiss Family Robinson*, and Johanna Spyri's *Heidi*. I eventually moved on to edited versions of Jack London's works (*Call of the Wild*, *Sea Wolf*, and *White Fang*) and those of Edgar Rice Burroughs (*Tarzan, Lord of the Jungle*) and many others.

The *Leather Stocking Tales* by James Fenimore Cooper was also available in editions for the young.

But by age twelve, I was into "adult" editions and began to read Sir Walter Scott. The first novel was *Ivanhoe*, followed by *Kenilworth*, *Quentin Durwood*, and *The Talisman*. I fell in love with the romantic vision of the medieval world depicted in these romances by Scott. That interest led me to the works of Thomas B. Costain (*The Black Rose*, *The Moneyman*, *The Silver Chalice*, *The Darkness and the Dawn*). Once I picked up *The Black Rose*, I almost couldn't put the book down. This was true as well for *The Moneyman* and *The Silver Chalice*. My knowledge of life in medieval Europe grew little by little and prepared me for a later year-long study of the literature of that period during graduate studies.

At some point, I discovered Alfred Leland Crabb, and thus began my strong interest in the American civil war. *A Mockingbird Sang at Chickamauga* made a lasting impression on me. It wasn't Crabb's story-telling ability, necessarily, but the heroism displayed by both sides in this battle. Crabb sparked an interest that led me to eventually write a civil war story of my own in 2006 entitled *Tramping with the Legion: A Carolina Rebel's Story*.

Some fifteen years after reading Crabb's novels, I met one of his nephews, George Crabb, who was acquisitions librarian at Eastern Kentucky University, where I was teaching at the time. We became good friends and often played racket ball and tennis together. We discussed some of Dr. Crabb's writings, but all in all, it seemed that George was a bit intimidated by his famous uncle.

The romance on the sea came alive for me early on with the discovery of *Robinson Crusoe*. Somewhat later I discovered C. S. Forester and began reading his series about Horatio Hornblower. *Two Years before the Mast* by Richard Henry Dana fed that interest. Other sea stories soon came along, in particular the trilogy about a real-life mutiny on the high seas by James Hall and Charles Nordhoff. After reading *Mutiny on the Bounty*, I could hardly wait to read the other two books in the sequence: *Men against the Sea* and *Pitcairn Island*.

An interest in detective stories came later. Sherlock Holmes was an early find, and I still return occasionally to his adventures. I read many of Agatha Christie's novels centering on the crime-solving abilities of the somewhat prissy Hercule Poirot. But by far the best of the detective stories (in my opinion) were written by the Belgian, Georges Simenon, especially his *Maigret* series, but these I read as an adult and in French.

Beginning in my teen years, I discovered the Kentucky writer, Jesse Stuart, and realized I had found something of a kindred spirit. Here was a man who made a success in life but who had started life on a hardscrabble farm in Kentucky. I really enjoyed *Taps for Private Tussie*, especially Stuart's use of dialect, but I felt that *The Thread That Runs So True* was a little mushy and at times too self-aggrandizing. I began to appreciate poetry when I read some of Stuart's poems in a collection titled *Boy with a Bull-Tongue Plow*.

I discovered Hemingway in high school as well as some other American "classical" writers such as Melville. When I was seventeen, I somehow ran across the author Somerset Maugham. Now that was a strange writer for a teen to be reading, but I was not following any particular plan and was thirsting for knowledge with no real guidance.

I struggled through *Of Human Bondage* and found it very depressing. Maugham's *Moon and Sixpences* and the *Razor's Edge* were much more to my taste. Then I stumbled onto his *Notebooks*. How challenging, how different, how risqué! The *Notebooks* were full of stimulating and controversial viewpoints. I recognized early on that Maugham was an agnostic, if not an atheist. I didn't pick up on his sexual orientation, not that it would have changed my admiration for his use of language.

I was trying to learn as many new words each week as possible. I was diligent in working through *Word Power Made Easy.* This was a hardback book with a simple black cover. It had a somber look, much less enticing than the more recent colorful editions. I worked through the exercises in the entire book and then started over to see how many of the words I could still remember. After the third time through the exercises, I had a good sight vocabulary, but in no way could I use all these words actively in conversation.

The Cullman librarian suggested that I read *Kim* by Rudyard Kipling. This novel opened the fantastic world of India to me. How exotic it all seemed.

I had to follow up with the *Jungle Book,* and afterward, with *Captains Courageous.* How I came upon Kipling's poem called "If," I cannot say. But I was totally fascinated with the verses and quickly memorized them. A good portion of the lines remain in some remote area of my brain. I can still remember the way the poem begins and ends.

> If you can keep your head when all about you
> Are losing theirs and blaming it on you.
>
> If you can fill the unforgiving minute
> With sixty seconds worth of distance run
> Yours is the Earth and everything that's in it,
> And–which is more–you'll be a Man, my son!

I found that a woman could write good historical fiction when I discovered Frances Parkinson Keyes. I read *Came a Cavalier* and other works in which the role of the female characters was much more developed than in most of the novels composed by the male authors I had been reading. It would be some time yet before I would try Daphne du Maurier. When I did make a stab, I was not very appreciative of *My Cousin Rachel.* I had some trouble also with the Brontë sisters, Charlotte (*Jane Eyre*) and Emily (*Wuthering Heights*), but Heathcliff is a tormented soul forever etched in my mind.

A school librarian tried to interest me in the works of William Faulkner, but other than *The Bear*, it took a college professor to lead me through

The Sound and Fury and *As I Lay Dying.* The latter was morbidly funny, but the first third of *Sound and Fury*, when Benjie is the narrator, was tough reading indeed.

When I seriously delved into Conan Doyle's series about the great detective Sherlock Holmes, I was hooked. Of all the Holmes adventures, the one that made the deepest impression was *The Hound of the Baskervilles.* After reading that story, I had a few nights when I had a hard time going to sleep. I could see that monster dog coming to our farm. However, the most loss of sleep came after reading Edgar Allan Poe's *Murders in the Rue Morgue.* It wasn't until college days that I read Poe's classic poems *The Raven* and *Annabel Lee. The Raven* became one of my all-time favorite poems.

I stumbled on T. S. Eliot's works at some point in my late teen years. I tried my best to read the *Waste Land*, but too many of the allusions escaped me. However, I was delighted to find *The Love Song of J. Alfred Prufrock.* Even as a teenager, there was so much about that elderly social misfit that I could identify with. Prufrock was so unsure of himself, so indecisive. *There will be time for a hundred indecisions/ And time for a hundred visions and revisions.../...Indeed there will be time to wonder, Do I dare? And do I dare?"* Prufrock wanted so desperately to be accepted, but he felt alienated. Though the mermaids sing, he does not believe they will sing for him.

I committed to memory many of the best lines from *Prufrock* and retain a few of them more or less intact fifty years later. There are some great lines, but how can they be used in a conversation? I have yet to be at a social event where I can speak the line *"in the room the women come and go talking of Michelangelo."*

I returned to Eliot in my last quarter of undergraduate coursework. I was enrolled in an independent study course in comparative literature and decided to write a paper in which I discussed certain aspects of the human condition as presented in Eliot's *The Cocktail Party* and Jean-Paul Sartre's plays, *Les Mains Sales* (Dirty Hands) and *Huis Clos* (No Exit). What is the origin of evil in the world? Can evil be overcome? Can we make decisions that bring about good?

According to Eliot, good and evil are both created in large measure by choices made by the individual. It is the individual who makes his or her own heaven or hell. For Eliot, "hell is oneself." In Sartre's view, good and evil, heaven and hell are created by the interactions of individuals. People make hell for themselves and for others: *"L'Enfer, c'est les autres."* (Hell is other people.)

In Sartre's play *Dirty Hands*, Hugo is an intellectual who is paralyzed into inaction because he thinks about all the options, all the what-ifs. He is called to be a man of action, but he cannot. Prufrock, Hugo, and Raskolnikov in Dostoevsky's *Crime and Punishment* suffer from the same malady—inability to make decisions. Do I dare? Or do I dare?

The hollowness of modern life was starkly portrayed by Eliot in his dark poem "The Hollow Men."

He showed great farsightedness when he wrote the closing lines: "This is the way the world ends/Not with a bang but a whimper."

Later in literature courses at the graduate level, I became fascinated by two symbolist poets of the second half of the nineteenth century, Baudelaire and Verlaine. I committed several of Baudelaire's poems to memory and eventually taught a seminar on his works.

Verlaine's innovative poetic forms, using uneven lines and his great musicality influenced the poetry of the twentieth century. One of his short but highly lyrical poems is titled "Chanson d'Autonne" (Autumn Song). I am sure it has been translated from French to English by many poets, but I was lured to try my hand.

The languid strings
of autumn
violins
pervade my tortured
soul
with mortal
monotones.

Feeble, pale and
fraught with cares
while yet another
hour blares
I dream of former years
and brush away
my tears.

THE VIEW FROM BRINDLEY MOUNTAIN

I stagger on
My aimless way
Through bitter breeze
Propelled with ease
Now here, now there
In likeness of
The autumn leaves.

Mural and Window Art

Art is long and time is fleeting.

—Henry Wadsworth Longfellow
A Psalm of Life

By the time I reached the third grade, I was the *de facto* "artist in residence" in the Cullman Elementary School. Word got around that I could draw almost anything. Soon I was doing murals for all the festive seasons of the years. This allowed me to escape a lot of boring and onerous activities in the classroom.

Most children are creative artists, but after a few years, they seem to move on to other activities. Some maintain that elementary teachers stifle the creative talents of young children by trying to make them conform to some rigid norm: "Color inside the lines. Sky is blue not green. Did you ever see purple grass?" Perhaps some budding artists were turned off by such rigidity, but I would hazard to guess that those really committed to creating just went ahead with their dreams.

I began to draw and color with crayons very early. At age five, I did a "freehand" drawing of one of our pear trees and colored the picture with crayons. When I proudly showed the finished product to my mother, she didn't believe I had done the drawing. She thought it must have been Glenn, who was almost eleven years old. Only after Glenn swore that he didn't draw the tree did my mother accept the truth of my ownership.

Being fascinated with the songbirds that populated our farm, I began to look them up in the elementary school copy of Audubon's bird book. I was able to check the book out and take it home. That gave me the opportunity to copy the birds that I knew best. Since I didn't have any unlined white paper, I filled a lined Bluebook with drawings of the birds and colored them with crayons. My mother kept the drawings for the next fifty years. After her death, while cleaning out her house, I found that old notebook.

Our family acquired a box of jigsaw puzzles from time to time as Christmas gifts. After putting a puzzle together, I would then copy and color the picture. When I was ten years old, someone gave me a little child's set of watercolors. This was a great new adventure. One of the first copies was of a street scene in the town of Strasbourg, France. The little *Ford Times* magazine that came to our house once a month was filled with great watercolor washes of scenes from around the US. I began to copy some of these as well.

After a year or two of doing graphite drawings, pen and ink drawings, and water color sketches, I gave a try at oil painting. This was more of a challenge for two reasons. First, having no lessons, I tried to paint with oils in the same way I had been painting with watercolors. Consequently, the work had no texture or sense of depth. One scene I did feel pretty good about was a Western landscape with snowcapped mountains in the background and a mother grizzly bear and her cubs in the foreground fishing in a small river. This scene was really fascinating to me. I had never seen mountains firsthand, and certainly not snow covered ones or grizzly bears in a river. This little oil painting now hangs in the house of my daughter Sabrina Tyrrell in Tampa, Florida.

When I was thirteen, I enrolled in an art course by correspondence. Lessons were assigned and sent by mail. I completed the assignment and mailed the work back for evaluation. I did the assignments diligently for about a year, but I was disappointed in the results. The course was geared more to commercial illustration than to creative art. There were lessons on how to illustrate men's and women's clothing in lamp black washes. I learned techniques for pen and ink sketches for cartoons. After the first year, I was sure I didn't want to be a commercial illustrator, so I abandoned the course.

During my high school years, I did illustrations for the yearbook and other school projects. In a geometry class taught by Professor Spencer Spiegle—who also taught graphic design—I spent hours drawing animals as geometric shapes. This caught the eye of the teacher, and he encouraged me to continue this sort of "cubist" endeavor. My grade in plain geometry was okay, but I don't think I got as much out of the class as I should have.

One of my classmates at Cullman High School, Ronald Wolf, was very good at decorative art. One Christmas season, he invited me to help him decorate one of the Lutheran churches. Ronald was a sophisticated city kid. He brought a record player to the church so we could listen to classical music while we worked. It was from him that I first heard the names of Bach, Mozart, and Beethoven. He was the friend who patiently explained to me the correct pronunciation of the latter composer's name after I had looked at the record label and called that composer *Beet-hoe-vin*.

In the fall of 1951, at not quite fourteen years old, I worked with a local artist named Clay Mann, who was the window decorator for Ponders Department Store. Clay was only a part-time decorator and was also responsible for the men's shoe department. That particular Christmas season, Clay decided to create elaborate, near life-size cutouts of human and animal figures in an effort to duplicate in a small way the figures he had seen in Macy's Department Store in New York City. Because of time constraints, Clay needed help in drawing and cutting out these figures. He asked me for help. I spent all day every Saturday for six weeks drawing the forms. My models were small sketches in a little brochure that Clay had gotten from somewhere. I drew and cut out the shapes of elves, reindeer, sleighs, and carolers dressed in nineteenth-century attire.

Clay would drop in on me every so often, but for the most part, he was busy on Saturdays selling shoes. My few weeks with Clay working on this window decoration project were the most fun I ever had with commercial art. I almost changed my opinion of the profession.

I continued to dabble in art during my undergraduate days. I took a class in oil painting, but I must confess that the teacher was not very inspiring. For the most part, I just did sketches for the literary magazine. Some of the male classmates pushed me to pledge Delta Sigma Phi fraternity. My budget was so limited that I could see no way to pay the fee to join. However, this problem was solved when the president of the fraternity, Jim Smyth, said he had a sister who needed a large oil painting to hang over a new couch she had just bought (the bane of all artists!) She wanted a scene with beach and ocean and sky with clouds.

I took on the project and was able thereby to join the fraternity. Later, a similar consignment came my way when I was asked to join the Jaycees. Another picture to hang over another couch, but it was equal to the fee required to join the Jaycees, so I wasn't complaining. I had never been willing to go the distance for the sake of art. There were just too many starving artists in the world. I knew I would not become wealthy with a career in higher education, but at least I would be able to feed my family.

Sacred Harp Singing

Music washes away from the soul
the dust of everyday life

—Berthold Auerbach

I n the eighteenth century, the South developed
a genre of music that remains popular in many
rural areas today. It is a four-part *a cappella* style
of singing called *Old Harp*, *Sacred Harp*, or *Fa Sol
La* singing. This music is also occasionally referred
to as Shape Note singing. One style of Sacred Harp
uses only four shapes: a triangle for Fa; a circle for
Sol; a square for La; and a square tipped on one
corner for Mi.

Another system of Sacred Harp uses seven
shapes, adding a shape for Do, Re, and Ti. This gives
the classical Do Re Mi Fa Sol La Ti Do scale heard in
the *Sound of Music*. In the South the /fa/ and /la/ are
not pronounced in the Italian way, but sound more
like /fauh/ and /lauh/. The /l/ is silent in /sol/ and
rhymes with /sew/.

Most Sacred Harp songs are religious in theme,
and many were written in the eighteenth and nine-

teenth centuries. The tenor and treble parts are sung by both men and women an octave apart. With no accompaniment (often not even a pitch pipe), a skilled leader pitches the various parts. The group then begins, first singing the sounds of the notes through the first verse, then starting again with the first verse but this second time singing the lyrics of the song.

In the summer months, Mother and Dad enjoyed attending the annual Sacred Harp Convention at the Cullman County Courthouse. This meeting was held the second weekend in July. We sat in the balcony and looked down on the singers, who were arranged in a hollow square with each side representing a part. Most of the singers appeared to know the songs by heart, but a few held oblong books entitled *Sacred Harp*.

Everyone had a paper fan in constant motion because no air-conditioning was available in the court house. Big ceiling fans buzzed above our heads in tune with the flies. My dad had a good appreciation for the music and could sing the tenor or treble parts, but I paid much less attention to the music. My entertainment consisted in watching the singers sway and pat their feet in time with their waving fans.

One of the most visible members among the Sacred Harp singers in North Alabama was Mrs. Ruth Denson Edwards. She was a fourth-grade teacher in our elementary school. Her father, Thomas Jackson Denson, was one of the great singing-school teachers and Sacred Harp composers of the first half of the twentieth century. Mrs. Edwards had a quiet, dignified, and stately presence. She was tall and had red hair. Her voice was quite powerful and often was heard above the others.

Thomas Jackson Denson is given credit for popularizing Sacred Harp singing. He was one of four sons of Methodist minister Levi Philip Denson. Thomas was born in 1863 in Arbacoochee, Alabama (Cleburne County). Thomas, affectionately called "Uncle Tom" by his students, taught Sacred Harp singing throughout the lower South from Georgia to Texas.

Thomas, along with his older brother Seaborn Denson, formed the *Sacred Harp Publishing Company*. In 1933 they purchased the rights to the J. S. James music book, simply called *Sacred Harp*. During revisions, both Thomas and Seaborn died and Thomas's son, Paine, completed and published the new edition in 1936 with the title *Original Sacred Harp (Denson Revision.)* At the centennial of the first publication of Sacred Harp Music (1844–1944), a monument to Thomas Denson was erected in the village of Double Springs in Winston County, Alabama, a few miles west of the city of Cullman.

My dad spent a couple of summers teaching singing schools in the small towns of Morgan and Cullman Counties just before he joined the US Navy during WWI. Shape-note singing is still very much alive in the twenty-first century. The style is taught in Virginia, Tennessee, Texas, Arkansas, Mississippi, Georgia, and Alabama. Buell Cobb Jr., grandson of

Joe Cobb, leader of the morning hymn sings at the Cullman Christian Church, is very active in disseminating Sacred Heart music and history. Through efforts of people like Buell, many recordings have been digitized in the last few years.

Naturally I grew up hearing so-called "country music" all around me. In our house, the music we listened to was not recorded as we had no turntable. The music we heard was via the radio. Much of the music on the airwaves was sung by household names like Ernest Tubbs, Hank Snow, Eddy Arnold, and Hank Williams Sr.

Williams often joked that to appreciate good country music a person had to smell a lot of mule manure. I sure was a good candidate if that be the case; however, I always felt that the subject matter of country tunes was rather narrow and repetitive. The lyrics told stories of whiskey, cheating, heartbreak, honkytonks, and wild, wild women. Among these themes, a young kid could find little to relate to. In the nineteen forties, gospel was the other principal musical genre broadcast by WBRC, the Birmingham station.

My family sat around the radio and listened to the Grand Ole Opry on Saturday nights. A few memories of that variety show remain: the comedy of Minnie Pearl, (an icon with her fancy hats with tags attached), the powerful voice of Kate Smith, the antics of Grandpa Jones, and the close harmony of the Carter family.

While we did the indoor chores on Sunday morning and prepared for church services, we keep one ear tuned to the Renfro Valley singers and their particular brand of Kentucky country music. Sunday mornings, gospel quartets filled much of the airwaves. Among the many groups were the Blackwood Brothers, the Oak Ridge Boys, and the Chuck Wagon Gang.

I enjoyed good lead singers (second tenors) and tried to imitate them when I went about my chores in the afternoon. A deep bass voice gave me chill bumps and made me wish I had such a range. I had no idea in those days before my voice changed that I would eventually be able to hit the low notes that seemed so impossible when I was young.

After a couple of hours of radio music on Sundays, we set out for church. A hymn sing always preceded the separation of age groups to attend Sunday School classes. During the hymn sing, someone would call out the number of a song in the hymnal and Joe Cobb would give the pitch and those present sang with gusto. That's when I began to memorize many of the old hymns popularized during the revivals, camp meetings and "awakenings." The first verse many are etched in my brain—classics like "Leaning on the Everlasting Arms," "The Old Rugged Cross," "Onward Christian Soldiers," "Washed in the Blood of the Lamb," "Just As I Am Without One Plea," and "Amazing Grace."

Even though I didn't own a record player, I was not oblivious to the pop music of the late forties and fifties. Anybody who was a teenager in those days will recall many of Elvis's lyrics. Others songs that come readily to mind are "Too Young to Be in Love" by Nat Cole, "Come On to My House" by Rosemary Clooney, "Mocking Bird Hill" by Les Paul and Mary Ford, "Shrimp Boats Are A-Coming" by Jo Stafford, and "On Top of Old Smoky by the Weavers." Other popular titles were "Good Night Irene" ('50), "Tennessee Waltz" ('51), "Rock Around the Clock" ('55), "Don't Be Cruel" (1956), "Volare" ('58), and "Mack the Knife" (1959).

Almost everyone learned a few lines of "You Are My Sunshine," "Good Night Irene," and the "Tennessee Waltz." In those days when the repertoire of recording studios remained low, the DJs played songs for months. We learned the words without even trying.

As a freshman in high school, I decided to learn to play a musical instrument and participate in the marching band. My dad suggested that I study the saxophone. I went to the band director, Mr. Pasquale Bria, a crotchety old gentleman with a heavy Italian accent. He pooh-poohed the idea of the saxophone. He already had a couple of sax players, and there were no more of those wind instruments in the band room. He looked around and found an old beat up trombone and handed it to me. *"Take zees horn eh stoodee zee musike,"* he said and tossed a book of beginning trombone music in my general direction. With that, he turned and began working with another student.

I proudly took the trombone and music home, but I soon discovered that the task was not going to be easy. The noises that came out of the trombone were worse than scratches on a chalkboard. I was working on making sounds while sitting on the back porch. These cacophonous noises created an uproar among the farm animals. The chickens that had been quietly lying under the porch went squawking off as fast as they could travel. Nell, the mule, started braying. My dad suggested that I practice in the woodshed and spare my mother and him severe headaches.

The following day, I asked Mr. Bria for some assistance. He spent a few minutes showing me how to form my mouth, how to oil the slide, how to vibrate my lips. Soon he was off to another part of the band room to help a more advanced student.

I kept practicing as best I could alone in the woodshed. I finally was producing some sounds that were remotely music-like, but from the drawings illustrating the slide positions, I was very unclear about what I was doing. One day I was sitting in the band room trying to play "Mary had a Little Lamb." All of a sudden, Mr. Bria appeared at my shoulder. *"Zat eez no correct! Zee slide eez no in zee rite positione."*

He took hold of the slide and moved it a little farther out. "Zees eez zee note you vant, joost heer. Now play zee note again and try to heet zee correct espot." I gave it my best shot. Obviously, it wasn't good enough. Mr. Bria angrily grabbed the slide and thrust it out. I lost my grip, and the slide came totally off and went skidding across the floor. *"Dio mio!"* he yelled. *You veel ruin zee #%&·*^@ trombone!"*

Sheepishly I went to retrieve the slide while the other students snickered at my chagrin. I put the trombone in its case, placed it in the storage room, and walked out the door. Since that day, I have never again held a brass instrument in my hands.

During my teen years, I wanted to learn to play the piano, but without one in the house to practice, this seemed a lost cause. However, in my freshman year in college, I heard that students could take beginning piano. I signed up and began to have private lessons with Miss Martha Stone. I signed up to practice on a piano in the music building in the evening. I was clumsy, and my fingers wouldn't move very fast. Miss Stone was very patient with my playing, and I eventually made some progress. I was reminded recently by our old dorm counselor that I "banged" a lot in the evenings on an old piano that was kept in the basement of Ewing Hall (the men's dormitory). I must have been a veritable irritant to those who could hear me.

I enrolled for piano lessons again for the second quarter and again for the third quarter. At the end of the term, I was required to give a recital for three of the music professors as part of the final grade. The piece was *An English Country Garden*. I panicked. I couldn't bring myself to go to the recital hall at the assigned time.

Miss Stone found me the following day and told me I could still play my recital piece if I wanted a grade above an F. The thought of an F averaged into my grade point was the incentive I needed to muster the courage to go before the three critics. My fingers seemed paralyzed. I forgot the music about halfway into the song. The whole episode was a disaster. Fortunately, Miss Stone had mercy on me and gave me a grade of C. That was the only grade below a B that I ever received in my college years. I decided that piano playing was not in my future. In the fall of my sophomore year, I did not re-enroll for more lessons.

Antics, Anxiety, and Acne

We don't see things as they are,
We see them as we are.

—Anaïs Nin

As young kids, most of us thought it was fun to imitate adults who smoked. One way was to buy candy cigarettes. From a distance, they looked like cigarettes but were mostly just white sugar. We could ruin our teeth while we encouraged a later tobacco addiction. Country boys could make corncob pipes with no trouble at all, stuff some ground-up leaves in the bowl and emulate smoking. Luckily the pipe usually would not stay lit.

The kids who wanted to be more adventurous searched the fields for wild rabbit tobacco. This is a single-stem weed that grows about a foot tall and has narrow leaves about an inch and a half long. When the leaves mature, they turn a silver or grayish green color—very easy to spot in an overgrown field.

When the plant is past its prime, the leaves curl as they dry. At that point, they can be stripped off the stem and rolled in the palm of the hand to break them into small pieces. These leaves could then be rolled in whatever paper was available, or they could be stuffed in the bowl of a corncob pipe. The leaves smoked very hot and usually caused a coughing spell.

In these teen years, my dad gave me the task of searching in Lessman's Woods for a suitable evergreen tree at Christmas season. This was more difficult than I had expected. My search for the perfect tree was always foiled. It seemed that every cedar or pine had some deformity. Finally, I was forced to chop a tree that was only partially perfect.

Once cut, getting the tree back to the house was no easy task. The tree had to be dragged along the ground for at least a quarter of a mile. This was not conducive to preserving all the limbs and needles intact. However, my parents never rejected any tree I brought home. It was always placed in the corner of the living room by the door leading to the porch. This meant that we had no ready access to the porch for a couple of weeks. This wasn't really a problem because our friends and family knew to come to the back door of the house at all times anyway.

Every year my mother brought out the decorations for the tree from a storage place in the spare bedroom. She kept a single string of lights, the balls, the rope, and even the tinsel from the past year. As far as I could tell, the only thing she ever bought for the tree was an occasional new box of tinsel. If a light burned out on the string, she just bought a replacement bulb, not a new string of lights. She was never tempted to suspend her frugality even for the Christmas season. I had no problem with using the same decorations. But it was a bit disconcerting to find my present enclosed in last year's wrapping paper! Regardless of these things, the season was always an exciting time. We had goodies in the house that were never there at any other time: assorted nuts, oranges, peppermint candy, fruit cake and mincemeat pie.

The social anxieties that plagued me became more acute in my teen years. I remember very vividly one anxiety attack when I was fourteen. I had been asked to give a talk at a Chi Rho Youth Fellowship regional meeting in Huntsville, Alabama. I prepared an overly erudite talk using the *Meditations* of Elton Trueblood. Several of us rode up to Huntsville in one car for the meeting. I was nervous and became more and more anxious as we neared the host-church in Huntsville. Soon I was feeling a great urge to pee, but I was too shy and embarrassed to ask the driver of the car to stop at a filling station with a restroom.

When we arrived at the church hosting the conference, I was in such great pain that I literally ran for the restroom. Things didn't get much better. When I was introduced at the podium and began my "speech"—much too serious for the occasion—the audience soon became restless. I lost them in short order. The kids began to talk among themselves. The whole affair was an absolute disaster, but I struggled through somehow and finished my remarks—a nerd to the bitter end.

That was the first of many talks I have given to groups large and small over the years, but I confess that it was a very long time before I could relax before one of these occasions. In every case, I always made sure a bathroom was nearby.

The Boy Scouts were very popular in the forties and fifties. I joined a Cub Scout Troop when I was ten years old. After Cub Scouts, I joined a Boy Scout troop. I took scouting very seriously. I worked diligently to earn as many merit badges as possible. I wanted to become an Eagle Scout, so I acquired all the requisite badges except the one for life saving. I was not a good swimmer, and I was afraid to try for that last badge.

When we acquired our first automobile in 1948, I was not yet eleven years old and could not foresee that in three years I would be driving. Dad was sent to the VA hospital in Birmingham to seek treatment for pernicious anemia, and Glenn had gone to Flint, Michigan, to work. Mother did not know how to drive and didn't want to learn. Thus, Dad taught me to drive before he left for the hospital. So at age fourteen, I drove Mother on all her errands around town, careful to obey all the traffic laws. Luckily, I was tall for my age, and I was never stopped by a city policeman.

After Labor Day in 1950, I began junior high classes. I was very glad because I wanted more challenging classes than we had in elementary grades. Those of us who had done well in arithmetic were put in a class of "pre-algebra" taught by an ancient gentleman called Mr. Gatlin—of course we nick-named him "Gatlin Gun".

Now, I confess that no course in elementary school had ever given me the slightest bit of challenge, but now prealgebra gave me fits. I really had to buckle down. Of course, there was no help at home. Neither of my parents knew anything about algebra. However, after an initial B in first term, I received As for the rest of the year.

By the age of fourteen I had developed a serious case of acne. I'm not talking about a few pimples. I'm talking about large swollen lumps that hurt and that could be characterized as *Job-size* boils (*Job* as in the Bible). Ole Doc Daves was puzzled about my case. He pulled out a huge tome from his bookcase and began to peruse it. After reading for a few minutes, he prescribed a pinkish liquid for me to apply each night. I was faithful with the application, but the results were nil. The Doc also had me stop eating anything containing chocolate and later, any dairy products.

A female relative suggested that I go to a women's beauty salon and have a cleansing mask applied. This was potentially very embarrassing, but I wanted results badly enough that I risked being seen by one of my peers. Indeed, I sneaked into the beauty shop several times for facials. No effect.

Apparently, acne is genetic and was passed down to me through my maternal side. Luckily, of all my cousins in that line, only one other had a major case. Unfortunately, this cousin was a girl. Her parents had sufficient funds to send her to a dermatologist in Birmingham, and she received the finest care available in the early 1950s. Her symptoms were lessened slightly, but she was not cured.

Someone suggested that antibiotic shots might be of help. This was not my idea of fun, but I was desperate. A physician in Cullman agreed to give these shots a try. Each week for six months I rode my bike to that office where a very nice nurse attempted to give me a shot in my shoulder muscle. I say *attempted* for good reason. In that period of time, needles were sterilized and reused. After a few punctures, the point of the needle became dull.

My shoulder muscles were rather well-developed from push-ups, chin-ups, and normal farm work. The nurse had to practically throw the needle like a dart to make the point penetrate the muscle. Being very self-conscious, I would not agree to shots in my hip where the tissue was softer. Pull my pants down in front of a woman! No way! I wanted the shots in my upper arm regardless of the number of needles I broke.

Several times the needle did break, and the nurse would have to try again. In any case, the night after each shot I had a difficult time going to sleep because of the pain in my upper arm. No pain, no gain, I thought. "This has got to work," I said. But, no! After six months, the project was abandoned. The results were nil. The only gain was sore muscles.

Ministers of the Gospel kept talking about the efficacy of prayer—how God answered prayer—how a person could take their cares and pains to God and receive relief. All that was required was faith in God's healing powers. Those who believed they could be cured were cured. It was time to try out this premise. I prayed long and hard each night for God to rid me of my acne.

I made all sorts of wild promises about what I would do for God in return. I would no longer lust after material things. I would cease to have sinful thoughts about the semi-nude women in the "girly" magazines. I would promise to study for the ministry. I would give half of my eventual fortune to charity. I would go to Africa like Dr. Albert Schweitzer and work among the poor and the sick. I would do whatever the Lord wanted me to do. I believed! I had faith!

Each morning when I awoke, I would hesitantly and gingerly feel my face. No change! I kept up this routine for several weeks. No change. I lost faith. I gave up on divine intervention. When I looked into a mirror, I was horrified, disgusted, turned off. I assumed that my face was viewed likewise by everyone else. I stayed away from people as much as possible. I was happy only when curled up with a book living some vicarious existence where I was a handsome young man with clear skin.

When I was with a group, I sought to draw the least attention possible. I avoided the limelight. I kept my head down as much as possible. Unfortunately, my actions were viewed by some as standoffish. Others accused me of having a superiority complex! I wondered how they could be so wrong.

Acne continued to plague me for several years but gradually became milder. By my late twenties, I had only rare outbreaks. In my teaching career, I was in front of students constantly and very soon overcame my sensitivity of being in the public eye. Gradually social anxiety faded into a much less traumatic memory.

The Carnival Peep Show

"Come on folks! Step right up! See the bearded lady. Right this way, folks. Get your tickets here. Only twenty-five cents!"

—A carnival barker

A carnival usually arrived in Cullman County once a year, in the spring. The crews who came to small rural towns were not top-of-the-line characters. They were a motley bunch, to put it mildly. But we kids didn't know and didn't care. We were thirsting for entertainment. Of course, the main feature for kids at a carnival was the rides.

We rode the Ferris wheel, the merry-go-around, and other assorted thrills which were often in dubious physical condition. However, these were the days before constant litigation. If someone got hurt, it was probably mildly, and the child was patched up and sent out to play again soon. No one seemed to be worried about the safety of the equipment. In the first place, at these small carnivals most of the rides didn't go very fast and weren't very high off the ground.

Every carnival or county fair had a midway. Here carnival personnel bet they could guess a person's weight or their age within a certain figure. The public could engage in a contest of strength by striking a wooden block with a mallet hard enough to send a ball up a shaft toward a bell. Most teenage boys liked to try to ring the bell to impress the girls with their strength.

Many midways had a hall of mirrors and a hall of horrors. Then there was the baseball throw, the ring toss, the shooting gallery with a row of ducks floating past, a fishing well (a magnet on a string attached to a short pole), a booth where for a dime or a quarter you could throw darts at balloons or baseballs through a small round hole. The successful contestant could claim a stuffed animal or some other souvenir. For those who didn't win a prize, there was plenty of cotton candy and soft drinks.

The midway also had a freak show section. Every carnival owner had to have a fat lady or a bearded lady, or a two headed snake, or a five-legged goat. The curious paid a quarter to see such anomalies. Finally, in a tent tucked back out of the limelight and the prying eyes of children was the "girly show." This was the tent where the rough-hewn men seemed to gravitate.

My parents had taken me to fairs and carnivals from time to time. But when I was thirteen and in the seventh grade, I visited the fair with a classmate named Lucius. Now Lucius was a city boy who was a bit effeminate in gestures and speech. He was a little pudgy—well, okay, he was fat. The kids in class made fun of him and called him "fatty" and "queer" and other unpleasant epitaphs.

This was the age when boys gave weaker kids the pink belly. Lucius was a perfect candidate—soft, fat, white belly. Now, on the contrary, I was the tallest boy in my class. I was wiry and tough and burned by the sun and hardened by farm work. No one attempted to give me a pink belly. I felt sorry for Lucius, and I came to his aid once when the boys held him down on the playground with his pants down and his shirt up. They were slapping on his belly pretty good, and Lucius was in a panic, crying like a baby.

I pulled a couple of my friends off Lucius and suggested they go after somebody a little more worthy of their efforts. From that time on for the rest of the year, I couldn't shake Lucius. He was like a leech, my constant companion.

Lucius loved to play canasta and wanted to teach me. Finally, I acquiesced. Lucius's mother drove him to our farm in the evening after supper at least once a week, and we played canasta in the kitchen. No matter how hard I tried, I could never beat him in that silly card game. When school was out that spring, Lucius and his family moved away, and I never heard from him again. I was not too disappointed.

The spring before he moved out of town, Lucius and I attended the carnival together. He had plenty of money to spend, and he was generous. As we strolled about the midway, we became curious about the invitation by one barker to come into his tent and see Miss Angel. The poster of her seminude body was very tantalizing.

"Come on, let's go in," Lucius said. My better judgment said no, but my willpower was weak. I had never seen a naked woman, and the thought of doing so was exhilarating. After a minute or two of hesitation, we paid one dollar each and entered the smoky, darkened tent. It was crowded with men in overalls and heavy brogans—the smell of tobacco, whiskey, and sweat created a pungent odor. The air was filled with blue haze, and I had trouble seeing the stage. No one paid the least bit of attention to Lucius and me. If they had, they would have realized that we were under-age.

The men seemed to be farmers and laborers. Despite the dim lighting, I saw over to my right, slightly behind some other men, my neighbor—the city's grave digger. He was not looking my way, and I quickly tried to get behind one of the larger men in front of me. I should not have worried that he might tell my dad. There was no way he wanted anyone to know he was visiting a peep show. I wasn't thinking rationally and scanned about to see if I recognized any of the other men. I didn't.

A platform about three feet high was set up at the far end of tent. A red drape hung in front of the platform. We all stood in anticipation. Finally, some soft, erotic sounding music began to play with a rather tinny sound. The barker came on the platform and told us we were about to see Miss Angel, the prettiest woman in the South.

Anticipation gripped the air as we waited for Miss Angel to appear on the makeshift stage. To our disappointment, she came through the red curtain fully clothed. We wondered if we had wasted an otherwise good dollar which would buy a ticket to the ring-toss plus a fluffy cotton candy. Angel had a big boa wrapped around her neck and bosom, so that I could see less flesh that I would normally see on a nun walking the streets of Cullman any day of the week. It's true that Angel's skirt was much shorter than the nun's habit, but she wore dark netted hose, so no leg flesh was visible.

The men began to whistle and hoot as Angel danced around the stage swinging her boa. After a half a minute, the men began to holler, "Take it off!" Slowly Angel began to unbutton her blouse. My heart picked up speed. I tried to muscle my way a bit closer, but the men in front were closing rank, their eyes riveted on Miss Angel. She swayed her hips and shimmied. Slowly she continued unbuttoning her blouse, but she didn't take it off—she just teased us with a view of her white bra and her abundant cleavage.

Angel gyrated around the platform in her ultra high heeled shoes, swinging her boa and tossing her head. After what seemed like several minutes, Angel tossed off the boa with a sensual gesture. She was teasing us, playing on our expectations and our anticipations. Eventually the blouse was off and tossed aside with a nonchalant gesture. This was some progress since I hadn't seen a woman wearing a bra before. In TV commercials, *Wonder Bra* used a manikin, not a real person. I was ready for more.

Just then, Angel retired behind the curtain. The barker came back on the platform and told us that the show was over. This was all a dollar bought, and we were free to leave. However, if we wanted to see more of Miss Angel, we would have to pay another dollar. Almost no one left. The barker came around and collected from everyone, barely hiding his glee.

Then Angel made a new and more provocative appearance. She danced and swayed to the music and gradually began to take off her skirt. My heart really started racing. With the skirt off, the target of our desire was still invisible behind black panties, a garter belt, and net stockings. More dancing followed. Finally, Miss Angel wiggled out of her garter belt. There she was, swaying around in bra, panties, silk stockings, and spikes. Suddenly she gave us a wink, a wave, and exited behind the curtain. The men began to boo and call for her return.

By now you have figured out the routine. The barker came back on stage to tell us that we had seen all we paid for. If we wanted more of Miss Angel, we would need to cough up some more dough—my words, not his. Lucius and I conferred. We decide that since we had come this far and spent two dollars already, we might as well stay to the end. After all, what we came to see had not yet materialized. We put one more buck each into the barker's greasy palm. Some of the men left the tent in disgust. Probably this was because they either didn't have enough remaining money or they had a wife who kept account of their expenditures.

Lucius and I waited for Miss Angel with renewed anticipation. Our goal of seeing a naked woman now seemed very near. Well, out came Miss Angel for the third time. She danced and swayed, lay on the floor, lifted her legs, arched her back, and went through any number of other gyrations.

By this time, the sweat was running down my face. It must have been a hundred degrees in that tightly closed tent. All the spectators were becoming agitated with impatience. Finally, Miss Angel took off her bra to expose two milk-white breasts. They were a delight but not what we had paid to see. After a few more erotic moves, Miss Angel took off her stockings and threw them into the crowd. Then she sashayed back behind the red curtain.

The men became angry and started to raise a fuss. The barker had a hard time restoring order. When the men became quiet, he promised that— for just one more dollar—Miss Angel would "take it all off."

I had no more money, but luckily, Lucius had two dollars remaining. He forked them over to the sweaty barker. We were ready and anxious for the last act. Out came Miss from behind the red curtain. After a couple of minutes of evocative dance moves, Angel dropped her panties. In that dim light, all I could make out was a patch of very dark hair. *Is that all there is?* I wondered. Miss Angel sashayed provocatively around the edge of the platform so we could all have a better view. She turned and showed us her cheeks, wiggled them for a few moments, then pranced back behind the curtain.

The men gave a loud applause and quickly exited the tent. Lucius and I sneaked out in the midst of the taller men hoping that no one who knew us would see us. Apparently, we succeeded. I never had any repercussions from this little episode.

However, on the radio two days later, during the police report, I learned that the peep show tent was raided by Police Chief Belt Edmiston and his boys the night after Lucius and I were present. The barker and Miss Angel were taken into custody. Several of the customers were named in the report. Whew! That was a close one!

White Sidewall Tires

By Cullman's northern border, reared
against the sky, proudly stands our
Alma Mater, as the years go by.

—Cullman High School Song

The courses in high school were not overly challenging, with the exception of typing where my fingers just wouldn't fly over the keys correctly as the teacher expected. However, my lowest grade did not come from typing, but came in physical education one term during my sophomore year. I had forgotten all about that low grade until recently. My mother (bless her heart) kept all my report cards from the first grade through undergraduate school. After her death, I was looking through those old reports and discovered a C grade in physical education!

During my freshman year, the Korean War was raging fiercely. President Truman's secretary of state, John Foster Dulles, was pressing the "domino theory." He was predicting the takeover of the world by Communists. Down in Southeast Asia, the French were struggling to resist an independence movement led by Ho Chi Minh. When the French army collapsed at Dien Bien Phu in 1955, containment of Communism was left to the Americans. Slowly, the US government added additional "observers" into the conflict, then support troops. Before long, the US had a fighting force engaged.

I was too busy being an adolescent to pay a lot of attention to the Korean conflict. But no one who was living at the time will forget the firing of General MacArthur by President Harry Truman. Most of us were pro-MacArthur at the time. Only later we realized that Truman was correct to assert his role as commander in chief and avoid a major clash with China.

On the domestic front, we couldn't help but notice McCarthyism and the "Red Scare." By 1953, the senator from Minnesota was investigating Communist influence in the US Department of State, the Army, Harvard University, the Methodist Church, Hollywood, and Little Orphan Annie. McCarthy was seeking out "fellow travelers" as well—that is, folks tainted by association. You were in for trouble if you had read *Das Capital!*

Much of the national and world events were now being shared with Americans via television—the idiot box, as some were now calling it. With only three networks and no cable channels, the entire nation was watching the same shows. Our family never owned a TV during the years I lived at home. However, no one could avoid hearing and learning about what was being broadcast on TV. The programs were the talk of the town. Sometimes I would catch a television program at a relative's or friend's house. Even without a TV, I knew something about the exploits of Lucy and Desi, Jackie Gleason, Arthur Godfrey, and Uncle Milty. In those days, the most talked about show was hosted by Arthur Godfrey.

For young teens in the nineteen fifties, music was the common denominator. With many fewer releases in those days, songs were played by disc jockeys on the radio for weeks on end. We all learned the words and could make a stab at singing them. The radio was reinforced by the jukeboxes in all the cafes and most restaurants. Teens could put in a nickel in the large console or in one of the little individual booth players and pick out their latest favorite tune. Most everybody could afford a little cheap turntable and could buy "singles" in an inexpensive 45 rpm vinyl format.

Boys' hair styles had rarely been so varied as they were in the early 1950s, fluctuating from flat tops and butches to long duck tails and heavy sideburns. To keep the flat top hair standing in place, most boys used butch wax. This was useful also in keeping duck tails in place. A variety of hair tonics and creams appeared on the market. *Brill Cream* was no doubt the most advertised. Anyone living at the time can probably remember the jingle: "*Brill Cream, a little dab'll do ya!*"

Friday and Saturday night most teens were out for fun. Roller skating rinks were constructed all over the US. One was built in south Cullman. This was one of the Friday night gathering places. Good and bad skaters and novices covered the floor. One had to be very careful not to kill or be killed.

Americans were deeply in love with their cars in the fifties. It was only natural that someone would figure a way people could stay in their cars, not just while driving, but while watching a movie, or necking, or eating. If the seats had been more comfortable, no doubt Americans would have taken to sleeping in their cars as well.

This was an era of great optimism despite the clouds of the Cold War and the atomic menace. Predictions for a magnificent future were in the air. The four-minute mile was about to be broken, as well as the sound barrier by the new jet planes. Some predicted we would be flying hundreds of people to Europe in three or four hours in new SSTs. Some futurists saw automatic cars that would travel safely down well-built highways without requiring a driver. Others predicted that we would all soon have little personalized jetpacks or tiny helicopters that would spirit us around above the treetops and make traffic jams obsolete.

The bravest of new worlds had us traveling to Mars and being able to communicate with other planets in galaxies light-years away. Some scientists proposed establishing a colony on the moon. On a more practical level, some predicted that women would soon no longer have to cook; food would be prepared and frozen. That food would be removed from the freezer at the housewife's convenience, micro-waved and served. Clothes would no long need to be ironed. Vacuum cleaners were going to replace the need for brooms and mops. Women looked forward to many hours of leisure time. Soon a television set would be in every home—in color, no less!

Having no TV in the house, I missed some of the pop culture. Rather than lying on the couch watching TV, I stretched out on the hay in the barn loft and read. The loft was my personal gym as well. The loft was the place where I did push-ups. I fixed a way to do chin-ups by taking a good, strong broom handle and wedging it between the rafters. Almost every day when I climbed into the loft to throw down hay, I took a few minutes to do ten chin-ups.

At the high school, we had little in the way of exercise equipment. However, a trampoline sat on a stage in the gym. I enjoyed jumping on it, until one day I was present when one of the students missed the mat and one of his legs fell between the springs and the trampoline. This student fell over the frame of the trampoline and broke his leg so badly that his tibia pierced through the flesh. That sight was so traumatic I never felt comfortable on the trampoline again.

My dad had been in poor health for over a dozen years, and while I was in high school, his condition gradually worsened. For years, he was treated for pernicious anemia, but the underlying cause—yet to be discovered—was a severely hypoactive thyroid condition was called *mexadema*. This condition, affecting the entire metabolic functioning of the body, was often misdiagnosed or missed entirely. The disease causes extreme fatigue, hair loss, coldness in the legs and feet. If unchecked, the problem can cause organ failure and eventual death.

The strenuous life on the farm was gradually hastening death. No matter how much responsibility I assumed, Dad still had to bear the brunt of the work, since I spent most of the day at school. Eventually Dad decided he had to sell the farm. One day in the January of 1954 Ira Patterson came to the door and asked my dad if he would like to sell the farm: house, barn, acreage, and all. It didn't take Dad long to settle on a deal. But this meant finding a suitable and affordable house in the town of Cullman.

Luckily, my parents found a very nice little house that was less than a half mile from the high school. The house was only about five years old and was built on land just east of the Cullman Hospital (the land I watched being plowed when I was recouping from a tonsillectomy in the spring of 1947).

Now, of course, the folks in the house Dad bought had to find a place to live, so we had to wait a couple of months before vacating the farm. Mr. Patterson was obviously very anxious to move into the new place. He had big plans for refurbishing the house. He came to see us every few days to check on the progress of the second family in finding a suitable place. He would come bounding up the steps on the back porch and "holler" through the screen door: "*Ye ain't heerd nuthin' yet, I don't guess.*"

This question was so amusing I immediately took a fancy to it. I mimicked Mr. Patterson in a joking way whenever possible. As I became more interested in dialects of the lower South, I often listened for similar expressions. The word *ain't*, of course, is ubiquitous, and the word *nothing* is almost universally pronounced /nuthin/. But /heerd/ is rare enough to be a bit jarring on the ear. As American English evolves, the so-called strong verbs are being reduced from three to two forms. The simple past tense is interchanged with the past participle. He has went (gone); I seen (saw); he's done went (gone). It appears that in many regions of the country the different uses of those two forms are blending into one. Students who had senior English with Mabel Bailey at Cullman High will agree that she did not permit us to make such "errors"—at least in her presence.

In the summer of 1955, between my junior and senior year, I made my first long trip out of Alabama. I accompanied my brother, Glenn, to Flint, Michigan, in his new 1955 Plymouth. He drove straight through except for a couple of hours when he pulled off the road and took a nap. I couldn't sleep in the car. The seats were too uncomfortable, and the noise of cars whizzing by kept me awake.

Glenn seldom ever had two nickels he could rub together. He couldn't afford a motel and barely had the funds for gas and a hamburger. I wasn't much better off, but I had saved a few dollars from chopping cotton for Woodrow Graham.

We spent time in Flint, Michigan, with Aunt Pearl and Uncle Claude Parrish and with Uncle Carlton and Aunt Grace Scruggs. At their houses, I discovered what folks were watching on night TV—wrestling, and more wrestling. I found this extremely boring and missed my novels.

After our visit in Flint, Glenn and I headed off to Rochester, Pennsylvania, to see Uncle Dewey and Aunt Ruth Scruggs. Uncle Dewey worked in a plant, but he also had a small farm out in the country away from everything. The family raised a few chickens, goats, and pigs, and had a milk cow. They cultivated a large garden and raised most of their own food. I remember the house and outbuildings being rather haphazard in appearance, with all sorts of "yard art" scattered about. By that I mean old buckets, wheelbarrows, boxes, and tools scattered about the house and barn.

The inside of the house was no neater than the outside. The furniture was a bit aged and ramshackle. Aunt Ruth was a very caring person, but Uncle Dewey seemed rather gruff. I must admit he had a really great sense of humor and was a gifted story-teller. He was happy to tell tales of the "olden" days when he and my dad were very young. Dewey and Dad spent a lot of time in a log cabin owned by their grandfather, Judson. This was a two-room cabin with a dog trot that Grandpa Jud built on one hundred and eighty acres homesteaded in northern Alabama in the early 1880s.

Dewey and Dad enjoyed spending nights with their grandpa. They climbed a ladder into the loft of the cabin and slept on straw. It was like camping out—a real adventure for them. Dewey often told about the varmints that came into the loft to keep them company. He especially liked to tell about the screech owls. He claimed he had to wipe the face of the clock each morning before he could see the hands because the little critters had roosted on it and left their calling cards.

Dewey fancied himself a bit of a poet and writer. Later in life, he retired and moved back near his birthplace in Morgan County, Alabama. Dewey seemed to be trying to find himself—to overcome disappointments in his life's journey.

This rather rapid journey with Glenn through five states with a quick side trip to London, Ontario, gave me an urge to travel. At the time, I was not able to envision the great distances my future journeys would take me. (I would eventually visit places in Asia, Europe, Africa, Central and South America.)

After the trip north, I returned for one more year of life on Brindley Mountain. The farm was sold, and I had more time for reading, and drawing and painting. Of course, I no longer had the barn loft to serve as a gym, but I continued to do push-ups and chin-ups. I was not impressive in size, but I was strong enough to take care of myself.

The only time I ever ran away from a fight happened one evening as I was walking home from a Boy Scout meeting. In one of the town alleyways, I was accosted by a gang of five boys whom I didn't know. They were looking for trouble, and I just happened along. They expected to take me down and give me a good fright.

I began to push my way through the circle of boys. One of them pulled a switchblade knife and threatened me. At that point, I felt that the better part of valor was to make a run for it. I charged through the group, fists flying. I broke free and put on the speed. I never looked back until I could no longer hear any sound behind me. Luckily the boys had given up the chase and had gone looking for easier prey.

The fifties were the years of "souped-up" cars, gaudy with chrome, soaring fins, fender guards, mud flaps, loud mufflers, and wide white-sidewall tires. This new style vehicle was anathema to Mr. Spencer Speegle, one of our high school teachers. All these unnecessary and nonfunctional frills were examples of how the US was moving away from traditional values. When few others were aware of this shift, Mr. Speegle realized that the US was in the throes of an out-of-control consumer age. In his own peculiar way, he was trying to warn us of the downside to such immoderate consumerism.

Prof. Speegle taught advanced math classes—solid geometry, trigonometry, and precalculus. He also taught drafting. He was rather idiosyncratic, and frequently drew a large circle "free-hand" on the black board that was almost perfect. At times, he wrote with both hands on the blackboard simultaneously. This ability was a constant source of amazement to the students. Most of us couldn't pat our heads and rub our stomachs at the same time. Mr. Speegle wanted to show us that we could learn to be ambidextrous.

Prof. Speegle's social conscience was unusually high both for the era and for the location. He would call attention to garbage men and street sweepers working outside the classroom window and would say, "One day those men should be among the highest paid workers because they are doing necessary work that few people will do." He could not foresee that blacks and immigrants would take over those jobs, and thus the pay would not shoot up as high as he forecast.

I believe that Mr. Speegle would have preferred to teach philosophy or sociology. He was very concerned about the gradual loss of solidarity with the world around us and the dangers of the "me generation," which he could foresee on the horizon. I think he felt a lot like William Wordsworth when that poet penned the following lines.

The world is too much with us; late and soon,
Getting and spending, we lay waste our powers.
Little we see in Nature that is ours.

Prof. Speegle used a metaphor to express rampant consumerism. This metaphor was "white sidewall tires"—one of the totally nonfunctional features of the cars of the 1950s. He could just as easily have spoken of the ridiculous fins that soared out behind the cars like Mercury's wings, but he always ridiculed white sidewall tire. Prof. Speegle seldom drove a car. He walked almost everywhere in town. He was acutely aware of the danger of American dependency on automobiles and concerned about our lack of mass transit. Of course, his caution fell on deaf ears. He was too far ahead of his time. Going green and caring for the environment is still controversial fifty years later in the second decade of the twenty-first century. We respected Mr. Speegle, but we thought he was mostly just weird. He seemed to enjoy being considered different. He would occasionally ask a couple of strong, athletic students to pick him up from his chair by the hair of his head. This was to show that his mind could shut out pain—an illustration of mind over matter.

Cullman High offered its first foreign language course in the fall of 1955. The course was Spanish taught by a young teacher, Miss Mary Rice, fresh out of college who had taken a minor (18 credits) in Spanish and had a Social Studies major. Miss Rice had to work hard to keep up with the Spanish grammar in the textbook, and I never heard her speak Spanish in a conversational manner. In the class we did a lot of translating and a lot of grammar exercises. I was very disappointed. I wanted to travel somewhere exotic, and knowing Spanish seemed just the thing to smooth the way. As the class terms continued, I became more and more frustrated and bored in the class.

My two favorite subjects in high school were English (with Mrs. Gilbert in eleventh grade and Mrs. Mabel Bailey in twelfth grade) and American History with Miss Alberta Bailey. The latter Bailey was a white-haired old maid but an excellent teacher who really enjoyed what she was doing. She dedicated her life to the subject of history. Later, as the study of history developed into an avocation for me, I gave Alberta Bailey credit for starting the process.

In the late 1950s societal changes were rapidly escalating, paving the way for the rebellions of the 1960s. In urban areas, students were losing respect for teachers. The blackboard jungle became more than a movie. I was soon to experience this clash between students and authority firsthand in 1959–60 when I taught at Dayton, Kentucky High School (across the river from Cincinnati, Ohio).

In my own high school years, while we white kids were living the "Happy Days," our country was continuing to experience the unbelievable disgrace of segregation. Blacks had fought for our country in Europe and Asia, but back in the American South, they were second-class citizens. They had "colored" bathrooms and drinking fountains, segregated schools, segregated movie theaters and separate public swimming pools (if any at all). All sorts of methods were used to prevent them from voting and taking full part in the civic life of their communities.

Blacks were required by law to ride in the back of buses and trains and to yield even those seats to healthy whites if the bus became crowded. At

Cullman High, we were only vaguely aware of this discrimination because no blacks lived in Cullman. Most of us did not think long or hard about these social issues. We were happy with our "received" traditional ideas.

In my senior year, I was Cullman High's winner of the *Birmingham News* "Profiles in Courage" essay contest. My essay was entitled "Charles Sumner— Black Man's Moses." This essay was written in 1956 for a contest in Alabama and judged by white jurors. What makes all this worth noting is that Senator Sumner was one of the most vocal and courageous of northern abolitionists. At one point, he was beaten almost to death on the floor of the US Senate by an advocate for slavery. In a state that elected George Wallace as governor two years later, it may seem surprising that an essay lauding an advocate of full rights for blacks would be judged a winner.

During commencement ceremonies in May of 1956, held in the high school gym, Superintendent Allen Hyatt, passed out 164 diplomas (98 to girls and 66 to boys), and we recessed out of the little gym and into the larger world. Many of us never again set foot in the buildings of old CHS, but the life lessons we learned in those halls would help us navigate the future.

The summer after graduation from high school, I needed a job in order to earn money to get a start on a college education. Part time work was very scarce in Cullman. My dad had the idea of going to talk to the mayor, Mr. W. J. Nesmith, about possible work with the city. The result was a job in the Public Works Division assigned to the road maintenance crew.

This meant working Monday through Friday from seven in the morning until five in the afternoon with an hour off for lunch. On Saturdays, the work stopped at noon, making a total workweek of fifty hours. The wage for temporary workers was fifty cents an hour. This meant a total of twenty-five dollars per week. I worked for twelve weeks that summer in the heat and dust using a shovel, a pick, and a scythe. I learned how to look like I was working while leaning on a shovel. In addition, I gave a try at chewing tobacco (and failed), and I heard many a raunchy joke.

As the end of the twelve weeks, I pooled my earnings with past savings and found I had four hundred sixty-three dollars to take with me to Lexington, Kentucky, to begin my college days at Transylvania University. This does not seem like much money today, but I had a tuition scholarship, a job in a cafeteria where I earned two meals a day, and a job on campus that paid fifty cents an hour. In the end, I graduated in three years and owed the university $500, which my wife and I paid off in one year.

Southern Cooking

In the rural South, one's social level determined
what parts of vegetables and animals a family ate.

N ot all Southern breakfasts include grits.
Never once was I served grits by my
mother or by any member of the extended
clan. We all ate oatmeal. Mother was well ahead of
her time in believing that a bowl of oatmeal each day
would keep a person healthy, if not wealthy. I did not
eat grits until I attended college in Kentucky. Grits
appeared in many homes in Cullman, and just naturally had to be served in every restaurant and truck
stop throughout the South—if for no other reason
than to give the Yankees something to talk about.

My mother was also a firm believer that the
most important meal of the day was breakfast. We
always had enough food on the table at that meal to
suffice for the entire day if worse came to worst. The
breakfast menu never changed in my eighteen years
at home. Mother made biscuits from scratch every
morning without fail. After the bowl of hot oatmeal,
we always had a plate of scrambled eggs (the only way
my mother ever fixed them); sausage, ham, or bacon

from the smokehouse; a bowl of milk gravy; plenty of butter, jelly, jam, or sorghum syrup; and a large pitcher of whole sweet milk.

I emphasize *sweet milk* because some farm families enjoyed drinking buttermilk with meals. For me, buttermilk had only one acceptable purpose—to be used in making biscuits or cornbread. The only item in our copious breakfast that was not grown by us on the farm was the flour used in the biscuits and gravy, Quaker rolled oats, the salt, pepper, and sugar used to season, and the black coffee my dad adored.

My mother cooked one other meal during the morning hours—dinner—which was served at noon on the dot. With the exception of Sundays, the noon meal consisted of vegetables, fruit, and dessert unless some special occasion caused a change—the arrival of guests, or hog butchering time, or a visit from the preacher, or Dad having a hankering for liver and onions, or Mother deciding to try her hand at a new meatloaf recipe.

Sunday was the day for fried chicken, no exceptions here. Mother caught one of the free-range "fryers" (young, tender roosters), wrung its neck, pulled off skin and feathers, and fried it in an iron skillet in about a half inch of hog grease (lard). Mother ate the back, the gizzard, and the liver. I ate one drumstick and Glenn ate the other. We argued over the wishbone. Once the meat was eaten off the wishbone, we made a wish, tugged at each side to see whose wish would come true—the one with the largest portion of bone. White meat was for guests (e.g., the preacher) or for Mother if there was no guest. Dad ate the thighs.

All the food served at the noon meal was raised on the farm with the exception of liver and ground beef (and the aforementioned flour, sugar, salt, and pepper). The choice of vegetables depended on the season. In the spring, "English" peas took the spotlight, along with tender leaf-lettuce, early turnip greens, and rhubarb. If you have only eaten canned green peas, you have no idea how good very fresh, early English peas can be, lightly stewed with butter, salt, and pepper.

A bit later in the season, onions and radishes grew large enough to eat. Turnip and kale greens could be supplemented with tender wild pokeberry leaves that thrive so well in the spring. Pokeberry leaves are sweet and take the sharpness off kale or turnip greens when mixed with them.

Later in the early summer, squash, okra, tomatoes, corn, and various beans made it to the table; still later came the potatoes (Irish and sweet), peaches, pears, apples, strawberries, dewberries, blackberries, and grapes.

It is important to note that all the food was fried, stewed or eaten raw. There was no steaming, broiling, baking, or grilling. Many of the stewed vegetables were very much overcooked by today's taste, but not the creamed corn and the early peas. The corn for creaming was cut thinly off the ear. The ear was then scraped to get the milky juice, which makes the dish so special. Butterbeans, field peas, and green beans were always cooked with a slice of bacon. Lard was the frying agent of the day.

The late summer and fall were times to serve field peas, turnips, sweet potatoes, collards, pole beans, and fruits such as muscadines and scuppernongs (wild grapes), fall apples, watermelons, cantaloupes, and pumpkins.

No dessert can surpass a good, juicy cobbler. The art of cobbler-making, unfortunately, seems to be disappearing. Rural women in the South had a special way of "fixing" cobbler. It was prepared in a deep tin dish. The dough was partially cooked before being added to the stewed peaches or other fruit. A layer of partially baked strips of sugar-coated dough were laid on top of the fruit. Hmm, exquisite!

All during the summer and fall, rural women were preparing for the winter months when no fresh vegetables or fruit would be available. Most of the vegetables were canned on the old cookstove: butter beans, green beans, beets, kraut, okra, tomatoes. Cabbage and cucumbers were placed in tubs of salt-water and vinegar and turned into kraut and pickles.

Some items could be dried: beans, apples, and corn. The dried corn could be soaked in a lye mixture to create hominy. The elementary school lunchroom staff loved to serve hominy even though it was seldom eaten by any but the poorest of students. The large flat area of our storm cellar was a perfect place to dry fruits. I especially enjoyed snitching a few handfuls of drying apples to eat while doing chores. Every few hours of the dying process produces its own special flavor. Apples are best after one full day in the sun. When totally dry the apples were stored in a burlap bag and hung from the ceiling in our spare bedroom. Why from the ceiling? To make sure no stray mouse could get at them. These dried apples made wonderful fried pies. In later years, I have tried fried apple pies from several venues, but none have had the taste I remember.

The one main aggravation with drying fruit outdoors is the flies, bees, and wasps. Not that they eat too much, but that they create such an unsavory atmosphere. It was always best not to pay them much attention. In any case, the fried pies were cooked so thoroughly that there was nothing unhealthy about them. All the germs were destroyed.

One of the best ways to describe Southern cooking is to note those foods that were *not* a part of the cuisine. When I was a youngster, there were no grills for steaks or burgers. Fried fish would appear on many tables the evening or day after a fishing trip; otherwise, fish and crustaceans (shrimp, lobster, crab, and crawfish) were seldom eaten except in regions near the Gulf, the Atlantic, and in a few upscale restaurants in Birmingham, Atlanta, and Nashville.

Lamb, veal, and duck were generally not on the family table but could be ordered in a "fancy" restaurant in large cities. The only cheese to appear on most rural table was American (e.g., Velveeta or perhaps Swiss). Hoop cheese was cooked with macaroni or eaten in slices with sugar on it. As a child, I only knew of two types of pasta, macaroni and spaghetti. Rice was rarely served except in areas of the South where the plants were grown. My mother considered rice a dessert. She boiled it and put sugar on it—making a sort of rice pudding.

You may have noticed that I have not talked about spicy food. In most rural farm families, few spices other than salt, pepper, cinnamon, and vanilla extract were used. A few farmers grew hot peppers, but the majority grew only bell peppers: green, yellow, or red. Hot food, spiced or temperature hot, was unlikely in most homes. My first encounter with pizza was in Lexington, Kentucky. Fraternity pledges were forced to eat hot and spicy pizza as part of the hazing process.

The following vegetables were generally not a part of the typical rural Southern cuisine: zucchini, cauliflower, broccoli, asparagus, Brussels sprouts, eggplant, and artichokes. The only homemade soups my mother fixed were tomato, chicken noodle, and potato.

Like the taco in Mexico, in the rural US, cornbread was the staple food that accompanied each meal except breakfast. Cornbread was crumbled in "pot likker" (juice left after stewing greens). Cornbread was crumbled in warm milk. Cornbread was crumbled in the "juice" remaining after cooking butterbeans and field peas. Cornbread and butter were eaten with sorghum molasses. The other bread staple was hot biscuits, which were essential to accompany fried chicken, ham, gravy, jelly and jam.

In the summer after the advent of refrigeration, iced tea became the drink of preference with meals (still is). Iced tea, usually very sweet, was used to wash down all the foods mentioned above. The only other likely drink (besides water) was cold sweet milk. Drinking sodas with meals came much later.

When an occasion was very special—a birthday, an anniversary, a reunion—homemade ice cream became the dessert of choice. During the summer, a typical refrigerator did not make enough ice to manage a whole freezer of ice cream. A trip had to be made to the local icehouse to buy a fifty-pound block—there were no *7-Elevens* where one could make a fast visit for a sack of crushed ice.

The block of ice (twenty or fifty pounds) was brought home in a burlap bag and quickly crushed while still in the bag on the concrete storm cellar using the flat edge of a double-bladed ax. The crushed ice was then placed around the metal container in the wooden freezer bucket. Inside the container was a mixture of eggs, milk, sugar, and vanilla extract. As the crank was turned, more ice and salt was added and the melting water was drained off. The crank of the freezer was turned until the mixture was so hard that turning became too difficult. At that point, the ice cream was ready to eat. It was never very hard and tended to melt rapidly. If fresh picked strawberries or dewberries were available, some was added on top of a bowl of cream. This could match up any day with the best *gelato* served in Italy.

Herman's Store

Every young child who entered Herman's store was invited to go to the candy case and pick out a piece or two—at no charge.

During the summer of 1955, I worked for my mother's youngest brother who operated a small grocery store in north Cullman. My job was *factotem*; that is, I did whatever I was asked to do at any given time: stock the shelves, answer the phone, serve customers, work the cash register, bag, sweep the floor, and deliver call-in grocery orders. No one had trouble remembering the store's phone number. I recall it to this day. It was only three digits—662.

The adding machine and cash register used in Herman's store are museum pieces today. The cash register was a huge and heavy affair with more buttons than fleas on a stray dog. It took several lessons to get the hang of the thing. The adding machine had a crank handle. First, you pushed in numbered buttons to equal the cost of an item and then pulled the lever in the fashion of the one-armed bandit in a casino.

The machine I enjoyed operating the most—it had a powerful aroma to accompany its crackling sounds—was the old-fashioned coffee grinder. You could pour a pound of *Eight O'Clock* coffee beans in the hopper and turn it on and revel in the wonderful fragrance that filled the air.

The shelving in Herman's store was eight feet high around the perimeter of the walls. To reach the nonbreakable items on these high shelves, we used a "grabber." This was a long pole with a lever that worked two metal "jaws." At first, try the box usually fell on the novice's head. But once a person got the knack, it was easy to pick off a box of cereal or cake mix with no spillage.

Aunt Vera, Uncle Herman's wife, was a stickler for keeping a dust-free store. She insisted that the shelves be gone over periodically with an old turkey-feather duster that had been used so much it looked more like the back end of a tired rooster. I couldn't see the point in moving all the cans and boxes for this useless activity. In the dry season, the dust blew back on the shelves in less than a day!

Even though this was a grocery store, Aunt Vera insisted on having a supply of thread for her lady customers. This was a time when clothes were repaired and patched, not thrown away or given to Goodwill as soon as it was ripped or torn or a button pulled off. Thread and buttons of all colors were essential. Consequently, the store had a little chest with shallow drawers holding any number of spools of thread from the factory of *Coats & Clark*.

Uncle Herman allowed his customers to buy groceries on credit, but not with credit cards, which didn't exist. He wrote down what they owed on tickets that were kept in an old wooden *Southern Gold Cheese* box. He hoped someday to be repaid, and a majority of clients eventually did so. No one was turned away from the store who needed food, no matter how much they owed.

This compassion and generosity irked some of Herman's brothers, who felt he should pay more attention to making a profit. Herman and Vera were very generous in other ways. They gave part-time jobs to young boys like me, even when the store could have survived without any extra help. One of the first teens to work was Tom Smith, son of Uncle T. A.

Tom made a name for himself because he didn't need to use the adding machine in the store to add up the costs of the purchased items. He just looked at what was placed on the counter by the customer and quickly added it all up in his head. Tom was valedictorian of his high school class, attended law school and returned to Cullman to practice. My parents held up Tom as an example for me to emulate, but I had my own ideas about success.

When kids came in the store, they were invited to make a beeline for the candy counter and the cold drink cooler. The cooler chest was two-thirds filled with water, which was kept cool by an electric motor. Soft drinks were five cents each. The candy counter was crammed with one cent items and bars for five cents. Since Herman was a great fan of local sports, when a member of a high school team came into the store following a winning game, that player was invited to have a "cold drink" on the house.

Ice cream cups were five and ten cents (half pints and pints, in flavors of vanilla, chocolate, and strawberry). You gave a little tug on a cardboard tab and the top came right off. Tampering was not yet a concern. If you licked all the ice cream off the top, you could see a photo of a Hollywood movie star. The ice cream in cups was eaten with a little wooden spoon which I hated. When wood or cotton touched my teeth or tongue, I got shivers from head to toe.

On the counter next to the adding machine sat a *Gregg* cookie jar. Anyone could reach in with their bare hand and grab a cookie. No one worried in the least about the transmission of germs. Hygiene concerns had not yet reached fanatical proportions. The counter opposite the adding machine was a very inviting space to hop up and sit and watch the activities. This was okay when no customers were checking out, but if you dared to sit idly on the counter during checkout, you risked a scolding from an otherwise easygoing Herman.

One other thing would throw Herman into a mild tantrum. The store had a public restroom (coed). Many of the workmen, as well as customers, used the facility. Graffiti "artists" and would-be poets could not resist leaving their talents behind. But Uncle Herman was not amused by the art or by the poetry, especially the scabrous type. He policed the privy as best he could; nevertheless, he had to spend valuable time with soap and water scrubbing off the latest versions.

The store was more than just a grocery; it was a place to socialize. A lot of people in the neighborhood found reasons to come to the store just to hang out. They would come in to buy a can of snuff, a pack of cigarettes, a spool of thread, or just to catch up on the neighborhood gossip. If they needed to know about the latest sports scores, Herman was a better source than the local radio station.

In the forties, there were no restaurants to speak of in Cullman. Herman cut meat to order rather than selling prepackaged items. For deli meats, he had an electric slicer which cut bologna, ham, liverwurst, and cheese to the thickness desired by the customer. Herman had a great old chopping block and the tools for sawing, carving, and chopping. A saltbox sat just behind the butcher's block. This box held salt pork items, fat back, and bacon.

If workers wanted lunch and hadn't brought their own from home, the best place for a sandwich was the local grocery. Herman would slice a piece of baloney, whip some mayonnaise on a couple of slices of white bread, and *voilà*, the worker had an inexpensive sandwich.

When no customers were present and Uncle Herman was resting in his house beside the store, we would sit around on wooden benches that were just outside the front doors. The store had a large overhanging portico to protect customers who might drive up to the front in bad weather. A few young boys inevitably would be hanging around tossing a ball or roller skating on the concrete flooring below the portico.

The younger ones enjoyed taking old discarded quart oil cans (which were made of cardboard except for the bottom and top) and stomp the can with their shoe. The can would curl up around their shoe, and a kid could clomp around like Frankenstein's monster until the can eventually tore to pieces.

For those folks who could not personally come to the store for health reasons or lack of transportation, Herman made sure that their food was delivered at no extra charge. Most of these clients lived within a half-mile radius.

The store had a gasoline pump in front that was serviced by the Gulf Oil Company. Gasoline was leaded at the time, there was only one grade. My parents used to irk Jerry because they would drive up on a Friday afternoon and buy one dollar's worth of gas! Of course, this was four gallons and was enough to do them for a week since they basically did only in-town driving.

In the nineteen fifties, many folks still had a need for kerosene. The big orange kerosene pump sat at the north edge of the store building. Clients brought large metal containers to be filled. From that container, they filled lanterns and lamps for use in times of storms when the electric power was sure to go out.

Herman and Vera practically raised a nephew, the son of one of Herman's sisters who died unexpectedly when the nephew was only five years old. Their generosity was never as evident as during Christmas season. I never saw the floor under a Christmas tree so loaded with presents as the floor in the living room of their house. The two children, Jerry and Judy, were showered with presents, and all the nephews and nieces received gifts as well. I was awed and amazed—and very jealous of Jerry and Judy. I really tried to avoid going to their house during that season. If envy is a sin, then I was quite the sinner.

Catty-cornered across the street from Herman's store was the home of a young boy who had an electric train set. My envy meter practically went off the scale when I happened to deliver groceries to their house. I always had to stay a few minutes and drool over the train as it traveled around a table filled with stations, trees, hills, tunnels, and other accessories.

The real payoff for my hours of work in the grocery store did not come with the four dollars I earned at the end of the day, but at noon when Aunt Vera would almost always serve fresh, hot tamales prepared by Mrs. Preiss who lived three blocks east of the store. Aunt Vera served pinto beans and slaw with the tamales and plenty of very sweet tea. She always had a freshly baked pie of some kind—coconut, chocolate, cream, or apple.

After lunch, Uncle Herman always took a short *siesta*. During this time of relaxation, he watched whatever sports program was on TV. If, for some reason, a caller had to speak with him, a button in the store alerted him to the call and he would pick up the receiver in the house. From about l: 30 p.m. to 4:00 p.m. a lull in the number of clients was usual. This was a good time to sweep the floor, which was concrete. Sawdust mixed with a small amount of oil was sprinkled around the floor. As this slightly oily sawdust was moved around, it picked up dirt and dust and prevented the lightweight material from becoming airborne. Without the sawdust, the air would have been thick with tiny dust particles, which would have lodged on the groceries and shelves.

As I recall, Aunt Vera did not work in the store at all on Saturday afternoons. She and daughter Judy busied themselves around the house. Cousin Jerry and I operated the store until siesta time was over. Around four o'clock in the afternoon, Jerry began to prepare for his big Saturday night date. The first item of business was to wash his car for thirty minutes or so. He was very meticulous with this chore. He even washed the tires until they gleamed. He vacuumed the inside and filled the tank with gas. Then he took a bath and got spruced up—shaved, sprinkled on some good-smelling cologne, and slicked back his hair in Elvis-like duck tails.

In the evenings, around 6:30 or 7:00, as we were about to close the store, I ate a can of Vienna sausages and a half-dozen saltine crackers washed down with an orange or grape soda. Sometimes I varied the menu and had a can of sardines. This satisfied me just fine. At home, the leftover supper was finished by six o'clock, and the kitchen was closed for the night.

Many times over the years since those Saturday workdays at Herman's store, I have revisited those moments in my mind. In comparison to farm labor, the work was easy. I met people of all ages and attitudes. The time spent in the store gave me an opportunity to make some progress on social skills. Good-hearted banter and teasing went back and both between Jerry and me and between us and the customers.

Several years later, after the store building had been sold and was no longer a grocery, I painted a picture of the south and east sides of the store at the request of Judy, who had a small photo of the store as it looked in the nineteen fifties. I painted in the big RC Cola sign on the south wall along with the head of Elsie the Cow (Borden's Milk Co. logo), the double doors with the Tip Top and Colonial Bread advertisements, the benches with the Buettner Brothers lettering, and the Gulf gasoline pump. Copies of this pastel painting were given to several individuals who hold fond memories of the store and of Herman and Vera. Apparently copies have spread all over the state. I should have claimed royalties!

"Transy" Years

When you set out on your journey…pray that the
road is long, full of adventure, full of knowledge.

—Constantine Cavafy, *Ithaca*

During the final year in high school, those
of us planning for college began to apply
to various institutions. Unfortunately,
at that time, Cullman High School had no career
counselor or anyone who had much to offer a student planning for college. I had no idea where to
apply, but I knew I wanted to journey beyond the
boundaries of the state.

Like many teens, I did not know what I wanted
to study in college, nor had any idea what I wanted
to do with my life. I enjoyed history and literature
and art, but I also achieved above average grades in
math and science. With no real planning, I thought it
would be great to study physics. I had no idea which
universities in the US had good programs in physics.
I did not know that reference guides were available.
Brother Gilbert, pastor of the First Christian Church,
and bee-keeper extraordinaire, was a graduate of

the oldest liberal arts college west of the Allegheny Mountains (founded in 1780)—an institution at one time the rival of Harvard, especially in natural sciences, medicine, law, and religion.

This former "Harvard of the West" is in Lexington, Kentucky, and is called *Transylvania* University—*across the woods*. Some rather legendary characters are connected with its traditions, but none were vampires and none were named Dracula. This Transylvania, unlike the one in Romania, is located in the heart of the Kentucky Bluegrass region, racehorse country, with rolling hills and pastures and immaculate white fences.

The university is loosely connected to Daniel Boone, who forged the Wilderness Trail through the Cumberland Gap into land that would eventually become the state of Kentucky. A short-lived trading and land development company was established in the little stockade village of Boonesborough on the Kentucky River, a few miles southeast of the present city of Lexington. The company was dissolved in 1778, but the new college, founded two years later, was graced in turn with the classical name *Transylvania*. (After all, classical Greek would be a basic course in the curriculum.)

The early history of the institution shows ties to several famous Americans, George Washington, Thomas Jefferson, and John Adams, who were early supporters. Henry Clay was a law professor at Transy before his election to the US Senate. Stephen Austin, instrumental in the creation of the State of Texas, was an alumnus. Other graduates became US senators, representatives, and state governors.

The most interesting character in the early years of Transylvania was a professor of Botany and Natural History named Constantine Rafinesque. He was something of a mad genius, very eccentric, even for a professor. The amazing part is that he was essentially self-taught. Born in Turkey, Rafinesque lived many years in France and Italy. He began collecting plant and animal specimens in whatever country he found himself.

Rafinesque made his way to America and was eventually appointed professor of Botany and Natural History at Transylvania—at no salary! He received room and board and an allotment of candles and wood. What more could a research professor want? To earn some hard cash, Prof. Rafinesque gave lessons in French and Italian on the side.

Rafinesque taught at Transylvania for seven contentious years. He wrote articles about specie variations that occur over long periods of time (the theory of evolution). These articles appeared some twenty years before Darwin published his famous work. Darwin even quotes Rafinesque in his *Origin of the Species.*

Eventually Rafinesque's eccentricities (and perhaps his too-advanced evolutionary theories) caused the university president, Horace Holley, to fire him. This is where the legend begins. When the president died of yellow fever, and the main building of the campus burned to the ground, the story quickly spread that Rafinesque had placed a curse on Transylvania. All beginning students are told some version of this legend during orientation, often embroidered a bit to add some excitement.

Transylvania barely survived the US Civil War. Old Morrison Hall still bears bullet marks from that conflict. For a time, the building served as a hospital. As the college made a slow return to financial stability, the medical and law schools and the seminary were dissolved. The school became essentially a liberal arts institution and remains so today.

Transylvania struggled through the first half of the twentieth century. Financial woes were compounded by two world wars and the Great Depression. Sound financial footing was reached in the mid nineteen fifties, in part due to the presidency of Dr. Frank Rose. Presently, Transylvania is on sound economic footing and is a highly regarded liberal arts university.

In January of 1956, I applied to Transylvania and was accepted for admission for the fall term. Tuition that year was one hundred and fifty dollars per quarter. A shared room was an additional fifty dollars a quarter, and three meals a day in the cafeteria cost approximately one hundred and thirty-five dollars per quarter. This totaled slightly over one thousand dollars for nine months. Almost every student acquired some financial assistance, and most worked a few hours on or off campus. The full cost at Transy in the twenty-first century is over thirty thousand per year. Most of the buildings are new, the dorm rooms are luxurious, the recreation facilities are wonderful, but I doubt if the dedication of the faculty is any greater.

I was awarded a full tuition scholarship along with a work-study grant for my first year of study at Transy. If I maintained a 2.5 grade point average, the scholarship and grant were to continue for each of the next three years. I decided Transy would be the place for me. Two other Cullman High classmates had entered Transy the prior year, Guy Waldrop and Nell Robinson. Another friend from high school and youth group, Josie Glascock, enrolled at Transy the same year as I. The four of us headed north by car from Cullman in September of 1956 with high anticipation. A great new adventure lay ahead.

We arrived at Transy late in the evening. I was directed to Ewing Hall, the men's dormitory, to obtain a room assignment. I was placed on the second floor in a room with four bunk beds stacked two and two. The room was not large enough to have four bunks on the floor and still have space to walk around. The bunks were military surplus and were made of metal with wire springs. The mattresses were about two inches thick. The room had two desks and two wooden straight chairs.

The one large window had no curtains or shade. The room had no bath facilities. Showers, commodes, and basins were at the end of the hallway. I was told we would have maid service, but I wondered why. It turned out that housekeepers came each day to make the bunk beds and sweep the floor. This practice was obviously a holdover from days when "gentlemen" scholars could not be expected to tidy up after themselves.

Even though I had grown up in the little clapboard house near Cullman with no facilities during the first six years of my life, I still felt that this dorm room was rather Spartan. But my reaction was nothing compared to that of the first of my roommates to arrive on campus after me. This was a young man raised on the Jersey Shore whose father was a banker. Both parents arrived with my roommate, and the mother immediately measured the window for curtains, the bunk for a nice spread, and the center of the floor for a rug. Soon the place looked halfway livable.

After one term in such tight quarters with two roommates, both from New Jersey, I was given permission to live off campus. This was rather unusual, but a well-to-do *grand dame* of Lexington, Mrs. Wiggington, who descended from wealthy hemp producers, needed someone to tend her coal-fired furnace. This relic had an automatic feed and only needed someone to fill the hopper each day and to make sure that the feed ran properly. The Dean of Men asked me if I would be willing to do this for free lodging. I jumped at the opportunity.

The Wiggington house was a two-story brick with a side room that had once been a porch. It was equipped with a shower, basin, and commode. The room was just large enough for a small chest of drawers, a desk, and a twin bed. The bed and chest were already in the room. I found an old wooden desk at a flea market/antique store for ten dollars and dragged it about ten blocks to the Wiggington house.

The little room was cozy, and it was all mine. I managed to stay alone for three terms; then I decided that for the fall term of 1957, I would rather put up with the inconvenience of bath facilities down the hall in order to have some social life. All I regretted leaving behind was the sherry decanter that Mrs. Wiggington kept filled. She loved to have a glass late in the afternoon and invited me for a "constitutional" if I happened to be in my little room.

Since I had arrived in Lexington with just over four hundred dollars in my pocket, I needed a couple of jobs each semester to keep from going into debt. I first worked at DeSha's diner, which served breakfast and lunch but not dinner. That facility was slightly above a "greasy spoon" and was located at Upper and Lancaster Streets. The twenty-first century version of DeSha's is an upscale bistro at the corner of Main and Broadway. Working at DeSha's meant that I had to buy my dinner. This was not something I could afford for very long. This meant eating lots of Vienna sausages and cans of sardines with soda crackers.

The faculty at Transylvania in the late 1950s was a dedicated lot. As noted, the president, Dr. Frank Rose, had advanced the college to its best position financially and academically since the US Civil War. Because of his success, Dr. Rose was hired to be the president of the University of Alabama in the summer of 1957. He was replaced at Transylvanian by the Academic Dean, Dr. Irvin Lunger, who served the institution admirably over many years.

Dr. Rose was an imposing figure with jet black hair and a dignified air. I remember meeting him during my first week at Transy when he held an open house at the presidential mansion. I had just been handed a cup of punch when Dr. Rose came over to greet me with a welcoming smile. He stuck out his hand to shake mine. I was so nervous my hands were shaking, and some of the punch had spilled out on my right hand. Nevertheless, I took his hand, and I mumbled something semi-intelligent. After shaking my hand Dr. Rose did not tarry, but left quickly, most likely in search of a napkin to wipe the punch off his hand.

My first quarter at Transy, I enrolled in the required "freshman" English course and earned a grade of A. This qualified me to be placed in "honors" English the following quarter. This course was taught by Dr. John Harrison. His no-nonsense approach had us writing rather lengthy papers each week. I pegged him from the beginning as a bit prudish and something of a stuffed shirt. Given his self-image, I figured he was not going to be impressed by a redneck Southern boy who didn't even own a suit.

The first week in this honors English class, the prim and proper Dr. Harrison tore my paper to shreds. I received an F for my pains. That was quite a wake-up call for someone whose all-time lowest grade was a C in physical education back in ninth grade! I did not panic but vowed to do better on the next theme.

The second week, I received an encouraging D for my efforts. The third week I received a C. Great! I was on a roll. I doubled my efforts, and the fourth paper received a B. Now if I could hold on, I had reason to hope for at least a B grade for the term. I redoubled my efforts, and sure enough, I was rewarded with an A on the fifth theme. I earned enough As in the next five weeks to merit a B grade for the course.

To win the struggle in this advanced English course was a major milestone. However, Dr. Harrison never became a fan of mine, nor I of him. Later when applying for graduate school I asked him for a letter of recommendation, and he flatly refused, indicating that he didn't believe I had what was required to succeed at graduate-level coursework.

Another professor was Mr. Monroe Moosnick, who taught general science and chemistry. I enrolled for his general science course, which was the last science class I ever attended. I had come to college expecting to study some field of science, but I had no concrete plans. I was just going with the flow. However, my reasons for leaving the field of science cannot be blamed on Mr. Moosnick, even though he had the irritating habit of catching students off guard when they were daydreaming or actually catching some shuteye during class.

Many times, Mr. Moosnick would stir me from some reverie. "Isn't that right, Mr. Scruggs?" He pronounced my name with something bordering on a sneer. He sometimes tried a few antics to keep students' attention. One device was to lie on his desk and lecture in a supine position. He was well-loved by science students. I believe he is the only Transy professor who has a commemorative stone planted on the campus lawn in his honor. It reads, "In memory of *Dr. Monroe Moosnick*," which means he evidently finished his doctorate sometime after I graduated and left Transylvania.

For me, the most influential professor at Transy was Dr. Edwin Alderson. He was the head of the modern language department. He taught French, Spanish, and German. Dr. Alderson received his *Doctorat de l'Université* from the University of Besançon, France, and his graduation tam and gown were colorful and quite debonair. He looked so suave and cosmopolitan marching in procession. When I watched him enter the chapel with the rest of the faculty, looking so "European and exotic," I wanted to someday wear a hood and tam just like his.

I enrolled for beginning French my first quarter at Transylvania—only because no Spanish course was open when it was my turn to register. Dr. Alderson was an excellent teacher and made learning French as close to fun as such a thing can be. We began the term learning the discrete sounds of French by repeating three sentences created by the famous linguist Dr. Pierre Delattre. Taken together the three sentences contained all the vowels and consonants sounds in the language. I am able to repeat these three sentences verbatim fifty years later.

Dr. Alderson noticed my southern nasal twang the first day. He said I would really do well when the class began the study of the French nasal vowels. In effect, my dialect made those vowel sounds even more difficult to pronounce correctly, since /m/ and /n/ and /ng/ are silent in French when closing a syllable. It is the preceding vowel that is nasalized. Since, like any Southerner, I gave a long glide to all the so-called long vowels in English, Dr. Alderson had me practice repeating the short, crisp French vowels while trying to pick up a heavy desk. The strain of attempting to lift a very weighty object caused all my muscles to tense, including the muscles in my neck, jaw, and cheeks.

After considerable practice, I could keep the un-wanted vowel glides reasonably in check. All of this effort paid off when Dr. Alderson invited me to participate in a ten-week summer intensive program in French studies. I, along with twenty-four future missionaries to the Belgian Congo, spent all day practicing French, eating and living in the same dorm. We made a vow to use only French among ourselves during the summer course.

Given the college's effort to hold costs down, Dr. Alderson also served as the Director of Admissions. Several additional professors filled other critical administrative positions. Even the dean of the college taught a course each term. These were the days when administrators and faculty trusted and supported each other and sacrificed time and energy for the good of the students. Such dedication to an institution is now a much rarer occurrence.

The two history professors at Transy were quite different, one from the other. Dr. George Emerson Dodds was an Eli, and he let everyone know he was Ivy League by the way he tied his tie. However, he tended to drone on when he lectured, and often he read from notes. This turned me off. I had trouble staying alert in his class. Now, history has always been of great interest to me and eventually became my avocation. I constantly try to increase my knowledge of the great themes of history and often lecture on various subjects to lay audiences—and I never use notes.

The more compelling of the two history teachers was Dr. John Wright. He specialized in American history and was quite animated in his lectures. He was able to catch the sweep of history and avoid becoming bogged down with minutia.

Ms. Martha Jane Stone was a member of the music faculty. She was very patient and long-suffering. I know this directly because she tried to teach me to play the piano over the course of three quarters. Unfortunately for her, no matter how hard she tried to make it easy and fun for me, I was unable to get my fingers moving as they should. She kindly gave me a grade of B for the first two quarters; however, when I totally choked at my little recital the third quarter, I received the only C grade during my college years (undergraduate and graduate levels).

The philosophy professor was Benjamin Franklin Lewis. With a name like that, how could he not be philosophical? Prof. Lewis gave stimulating lectures and could make Plato and Aristotle come alive. He had a great interest in logic and was fond of asking naïve students whether God could make a rock so big that God would be unable to lift it. He was trying a little shock treatment on us. At this time, Transy was loosely affiliated with the Disciples of Christ. Once a week, attendance at chapel service was compulsory.

Another little exercise in semantics by Prof. Lewis stuck in my mind always. One day he wrote on the blackboard: "*Time flies. We cannot. They go too fast.*" He asked us to re-order these three short sentences to make a more logical statement. All that was necessary was to put the phrase "We cannot" before "Time flies" in order to get: *"We cannot time flies, they go too fast."* The lesson was apparently to show how in English a word may function one time as a noun and another as a verb with no alteration in spelling.

The second year at Transy, an exchange professor from the Alliance Française in Paris came to teach upper level French. Her name was Anne-Marie Hameau. She had authored the textbook we used in first-year French. Mme Hameau, as we called her, was a very gifted teacher and exuded that cool suaveness and aloofness we associate with Parisians.

Dr. Alderson and Mme Hameau encouraged me to enroll for a speech course to see if I could whittle down my Alabama drawl and nasal twang a bit more.

I took their advice and enrolled for a speech class led by George Williams. He was more of a drama coach than speech teacher. He gave me monologues from Shakespearean plays to recite at the top of my voice in an auditorium of empty seats. At least he didn't require me to put stones in my mouth and yell at the wind in the manner of Demosthenes—nor did he hang a sword over my head.

By the end of my second year of study, I had a goodly number of credit hours in French, English, history, and philosophy. Belatedly, I began to think of a major. I noticed that one possible major was comparative literature. It seemed that all the courses I had taken to that point would be counted toward such a major. In the end, without thinking at all of what I might do with such a major, I settled for comparative literature.

Luckily, at the beginning of my second year at Transy, I found that I could work in the cafeteria at the YWCA in the center of town and receive lunch and dinner. I began to wash dishes at the "Y" and received the two main meals of the day. It was easier to skip breakfast than to skip dinner. It was at the YWCA that I met my future wife, La Donna Loescher. Our first date was to a Sadie Hawkins Day dance. The second was to see the movie *Around the World in Eighty Days*. We agreed to "go steady" and have been inseparable from that time on.

Transylvania had a psychology professor who lived in a house overlooking Gratz Park. This park was just across Third Street from Morrison Hall. This balding near-sighted professor was a German named Hans Hahn. He was Freudian to the nth degree. Dr. Hahn was a diminutive man who asked the girls in his class to raise their arms and put their hands behind their heads and arch their backs as they sat in their desks. Most of the coeds wore tight sweaters, which tended to enhance their natural endowments. But Prof. Hahn desired the extra enhancement that came with the little posture trick he had devised.

Dr. Hahn would enter Psychology 101 class on Monday mornings and invariable greet the class with: *"Gut mornink, little Susies* [even though a few male students took his class]. *Are you avake yet dis mornink? I saw you in zee park last night. Vat ver you doink?"*

The park Dr. Hahn spoke about was Gratz Park. It was a lovely place where couples who didn't own a car could sit and talk and neck a bit. Thus, Dr. Hahn's inquiry *"Vat vere you doink?"* La Donna and I spent considerable time on one of the benches in the park, leading me to write the following poem for our thirty-fifth wedding anniversary.

Gratz Park

Not at all unusual, this quaint old park
That conjures mighty memories
For those who felt its warm embrace.

Scarce an acre square, a residential jewel,
Tree-lined paths through well-worn grass,
Wooden benches near an antique fount.

THE VIEW FROM BRINDLEY MOUNTAIN

A place and space in time—in seeming isolation
Where lovers dared to dream their future,
Hold hands and kiss, and blush for more,
While unbeknownst the German prof. of psych
With Freudian eye observed from
nearby window ledge.

> *Vake up little Susies!!*
> *I saw you in zee park last night!*
> *Vat vere you doink?*

What fortitude's required in wintry months
To warm a bench as flowing fountain morphs
Into bizarre and glistening ice-caked shapes!
Where breathing intertwines in clouds of steam
And love begins to grow through
mittens, topcoats, jeans.

Those images remain in testament
to love grown strong
Where many nights 'til nearly curfew past
We nourish our majestic youthful fantasies.

With pins exchanged, rings given, vows expressed
Imagined voyages out to Africa and Philippines,
Brilliant careers envisioned, and children named.

No, not a simple square of shaded green expanse—
Gratz Park—a solemn space in place and time.
A cradle for a wealth of ever-lasting memories.

Since I needed money as well as food, I was lucky enough to be hired by Miss Roemel Henry, head librarian, to serve as custodian of the library building. My first job was to keep the building clean and empty the trash. During quarter breaks I buffed the floors, vacuumed the blinds, and washed the windows. (Miss Henry, like my mother, was a stickler for cleanliness!) The work I did pleased Miss Henry, who was noted for being a bit harsh and domineering. She eventually trusted me to serve as the evening circulation desk manager, which paid a whopping one dollar an hour. In comparison to sweeping floors and cleaning commodes, this was a "cushy" job, even though it was stress-filled. This job afforded me the money to take La Donna out on "big" dates on weekends to the lunch counter at Walgreens and to the local movie theater.

In foreign language classes in the nineteen fifties, a reel-to-reel tape recorder was an essential piece of technology. I needed one of my own to work on French pronunciation in my dorm room. I was able to obtain a high-quality tape recorder that had been donated to the library. Miss Henry didn't envision a use in the library for the machine, so she gave it to me. I used this machine to play and record French lessons until the spring of 1958.

La Donna and I were planning for an eventual marriage, so I desperately needed money to purchase an engagement ring. Reluctantly, I took the recorder to a pawn shop and hocked it for a hundred and fifty dollars. Combined with the little money I had managed to save, I now had enough to buy a quarter-karat engagement ring. Unfortunately, I was never able to return to the pawnshop and retrieve the recorder. Despite this, gaining a fiancée was worth the sacrifice!

We set a date for marriage, June 13, 1959. La Donna thought we needed money to set up a home. (What a novel idea!) A friend of her parents was the superintendent of Dayton, Kentucky schools. This steel-mill town was a very economically depressed area. The superintendent was having great difficulty finding grade-school teachers. La Donna applied for an opening as a third-grand teacher and was accepted. She quickly enrolled for summer course-work in primary education at the University of Cincinnati.

I continued my student-aid position in the library at Transy. By working through three summers, I accumulated the quarter-hours needed to graduate after three years. La Donna and I were married as planned on June 13th, 1959. We attended bacca-laureate ceremonies the next day. The following day, I participated in graduation ceremonies, but only received a blank piece of paper. Then, in late August, I received the BA degree in comparative literature, *cum laude*.

Needing to earn money, I also began teaching in the high school at Dayton—French and English. The salary was abysmal. To make a few additional dollars, I agreed to serve as the yearbook advisor and the varsity tennis coach. This very stress-filled year convinced me I would do much better teaching at the college-level. We returned to Lexington, and I enrolled in the Foreign Language Department at the University of Kentucky. I was granted a teaching assistantship and completed an MA in French Studies. Because teaching assistantships did not pay very much, La Donna took a job as assistant to the university archivist that allowed us enough funds to eat and put gas in the car. We even had our first child in the middle of those two years.

After receiving the MA degree, my wife, one-year-old daughter, Melana, and I moved to Boone, North Carolina, where I took a position at Appalachian State University as instructor of French and director of the audio-visual laboratory. After three years in North Carolina, the four of us (a second daughter had joined the family) returned to the University of Kentucky. Serendipitously, I had been offered the remaining two years of a three-year National Defense Education Act Fellowship that had been abandoned by its first recipient.

I completed course work for a PhD in French studies and general linguistics in the two years remaining on the fellowship. The UK graduate school awarded me a travel grant to conduct research in Paris, France. The four of us packed up and spent six months in the city of lights, where I pursued my work at the various libraries and archives.

The unexpected financial support from the NDEA Fellowship and the travel grant allowed me to achieve the goal of obtaining a PhD degree and launched me on a career in teaching and administration at the university-level. The path from Brindley Mountain was carrying me further than I had dared to dream.

Paris Sojourns

Life isn't measured by the number of
breaths you take, but by the moments
that take your breath away.

—Chinese proverb

After passing comprehensive exams for the doctorate in French Studies, I needed to find a dissertation topic. I wanted to do my research under the direction of Dr. Jean Charron, who was a specialist in seventeenth-century literature. In my search for a suitable subject, I ran across a bibliography of the works of Charles Dassoucy. No doctoral dissertation had been dedicated to this writer-musician and very little secondary research. I proposed Dassoucy's life and works as my topic, and this was accepted by Dr. Charron and my doctoral committee.

With the UK travel grant and the NDEA Fellowship, La Donna and I decided to take our young daughters (ages three and five) and travel to France so I could complete research there. The four of us left for France on Icelandic Airline's "Heart of Europe" flight, which flew from JFK airport in New York to Luxembourg via Rekjavik, Iceland. The round-trip fare cost ninety-nine dollars per person. The voyage was by turbo prop plane that shook and rattled the entire trip. The girls slept all the way, but La Donna and I could not sleep a wink.

We arrived in Luxembourg in the afternoon of the following day. After an overnight in the Haas Hotel, we took a train to Paris and were met at the Gare de l'Est station by a fellow French graduate student, Howard Hanson, who was also doing research for his dissertation. Howard had reserved rooms for us in the same hotel where he was staying—Hôtel du Piémont, Rue de Richelieu—very close to the *Bibliothèque Nationale.*

After a couple of days of orientation in Paris, La Donna, the girls and I headed south by train to the village of Ussel. At that time, Ussel was a middle-level village in the department of Correze in the central mountains. My mother's uncle, Nelson Creel, was wounded in France during WWI and married his nurse. The couple raised two sons in France, Avery and Roland. Each of these sons married and had four children. Avery was married to Angèle, who was an angel indeed. By the time we arrived in France, I had two first cousins-once removed, and eight second cousins, all living in Ussel. Nestled in the *Haute Correze,* Ussel is best noted for its favorite son, Jacques Chirac, president of France from 1995 to 2007.

We were feted by our relatives for a couple of weeks, and then we returned to Paris. Angèle Creel had acquaintances who owned a small furnished apartment for rent in the Levallois-Perret district of Paris. We moved into this flat on Rue du Villier, two floors above the auto repair garage run by the owner of the building. This mechanic was from the rural mountains in central France. He spoke a French idiom that could be compared to an Appalachian dialect in the US. Until I could train my ear, I had almost no idea what he was saying. Luckily his wife spoke a more "educated" variety of French and was easier to comprehend.

I quickly realized how much I still needed to learn about French street culture and how much I needed to train my ear for the many dialects and idiolects of French. No one, it seemed, spoke the so-called "pure" Parisian French that I had studied in phonetics class back in the States. I had no idea the extent that street French could vary from textbook French. Of course, the same is true for English.

As an example of my experience, imagine a foreigner who has studied the Queen's English and then comes to the US and hears *"Geet jyet? Noddjou? Nolsqueet."* These phrases look like nonsense when written, but any American will understand them when they are spoken orally. *"Did you eat yet? No, did you? No, let's go eat."* A simple example in French is the phrase: *"Shaipa"* for *"Je ne sais pas,"* meaning *"I don't know."*

I began research for my dissertation topic at the *Bibliotheque National* in Paris. This facility was an experience to behold. Twenty years before computers, the catalog was in dozens of "fichiers" (three by five cards in drawers). Researchers could only request ten books a day to be used in the General Reading Room. The stacks were closed and "*chargeurs*" (porters) searched for the books requested and brought them to the large reading room. These *chargeurs* were all mostly hefty men, similar in build to *les gros* (big guys) who worked at *Les Halles,* the central marketplace for all of Paris at that time.

These lowly civil servants did not seem to enjoy their work. They took their own good time in searching for a book in the bowels of the library and bringing it to the reading room. Sometimes they would be carrying several heavy tomes and would come to a researcher's location and literally slam the books down on the reading table with a sullen grunt and walk away.

The main reading room of the *Bibliothèque Nationale* was huge with a high glass domed ceiling. The building dated from the eighteenth century. The reading tables were long and wide, and several scholars sat at each table. During the winter months, the only heat available was from hot water that ran through a pipe which passed beneath the tables at foot level. You could take off your shoes and put your sock feet on the pipe and after a certain amount of time, the heat would percolate up your legs perhaps as high as your knees. But the body, arms, hands, ears, and nose remained cold. Some scholars worked with cotton gloves with the fingers cut out. Today's researchers in Paris do not have this "quaint" experience. France has a new state-of-the art library, built during the presidency of François Mitterrand, east of the *Gare d'Austerlitz.*

I also conducted research at the *Archives Nationales,* the *Bibliotheque de l'Arsenal,* the *Bibliotheque Mazarine* at the Institute de France, and at the "*Minutier Central de Paris* (containing minutes from court proceedings).

During the long hours when I was working at the BN, La Donna learned to cook French style. She tried many new recipes. Some of my favorites were and are *Coquilles St. Jacques, Iles flottantes, assiette de crudités,* and *boeuf Bourguignon.*

By the middle of June 1967, I had taken notes from all the primary sources I could find in Paris, and we began to plan our trip back to the US. I had a teaching job waiting at Eastern Kentucky University in Richmond, which was only about twenty miles from UK and my dissertation committee. In the fall academic term of 1967, I began teaching four classes and managing the foreign language laboratory and writing the dissertation.

By the following summer, I had finished the final draft. I had no problems with my committee. Dr. Charron was quite savvy and was good at paving the way for me. The approval of the dissertation: *Charles Coippeau Dassoucy, Seventeenth-Century Troubadour,* was given by committee and the Graduate School, and I applied for a December graduation. My thirty-first birthday was in November of 1968, and I received the PhD degree in December. The entire process of course-work, research, and writing took three years and four months.

Working at EKU gave me invaluable experi-ence. I functioned as surrogate chair of the depart-ment (Dr. Charles Nelson, the chair was a retired colonel who was unsure of himself in the world of academia). I was able to propose a program for an MA in French, which the graduate council accepted. This program began in 1970. In 1971 I proposed a student program to France for the intersession (month of May). This program was approved, and I took a group of ten students to Paris. Fortunately, I had a very understanding wife who stayed behind with our two children, who were then ten and eight years old.

This immersion program was twenty days in length. The student group was lodged on Rue Mouffetard, not far from the Pantheon in the Latin Quarter. After a week of visiting major sites in Paris, we took a small bus with chauffeur and began a ten-day excursion into the provinces. We left Paris and drove to Rouen and began a counterclockwise circuit around France. We traversed the coast of Normandy, visited Mont-Saint-Michel, Saint-Malo, and many quaint villages in Brittany, including Locronan, called the *ville d'art.*

We saw hundreds of *menhirs* at Carnac (prehis-toric standing stones) and followed the Loire River from Nantes to Angers, Saumur, and Tours. On the way, we visited six of the most historic renaissance chateaux. Afterward, we drove to Orleans and then east to Vézelay (the location of the most beautiful of Romanesque churches). From Vézelay, we drove to Clermont-Ferrand. In that mountain location, the students were lodged in a convent, which had a 10:00 p.m. curfew. All the students arrived back in their rooms well before curfew. Unfortunately, I was out with several cousins at a nightclub and was not back to the convent until after midnight. I had to ring a bell and awaken one of the good sisters out of bed to unlock the gate. The students didn't let me forget that embarrassment for a good long while.

From the central mountains, we headed down to Provence and visited many of the Roman ruins in Nimes, Arles, Oranges, Avignon, and Aix. Afterward, we visited the beach at Saint-Raphaël. A good friend with his tiny car met me, and we drove around the *Corniche* to Nice and on to Monaco. After the sojourn in the Midi, our bus headed north, and we stopped at the Marquis de Lafayette's little château; then we traveled on to Le Puy, and finally on to Paris.

The hotel owners at Rue Mouffetard in Paris were happy to welcome us back. They enjoyed the students and wanted to serve us a treat. They prepared one of the "delicacies" of Auvergne—*les andouilles* (a dish made of tripe, a.k.a. pork intestines). I tried to give the students courage to at least try this dish to make the owners happy, but most could only swallow a few bites. Unfortunately, the situation was just not salvageable.

In the fall of 1976, I was able to convince the dean of the college of Language and Literature at the University of South Florida where I was now teaching to support my proposal for a study program to France. The program had to be approved by the Director of International Studies at USF, Dr. Mark Orr, and also approved at the State Board of Regents level. All this approval was achieved and in the late winter of 1977, I began to recruit students for a program of six weeks of study of French language and culture—three of intensive work on the campus and three weeks in France on tour. Seventeen students enrolled.

I continued to take students to France, expanding the program to six weeks in France, and at times, adding a week in England, Belgium, Holland, or Germany. I continued this study-travel program through the summer of 1990. During two fall terms (1984 and 1985), I recruited students to attend the *Alliance Française* in Paris and also to take a couple of culture and history courses taught by me using *Alliance* classroom space. In addition, in 1984 I taught English phonology as visiting professor at the University of Paris.

In total, I led more than three hundred students on study programs to France from 1977 to 1990. The students always complained that I moved too fast on city walking tours. But staying ahead and encouraging them onward was the only way to keep fifteen to twenty-eight young people together in the streets of Paris with all the congestion and the distractions—patisseries, designer boutiques, crèpe stands, heavy traffic, and games of *boules* (similar to lawn bowling) on every sandy, level plot of land in the various parks.

One young lady who was something of a poet once wrote a few lines about each of the participants and about me. Her little ditty about me went something like this:

> Papa! Will you please slow down!
> Our legs and feet will never last!
> You keep on goin', you'll leave this town.
> Then you'll know you're movin' too fast.
>
> Now, if by chance we lose Papa
> We needn't look so very far.
> We only need to ask the "gens là-bas"
> Where can we find the nearest bar!

A lot of funny things occurred over these years of student tours. I should have kept a list of the strange and sometimes silly questions the students asked me. The most frequently asked questions dealt with the weather: *"Is it going to rain today? Will it be hot today?"* And of course, at breakfast: *"What time are we leaving today"* even though the answer was clearly noted in the schedule of activities.

"How long does it take to get there?"

"Where can I find refills for my ball point pen?"

"Why don't the French celebrate the Fourth of July?"

"Do I have time to stop at the bank/bureau de change before we take the metro?" These were the days before ATM machines. What a boon the new ATMs are for today's travelers who need funds quickly. French banks were/are notorious for their heavy-handed bureaucracy, their slowness, and their surly service. The only service more aggravating and exasperating was at the old PTT (Poste, téléphone, télégraph).

Of course, as program director on these trips, I was the person to contact when things were not perfect in the one and two-star hotels and in student pensions.

"Dr. Scruggs, my bed has been slept in!!"

"Dr. Scruggs, I found a pubic hair on my sheets!"

"Dr. Scruggs, there are no towels/toilet paper/light bulb/clothes hangers in my room."

I had to face down angry management when students caused them problems.

"Your students have stolen the towels from room 204."

"Students in room 378 have burned a hole in the carpet while ironing on the floor."

"The students in room 507 are disturbing the clients in the room next to them."

Occasional illness and accidents caused me passing problems. One young male student miss-stepped while playing Frisbee in Toulouse and twisted an ankle and had to be placed in a cast. Another male student drank too much wine at dinner and fell into the Seine River while showing off for some girls by walking the concrete wall above the water. A male senior citizen, taking medication for anxiety, shoved his hand through the glass of an upstairs hotel window in Paris and required fifteen stitches in his wrist and arm. Once, a female student had Montezuma's (or Napoleon's) revenge, which lasted not one or two days, but weeks.

But by far and away, the best laughs came in 1983 when a young lady from New Jersey kept the whole group in stitches. When passing through French farmland, I often called the students' attention to windbreaks made of poplar trees. After two or three such occasions, the young lady in question asked very seriously, *"Dr. Scruggs, why are those trees so popular?"*

Another time I spoke of ways the French used to dispose of the bodies of dead criminals, indigents, and ex-communicants in earlier centuries. Often these bodies were tossed into a lime pit on the outskirts of the city. The young lady asked with a puzzled look on her face, *"Dr. Scruggs, why did they throw bodies in the lion pit?"*

Now, you might think the girl had a serious hearing problem. In a way she did. Linguistically speaking, she was discriminately deaf. She associated new sounds with words she already knew and that were very similar phonetically. However, there was more to her naiveté. While we were at the Conciergerie in Paris, a fifteenth-century building use as a prison, I spoke about the imprisonment of the young Dauphin and Marie-Antoinette in that facility in 1792 during the French Revolution. Our young lady had a follow-up question: *"Dr. Scruggs, are they still there?"*

Later, while walking in the wooded area around the *Hamlet of Marie-Antoinette* on the grounds of the Versailles Palace, our young lady asked innocently, *"Why are we the only ones here?"* She was not the only person a bit linguistically challenged. While at the hamlet, we overheard a French-speaking guide telling a student group all about the *"omelet"* of Marie-Antoinette.

Once in the *Bourbon Palace*, the Senate Chambers, I called attention to the distinctive noses of Henri IV, Louis XIII, and Louis XIV on some low-relief sculptures. I spoke of their Bob Hope-like proboscises as "bourbon noses." The men were scions from the Duchy of Bourbon. The immediate question was, of course: *"Did they get their noses from drinking too much bourbon?"*

Père Lachaise Cemetery in northeast Paris is quite a good place to talk about famous individuals of French culture. Peter Abelard and Heloise are buried there. The tombs of Moliere, Jean de la Fontaine, Chopin, and Sarah Bernhardt can be located there. But what grave do students want to seek out first? Well, Jim Morrison's, of course. A cult of worshippers continues go to his grave with flowers and pot (not one to put the flowers in!). One student once asked me as we were standing in front of Gertrude Stein's tomb: *"Didn't Gertrude Stein party a lot with Shakespeare?"* Can't believe it?

Well, none of these little pearls are invented. They were all uttered, so help me God!

Once when I was with a student group in England, we took a bus trip out of London to Oxford, Stratford-upon-Avon, Warwick Castle and back to London. This was just after the British/Argentine conflict over the Falkland Islands. Our hair-brained young lady wanted to know where the "F——king Islands" were. Honest! Did we all talk funny, except her? At some point, a question or statement about satyrs came up. Our young lady was quick to explain the meaning of satyr: "It's a half-man, half-horse who chases nymphomaniacs through the woods." (!!)

At Anne Hathaway's house, we had a local guide who explained the construction of the building. It was made of half-timbers with slats between the beams. The slats were then covered with a mixture of straw, manure, clay, soil, etc., which was called daub. Our young lady listened intently and with evident concern. When we returned to our tour bus she whispered to me with a pained voice, "Dr. Scruggs, why did they put *dogs* in the walls of that house?"

On another bus tour out of London, I took the students to Canterbury to visit the cathedral. On the way I spoke of the *Canterbury Tales*: Our dear young lady quickly responded, "Didn't Ray Bradbury write the *Canterbury Tales*, Dr. Scruggs?"

I am almost afraid to mention one last bit of humor out of our young lady's mouth, but I will. As we drove southeast toward Canterbury, she noticed the water of the English Channel on a map. This led her to ask: "Are we anywhere near the British Isles?" As you can see, with these student groups, there was seldom a dull moment. In effect, the material is there for another book.

About the Author

D r. C. Eugene Scruggs retired following a long career as professor and administrator in higher education. Dr. Scruggs's career covered forty years at four US universities and two European. He was visiting professor at the University of Paris and a tutor for a summer program at Cambridge England. During his career, Scruggs led many study tours to Europe, Central and South America. He served two terms as chair of the Department of Foreign Languages at the University of South Florida in Tampa. Following his retirement, Scruggs published three books and coedited one other. His lifelong hobby has been art. He has created several hundred watercolor and pastel painting. More recently his passion has been vocal music, from Barbershop to Gospel, to Western. Scruggs currently lives in a retirement community in Lakeland, Florida, where he is actively involved in educational and enrichment programs for senior citizens. He welcomes comments from readers via e-mail at scruggsgene@aol.com.